THE GRANGE
DESSERTS
Cookbook
INCLUDING CREATIVE HOMEMAKING TIPS

I've had this for sometime but don't bake any more! maybe you and the girls will enjoy it! But it is for your birthday "Rachel Marie" with "delicious" memories of other years! ha —

your mom.

Favorite Recipes of ® The Grange Members

1981

Dear Homemaker:

With sincere personal pleasure, I introduce to you this outstanding book of recipes and homemaking ideas from Grange families throughout the nation.

Our Grange ladies, well known for their creative homemaking talents, have generously contributed their favorite dessert recipes and homemaking tips to make the publication of this book possible. We deeply appreciate the splendid cooperation and enthusiasm shown by members everywhere.

The Grange, a national organization over 100 years old, serves rural America through Granges on the state, county and local levels. The fraternal program of The Grange embraces the entire American family. Over 800,000 Grange members include all ages, from youth to senior citizens.

With the publication of this cookbook, we are striving to carry out part of the purpose of The Grange in enlarging the horizon of the American family for service and abundant living.

The homemaker who purchases this book from a Grange member will not only find a wealth of recipes and new ideas for her family, but she will also help support the important work of The Grange in her community.

Fraternally,

John B. Burgess, Master
VIRGINIA STATE GRANGE

COOKBOOK COMMITTEE

Mrs. Norene G. Cox, Chairman
Cox's Chapel Grange
Mouth of Wilson, Virginia

Mrs. Zollie Cornette
Goodwill Grange
Mouth of Wilson, Virginia

Mr. Joe B. Cox, Advisor
Cox's Chapel Grange
Mouth of Wilson, Virginia

Mrs. Fred Jackson
Carsonville Grange
Independence, Virginia

©Favorite Recipes Press MCMLXXIII
Post Office Box 3396, Montgomery, Alabama 36109
Library of Congress Catalog Card No. 73-85365
ISBN 0-87197-054-6

Preface ———————

Dessert is the grand finale of any meal. Your efforts become worthwhile when your family and guests praise a scrumptious dessert.

Dessert is more than just the last course. It's the personal touch of an elegant meal. Whether you choose an exotic new recipe or an old family favorite, you strive to give it that something special . . . the personal touch!

In the following pages you will find a wealth of trusted dessert recipes. Choose from delectable tortes, dessert beverages, cakes, fruit desserts, chilled desserts, pies, pastries, candies, cookies, dessert breads, or custards and puddings . . . any of which will assure you the dessert you serve will add that something extra . . . that special ingredient so necessary to a successful meal.

Because Grange homemakers are also well known for their creative homemaking arts, not only in the kitchen, but throughout the home, this book contains a special section on homemaking ideas. It includes all kinds of household tips and suggestions, ranging from home decorating to how-to-make-it instructions.

FILBERT CARAMEL PIE

1 1/3 c. sifted all-purpose flour
3/4 tsp. salt
1/2 c. vegetable shortening
3 eggs
1/2 c. (firmly packed) dark brown
 sugar
1 c. light corn syrup
1 tsp. vanilla
1/2 c. butter or margarine,
 melted
1 1/2 c. toasted filberts, coarsely
 chopped

Combine flour and 1/2 teaspoon salt in bowl; cut in shortening until of coarse consistency. Sprinkle with 3 tablespoons water; toss with fork. Press into ball. Roll out pastry on lightly floured surface 1 1/2 inches larger than inverted 9-inch pie plate. Fit into plate; trim 1/2 inch beyond edge of plate. Fold under to make double thickness around edge. Flute or trim even with edge; decorate with small pastry cut-outs. Beat eggs, sugar, syrup, remaining salt and vanilla together. Stir in butter and filberts. Pour filling into pie shell. Bake in a preheated 375-degree oven for 45 minutes or until set in center. Cool.

Photograph for this recipe on cover.

CANDY APPLE PIE

7 c. pared cooking apples, sliced
1 1/4 c. sugar
1 tsp. cinnamon
1/8 tsp. nutmeg
1 double crust pie pastry
2 1/2 tbsp. butter or margarine
3/4 tsp. light corn syrup
1/3 c. toasted filberts, chopped

Mix apples with 3/4 cup sugar and spices. Roll out half the pastry on lightly floured surface to 1 1/2 inches larger than inverted 9-inch pie plate. Fit into plate; trim edge.

Add apple filling. Dot with 1 tablespoon butter. Roll out remaining pastry to 9-inch circle; cut into 6 wedges. Arrange wedges on pie; flute edge. Bake in a preheated 400-degree oven for 45 minutes or until apples are tender. Place remaining sugar in large heavy skillet. Cook, stirring, over medium heat until melted and deep golden brown. Stir in corn syrup. Remove from heat; mix in remaining butter and filberts. Spoon over pastry wedges on pie; cool.

Photograph for this recipe on cover.

FILBERT MINCE CREAM PIE

2 c. sifted all-purpose flour
1 tsp. salt
3/4 c. vegetable shortening
2 c. mincemeat
2 tbsp. cognac
1 1/2 c. toasted chopped filberts
1 c. sour cream
1 egg
1/2 c. (firmly packed) light brown
 sugar
1 tsp. vanilla

Combine flour and salt in mixing bowl; cut in shortening until of coarse consistency. Sprinkle with 1/4 cup water; toss with a fork. Press into ball; divide ball in half. Roll out bottom crust on lightly floured surface 1 1/2 inches larger than inverted 9 inch pie plate. Fit into plate; trim crust 1 inch beyond edge. Fold under; pinch together to make high standing rim. Mix mincemeat, cognac and 1 cup filberts together; spoon into pie shell. Combine sour cream, egg, brown sugar and vanilla; beat until blended and smooth. Fold in remaining filberts. Spoon over mincemeat filling. Roll out remaining dough; cut into 1/2-inch strips. Twist strips slightly; arrange over filling crisscross fashion for lattice top. Seal strips at edge; flute crust. Bake in a preheated 400-degree oven for 45 minutes. Cool.

Photograph for this recipe on cover.

Contents

This edition of the Grange Cookbook series contains hundreds of exciting dessert recipes from Grange members. Beautiful full-color photographs, chosen by the editors of Favorite Recipes Press, expand the book into other food subject areas. Located throughout the volume, the photographs — along with their accompanying recipes — offer menu ideas to add to your cooking enjoyment.

Introduction to Desserts

Everyone loves desserts. They are the most exciting and creative area of cooking — and often a family's favorite part of each meal.

Delicious pies, bursting with fruit; light, luscious cakes frosted with extravagant icings; rich candies for tasty between-meal snacks or holiday gift-giving; cookies to keep the cookie jar full — all this and more are in this dessert-packed cookbook. You can prepare a different dessert each time for hundreds of meals if you choose. Or, more likely, you'll find favorites that you and your family will want to enjoy again and again.

The list of dreamy desserts in this book is endless in its variety and imagination. Such desserts tempt us beyond resistance . . . as the recipes that follow will prove.

Cakes

Can you imagine celebrating a birthday, wedding or anniversary without a cake? Cakes are practically a part of American tradition!

Cake baking is an art that homemakers have practiced with pride since the days of ancient Egypt. There is nothing like the praise and appreciation you receive when you prepare a fragrant, delicious, beautiful cake.

And there are so many *kinds* of cakes — layered, sponge, angel, chiffon, pound, and fruitcakes are but a few. And there are as many frostings as there are flavors. You'll find a wealth of marvelous recipes in this chapter, many of which are decorative and unusual.
You and your family will want you to try them all!

ARAH'S LITTLE ANGEL CAKE

4 egg whites
1/2 tsp. cream of tartar
1 c. (scant) sugar
Flour
1/4 tsp. vanilla

Beat egg whites until frothy; add cream of tartar, beating until soft peaks form. Add sugar gradually, beating until stiff peaks form. Sift flour 4 times; measure 2/3 cup. Fold flour into egg white mixture gently. Add vanilla. Spoon batter into small ungreased tube pan. Bake in a preheated 350-degree oven for 40 to 50 minutes or until cake tests done.

Mrs. Genieva T. Wakely, Flora
Riverview Grange No. 449
Lisbon Falls, Maine

MOCK ANGEL FOOD

1 c. flour
1 c. sugar
2 tsp. baking powder
1 c. hot milk
1 tsp. almond extract
2 egg whites, stiffly beaten

Combine flour, sugar and baking powder; sift 4 times. Stir hot milk into flour mixture. Fold in almond extract and stiffly beaten egg whites. Spoon batter into small ungreased tube pan. Bake in a preheated 350-degree oven for 1 hour or until cake tests done. Invert tube pan; cool cake.

Sandra Pearce, Sec.
Golden Gate Grange No. 451
Golden, Colorado

ANGEL FOOD CAKE

1 c. sifted cake flour
1 1/4 c. sugar
1 c. (8 to 10) egg whites
1 tsp. cream of tartar
1/2 tsp. salt
3/4 tsp. vanilla
1/4 tsp. almond extract

Sift flour and 1/4 cup sugar together 4 times. Beat egg whites, cream of tartar and salt until frothy. Add remaining sugar in small amounts, beating well after each addition until stiff peaks form. Add flavorings. Sift 1/4 of the flour mixture at a time over egg white mixture; fold in lightly. Pour into large ungreased tube pan; cut through batter with spatula to remove air bubbles. Bake in a preheated 350-degree oven for 45 minutes to 1 hour or until lightly browned. Invert pan; let cake cool.

Mrs. Kenneth Palmer, Sec.
Adirondack Grange No. 1019
St. Regis Falls, New York

ORANGE ANGEL FOOD CAKE

5 eggs, separated
1/2 c. orange juice
1 1/2 c. sugar
1/4 tsp. salt
1 1/2 c. cake flour
1/2 tsp. (scant) baking powder
3/4 tsp. cream of tartar

Beat egg yolks until lemon colored; add orange juice. Beat until foamy. Add sugar gradually, beating well; stir in salt, flour and baking powder. Whip egg whites slightly; add cream of tartar, beating until stiff peaks form. Fold egg whites into orange juice mixture. Spoon batter into an ungreased tube pan. Bake in a preheated 350-degree oven for 1 hour or until cake tests done.

Mrs. Mary Marlatt, Sec.
Souhegan Grange No. 10
Merrimack, New Hampshire

CHERRY TIPSY PARSON

3 c. milk
6 egg yolks
2/3 c. sugar
2 tsp. flour
2 tsp. vanilla
1   10-in. angel food cake
1 1/2 c. coarsely slivered toasted
    almonds
1   8-oz. jar red maraschino cherries
1/2 c. cream sherry
2 c. whipping cream

1/4 c. confectioners' sugar
Red maraschino cherries, with stems

Scald milk in top of double boiler. Beat egg yolks in bowl until light. Add sugar gradually; beat until smooth and creamy. Stir in flour. Stir a small amount of scalded milk into egg mixture gradually; return to top of double boiler. Cook over simmering water, stirring constantly, until mixture coats a metal spoon. Cool custard, stirring occasionally. Stir in vanilla; let chill. Cut cake into 3 horizontal slices; place top slice, cut side up, on cake plate. Sprinkle 1/4 cup almonds and about 2 tablespoons slivered cherries on slice. Stir sherry into custard; pour about 1/2 cup custard over cake slice. Repeat cake, almonds, cherries and custard layers; top with third cake layer. Pour about 1/2 cup custard over cake; refrigerate overnight. Whip cream with confectioners' sugar until stiff; frost top and side of cake. Spoon remaining whipped cream into pastry bag; pipe large rosettes on top of cake. Dry remaining slivered cherries well on paper towels; sprinkle side with cherries and remaining almonds. Serve remaining custard with cake. Garnish with whole cherries.

Photograph for this recipe on page 8.

EASY APPLE CAKE

1 c. salad oil
1 1/2 c. sugar
1 egg, well beaten
2 c. flour
1 tsp. salt
1 tsp. soda
1 tsp. cinnamon
4 to 6 apples, diced
1 c. chopped nuts

Combine oil and sugar; mix well. Blend in egg thoroughly. Sift flour with salt, soda and cinnamon; add to egg mixture. Blend well; stir in apples and nuts. Pour batter into greased and floured 11 x 15-inch pan. Bake in a preheated 350-degree oven for 50 minutes or until cake tests done.

Marie Wetter, Ladies' Act. Com.
Economy Grange
Sewickley, Pennsylvania

GAYLE'S FRESH APPLE CAKE

1 c. flour
1 tsp. baking powder
1/2 tsp. salt
3/4 tsp. cinnamon
1 c. sugar
1/4 c. shortening
1 egg, well beaten
2 c. chopped apples
1/2 c. chopped nuts

Sift flour, baking powder, salt and cinnamon together. Add sugar to shortening gradually, beating well. Add egg; mix well. Stir in dry ingredients and apples, beating just until mixed; blend in nuts. Turn into greased loaf pan. Bake at 350 degrees for 45 minutes or until cake tests done. Serve plain or frost with confectioners' sugar icing when cool.

Ruth E. Steger, Pianist
Scotts Mills Grange No. 938
Scotts Mills, Oregon

APPLE-SPICE CAKE

3 1/4 c. apples, diced
2 c. sugar
1 c. salad oil
2 eggs, well beaten
3 c. flour, sifted
2 tsp. soda
2 tsp. cinnamon
1 tsp. cloves
Dash of allspice
1 tsp. salt
1 c. chopped nuts
1 c. raisins

Sprinkle apples with sugar; let stand for 10 to 15 minutes. Add oil to apple mixture; blend in eggs thoroughly. Sift dry ingredients; stir into apple mixture, blending well. Fold in nuts and raisins. Pour mixture into greased and floured 8 x 12-inch pan. Bake in preheated 350-degree oven for 55 minutes or until cake tests done. Dates may be substituted or combined with raisins, if desired.

Mrs. Irene Rogers, Treas.
Hudson Grange No. 11
Nashua, New Hampshire

APPLE-NUT CAKE

3 eggs
1 tsp. vanilla
1 3/4 c. sugar
1 c. oil
2 c. flour
1 tsp. soda
1/2 tsp. salt
1 tsp. cinnamon
2 c. diced apples
1 c. ground nuts

Beat eggs, vanilla and sugar until thick and lemony; beat in oil. Sift flour, soda, salt and cinnamon; beat into egg mixture. Stir in apples and nuts. Pour into tube pan. Bake in preheated 350-degree oven for 55 minutes or until cake tests done.

Helen L. Chandler, Master
Quinnatissett Grange No. 65
North Grosvenordale, Connecticut

APPLE DAPPLE CAKE

3 eggs
2 c. sugar
1 1/2 c. salad oil
3 c. flour
Dash of salt
1 tsp. soda
2 tsp. vanilla
3 c. finely chopped apples
1 c. chopped nuts
1/2 c. margarine
1 c. (packed) brown sugar
1/2 c. milk

Beat eggs well, adding sugar gradually, until thick and lemony; beat in oil. Sift together flour, salt and soda; beat into egg mixture. Stir in vanilla, apples and nuts. Pour into greased 9 x 13 x 2-inch pan. Bake at 350 degrees for 50 minutes or until cake tests done. Melt margarine in small saucepan, stir in brown sugar and milk. Cook, stirring constantly, over medium heat for 3 minutes. Pour over hot cake.

Mrs. Vera Foland
Sanitaria Springs Grange
Binghamton, New York

COFFEE-APPLESAUCE CAKE

2 c. flour
1 tsp. soda
1/4 tsp. salt
1/4 tsp. cloves
1 tsp. cassia
1/2 c. shortening
1 c. sugar
1 egg
1 c. chopped raisins
Chopped nuts (opt.)
1 c. thick applesauce

Sift flour once and measure. Add soda, salt and spices; sift 3 times. Work shortening until creamy; add sugar gradually, beating after each addition until light and fluffy. Add egg; beat well. Add raisins and nuts. Add flour alternately with the applesauce, a small amount at a time, beating well after each addition. Pour into well-greased cake pan. Bake in preheated 350-degree oven for 1 hour and 15 minutes or until cake tests done.

Coffee Frosting

1/4 c. butter
2 tsp. vanilla
3 c. confectioners' sugar
1/4 c. strong coffee

Mix butter, vanilla and sugar together in a bowl. Add cooled coffee; mix until smooth and creamy. Add more sugar, if needed, to thicken the frosting. Spread over cake; sprinkle nuts on top, if desired.

Evelyn H. Pressey, Ceres
Deering Grange No. 535
Portland, Maine

APPLESAUCE-FRUITCAKE

2 c. flour
1 1/2 c. sugar
1 tbsp. cornstarch
2 tsp. soda
1 tsp. cinnamon
1 tsp. nutmeg
1/2 tsp. allspice
1 tsp. salt

1/2 c. oil
2 c. applesauce
1 c. raisins
1 c. chopped dates
1 c. chopped nuts

Combine flour, sugar, cornstarch, soda, spices and salt in mixing bowl. Stir in oil and applesauce, mixing well. Fold in raisins, dates and nuts. Spoon batter into a tube pan. Bake in a preheated 350-degree oven for 1 hour or until cake tests done.

Pearl L. Briggs, CMA Chm.
Manteca Grange No. 507
Manteca, California

EASY APPLESAUCE CAKE

1 c. sugar
1/2 c. butter
1/2 tsp. cassia
Dash of nutmeg
Vanilla to taste
1 tsp. soda
1 c. unsweetened applesauce
1 c. raisins
2 c. flour

Blend sugar, butter, cassia, nutmeg and vanilla together, creaming well. Dissolve soda in small amount of warm water. Add soda mixture to applesauce. Add applesauce mixture and raisins to creamed mixture, mixing well. Beat in flour gradually. Spoon batter into a greased cake pan. Bake in a preheated 350-degree oven for 45 minutes or until cake tests done.

Mrs. Hazel Libby, LA Steward
Somerset Grange No. 18
Norridgewock, Maine

APPLESAUCE SPICE CAKE

1/2 c. shortening
1 c. (firmly packed) brown sugar
1 egg
1 c. applesauce
2 c. flour
1 tsp. soda
1/2 tsp. cinnamon
1/2 tsp. ginger
1/2 c. raisins

1/2 c. chopped nuts
1/4 tsp. salt

Cream shortening and sugar together; stir in egg and applesauce. Sift flour, soda and spices together; mix in raisins, nuts and salt. Add to applesauce mixture; mix well. Pour batter into well-greased 8 or 9-inch square pan. Bake in a preheated 350-degree oven for 40 minutes or until cake tests done. Let cool.

Royal Frosting

3/4 c. confectioners' sugar
1/4 tsp. cream of tartar
1/4 c. boiling water
1/2 tsp. vanilla
1 egg white

Combine all ingredients in large bowl; beat with electric mixer at high speed for 10 minutes or until frosting holds a peak, stirring constantly. Spread over cake.

Mrs. Walter Davis, Women's Activities Chm.
Goehnor Grange No. 371
Seward, Nebraska

SPICY APPLESAUCE CAKE

1/2 c. shortening
1 1/3 c. sugar
1 tsp. soda
2 eggs, well beaten
1 tsp. cinnamon
1/2 tsp. nutmeg
1/4 tsp. ground cloves
1 c. seedless raisins
1/3 c. chopped walnuts
2 c. flour
1 c. hot applesauce, strained

Cream shortening; beat in sugar, soda, eggs and spices. Add raisins, walnuts, flour and applesauce alternately. Spoon batter into greased cake pan. Bake in a preheated 350-degree oven for 1 hour or until cake tests done.

Mrs. Mary Engelhardt, Master
Petaluma Grange P of H No. 23
Petaluma, California

FRESH APPLE CAKE

2 c. sugar
1 1/2 c. Wesson oil
3 eggs, well beaten
3 c. chopped apples
1 tsp. salt
2 1/2 c. flour
1 1/2 tsp. soda
1/2 tsp. cinnamon
1/2 tsp. nutmeg
1 tsp. vanilla

Cream sugar and oil. Stir in eggs and apples. Sift dry ingredients; add gradually to oil mixture, blending well after each addition. Stir in vanilla. Pour into greased and floured tube pan. Bake in preheated 275-degree oven for 2 hours and 30 minutes or until cake tests done.

Betty Page, Sec.
Ridges Grange No. 1616
Bronson, Kansas

GRATED APPLE CAKE

2 c. margarine
1 c. sugar
1 egg
1 tsp. rum flavoring
4 med. apples, grated
1 c. hot coffee
1 c. raisins
3 c. flour
1 tbsp. soda
1 tbsp. cinnamon
1 tsp. salt

Melt margarine; cream with sugar. Beat in egg and rum flavoring; stir in apples, coffee and raisins, blending thoroughly. Sift flour, soda, cinnamon and salt. Add flour mixture gradually to apple mixture, blending well after each addition. Pour into greased and floured tube pan. Bake at 325 degrees for 1 hour and 15 minutes. Nuts may be added, if desired. May be baked in loaf pans or muffin tins.

Mrs. Clifford L. Smart, Women's Act. Com.
Bee Hive Grange No. 385
Wenatchee, Washington

APPLE UPSIDE-DOWN CAKE

1/4 c. butter
1 c. (packed) brown sugar
2 1/2 c. diced apples
2 eggs, separated
1 c. sugar
1/3 c. fruit juice or milk
1 1/2 c. flour
2 tsp. baking powder

Melt butter in large shallow baking pan. Add brown sugar, stirring until mixture is smooth. Arrange apples over sugar mixture. Beat egg yolks, adding sugar gradually, until thick and lemony; beat in fruit juice. Sift flour with baking powder; beat into egg mixture. Beat egg whites until stiff peaks form; fold into batter. Pour batter carefully over apples. Bake in preheated 375-degree oven for 30 to 35 minutes or until cake tests done. Yield: 8 servings.

Mrs. John N. Newcomer, Past Master's Wife
Leitersburg Grange No. 361
Hagerstown, Maryland

BEST-EVER APPLE CAKE

3 eggs
2 c. sugar
1 1/2 c. salad oil
3 c. flour
1 tsp. soda
1 tsp. baking powder
1/2 tsp. salt
1/2 tsp. cinnamon
1 1/2 tsp. vanilla
3 c. diced peeled apples
1 c. chopped walnuts
1 c. grated coconut

Beat eggs, sugar and salad oil together. Sift flour, soda, baking powder, salt and cinnamon; beat into egg mixture. Stir in vanilla; fold in apples, walnuts and coconut. Spread in 9 x 13-inch pan. Bake at 350 degrees for 50 minutes or until cake tests done. May be served plain or with whipped cream or ice cream. This cake freezes very well.

Mrs. Marion Altemus, CWA Chm.
Rocksburgh Grange No. 116
Phillipsburg, New Jersey

KNOBBY APPLE CAKE

3 tbsp. shortening
1 c. sugar
1 egg
1 c. flour
1 tsp. soda
1 tsp. cinnamon
1 tsp. vanilla
3 c. coarsely diced apples
1 tbsp. orange juice
1 tbsp. margarine
1 tbsp. (packed) brown sugar
Confectioners' sugar

Cream shortening and sugar; beat in egg. Sift dry ingredients; beat into egg mixture. Stir in vanilla and apples. Pat into greased 8 x 8-inch pan. Bake at 350 degrees for 50 minutes or until cake tests done. Combine orange juice, margarine and brown sugar in small saucepan; bring to a boil, stirring until margarine is melted. Stir in confectioners' sugar until of spreading consistency. Spread over cooled cake.

Lillian M. Overmyer, Fund Raising Com.
Cleon Grange No. 633
Copemish, Michigan

BANANA-NUT CAKE ROYALE

1 c. shortening
2 c. sugar
2 eggs
1 c. mashed bananas
2 c. cake flour
1/2 tsp. salt
1 tsp. soda
1 tsp. baking powder
1/2 c. buttermilk
2 tsp. vanilla
1 c. nuts
1 c. flaked coconut
2 tbsp. flour
1/2 c. cream
2 tbsp. butter
1 egg white
1/2 tsp. coconut flavoring
2 c. sifted confectioners' sugar

Cream 3/4 cup shortening with 1 1/2 cups sugar until fluffy. Add eggs, one at a time, beating well after each addition. Add bananas; beat for 2 minutes. Sift dry ingredients together; add alternately with buttermilk to banana mixture. Stir in 1 teaspoon vanilla; beat for 2 minutes longer. Stir in 1/2 cup nuts. Pour into 2 greased layer cake pans; sprinkle half the coconut over each layer. Bake in preheated 350-degree oven for 30 minutes or until cake tests done. Remove from pans; cool, coconut side up, on wire racks. Prepare filling by combining remaining sugar, flour, cream and butter in small saucepan; cook over medium heat, stirring constantly until smooth and thickened. Stir in remaining nuts and vanilla. Prepare frosting by creaming remaining shortening with egg white and coconut flavoring until thoroughly blended. Beat in confectioners' sugar until fluffy. Place 1 layer of cake, coconut side down, on cake plate; spread with filling. Place second layer over filling, coconut side up. Frost side of cake, building up side 1 inch high; leave center unfrosted.

Mrs. Berlin Hinton, WAC Chm.
Elmdale Grange No. 2162
Chillicothe, Ohio

BANANA-NUT PARTY CAKE

2 c. sugar
1/2 c. shortening
2 eggs
3 c. flour
Dash of salt
1 1/2 tsp. soda
1/2 c. (about) buttermilk
3 bananas, mashed
1/2 c. chopped nuts
1 c. diced mixed candied fruit

Cream sugar with shortening until fluffy; add eggs, one at a time, beating well after each addition. Sift flour and salt together; beat into egg mixture. Add soda to buttermilk; blend well. Add buttermilk and bananas to flour mixture. Fold in nuts and fruit. Turn into greased tube pan. Bake in preheated 350-degree oven for 1 hour or until cake tests done.

Rosanna Mitchell, CWA Com.
Somerset Grange No. 18
Norridgewock, Maine

BEET CAKE

2 oz. semisweet chocolate
2 jars strained baby food beets
1 1/2 c. sugar
2 c. flour
1/4 tsp. salt
1/2 tsp. soda
1/2 tsp. vanilla
3 eggs, lightly beaten
1 c. salad oil

Melt chocolate in double boiler; pour into mixing bowl. Let cool. Add beets, sugar, flour, salt, soda, vanilla and eggs; add oil, blending well. Pour into an oblong pan or 2 layer cake pans. Bake in a preheated 350-degree oven for 25 minutes for layer cake pans or 35 minutes for oblong pan.

Icing

1 pkg. powdered sugar
1 3-oz. package cream cheese, softened
1/4 c. margarine, softened
2 tsp. cream
1 tsp. vanilla

Combine all ingredients, blending until smooth. Spread Icing over cake.

Mrs. Hazel Bryant, CWA
Marion Grange
Logan, Ohio

CARROT CAKE

2 c. flour
2 tsp. soda
2 c. sugar
2 tsp. cinnamon
4 eggs
1 1/2 c. salad oil
2 c. grated carrots
1 8-oz. package cream cheese
1/2 c. butter
2 2/3 c. confectioners' sugar
1 tsp. vanilla
1 c. chopped nuts

Sift flour, soda, sugar and cinnamon into large mixer bowl; add eggs and oil. Beat thoroughly; stir in carrots. Pour batter into 2 greased and floured layer cake pans. Bake in preheated 350-degree oven for 30 minutes or until cake tests done. Combine cream cheese, butter, confectioners' sugar and vanilla in small mixer bowl; beat until thoroughly blended. Stir in nuts. Spread mixture between layers and over top and side of cake.

Marie Wagner, Eco. Chm.
Eno Grange No. 2080
Bidwell, Ohio

BLACK WALNUT CHIFFON CAKE

2 c. sifted flour
1 tsp. salt
1 1/2 c. sugar
3 tsp. baking powder
1/2 c. salad oil
6 eggs, separated
1/2 tsp. walnut extract
1 c. chopped black walnuts
1/2 tsp. cream of tartar

Sift flour, salt, sugar and baking powder together into a mixing bowl. Make a well in the center of the dry ingredients; add oil, unbeaten egg yolks, 3/4 cup cold water, walnut extract and black walnuts. Beat with a spoon until well blended. Combine egg whites and cream of tartar in mixer bowl. Beat with electric mixer until stiff peaks form. Pour egg yolk batter over egg whites. Fold in gently with a spatula until just blended. Spoon batter into an ungreased tube pan. Bake in a preheated 350-degree oven for 1 hour and 30 minutes or until cake tests done.

Icing

1/4 c. butter, softened
2 egg yolks
1/4 tsp. black walnut extract
Pinch of salt
2 tbsp. cream
2 c. confectioners' sugar

Combine all ingredients; beat until smooth. Frost.

Margaret Thomson, Master
El Camino Grange No. 462
Gerber, California

FLORIDA GRAPEFRUIT BASKETS

3 Florida grapefruit

Cut grapefruit in half. Insert 2 wooden picks 1/2 inch apart on each side of grapefruit. Cut through the peel 1/4 inch below the top of the half to make handle; do not cut between the picks. Cut around each section of fruit loosening from membrane. Cut around entire edge of grapefruit. Remove picks. Lift handles and tie together. Attach flower to handle.

Photograph for this recipe on page 17.

ROAST TURKEY
WITH ORANGE-RICE STUFFING

1   12 to 14-lb. turkey
Salt and pepper to taste
Orange-Rice Stuffing

Wash turkey in cold running water. Pat inside dry with paper toweling, leaving outside moist. Sprinkle turkey cavities with salt and pepper. Stuff turkey with Orange Rice Stuffing. Fasten neck skin to body with skewer. Push legs under band of skin at tail or tie to tail. Place turkey, breast side up, on rack in shallow open roasting pan. Cover with a loose covering or tent of aluminum foil, if desired. Bake in a preheated 325-degree oven for 4 hours and 30 minutes to 5 hours or until tender.

Orange-Rice Stuffing

1 c. butter or margarine
1 c. chopped onion
4 c. water
2 c. Florida orange juice
3 tbsp. grated orange rind
4 c. chopped celery
2 tbsp. salt
1 tsp. poultry seasoning
5 1/3 c. packaged precooked rice
1/2 c. chopped parsley

Melt butter in a large saucepan; add onion and cook until tender but not brown. Add water, orange juice, orange rind, celery, salt and poultry seasoning. Bring to a boil; stir in rice. Cover; remove from heat and let stand for 5 minutes. Add parsley and fluff with fork. Any leftover stuffing may be wrapped in foil and placed in oven last 30 minutes of baking time.

Photograph for this recipe on page 17.

BAKED TANGERINES
WITH ORANGE-CRANBERRY RELISH

6 Florida tangerines or Temple oranges
2 tbsp. sugar
2 tbsp. butter or margarine
2/3 c. Florida orange juice
Orange-Cranberry Relish

Make 8 vertical cuts in the tangerine skin from the blossom end to about 1 inch from the bottom. Pull peel down and turn pointed ends in. Remove white membrane. Loosen sections at the center and pull apart slightly. Fill each center with 1 teaspoon sugar and dot with 1 teaspoon butter. Pour orange juice over tangerines. Bake in preheated 325-degree oven for 30 minutes. Garnish center with a small amount of Orange-Cranberry Relish. Serve with turkey.

Orange-Cranberry Relish

2 Florida oranges, quartered and seeded
4 c. fresh cranberries
2 c. sugar

Force orange quarters with peel and cranberries through food chopper. Add sugar and mix well. Chill in refrigerator for several hours before serving. This relish will keep well in refrigerator for several weeks.

Photograph for this recipe on page 17.

ORANGE CREPES
WITH ORANGE SAUCE

3 eggs
2 egg yolks
1/2 c. milk
1/2 c. Florida orange juice
2 tbsp. salad oil
1 c. all-purpose flour
3/4 tsp. salt
1 tbsp. sugar
1 tsp. grated orange rind

Beat eggs and egg yolks together. Add remaining ingredients and beat until smooth. Let stand at room temperature for at least 1 hour. Brush hot 7 or 8-inch skillet lightly with additional salad oil. Add 2 tablespoons batter to skillet; turn and tip skillet so mixture covers bottom evenly. Batter will set immediately into thin lacey pancake. Loosen with spatula and flip over in about 15 to 20 seconds or when browned. Brown other side and turn crepe out onto foil or waxed paper. Repeat with remaining batter.

Orange Sauce

1/2 c. soft butter
1/2 c. confectioners' sugar
1 tbsp. grated orange rind
3 tbsp. orange liqueur
1/3 c. Florida orange juice
1 c. Florida orange sections

Cream butter with confectioners' sugar and orange rind. Blend in orange liqueur gradually. Spread about 1/2 teaspoon mixture over side of crepe that was browned second. Roll up crepes. Place remaining mixture with orange juice in large skillet or chafing dish; heat until bubbly. Add rolled crepes and heat, spooning sauce over tops. Add orange sections; heat for just 2 to 3 minutes longer. Yield: 6 servings.

Photograph for this recipe on page 18.

LAMB CHOP AND TOMATO BROIL
WITH HORSERADISH SAUCE

6 1-in. thick loin lamb chops
3 med. tomatoes, halved
1/4 c. butter, melted
1/2 tsp. salt
1/8 tsp. pepper
12 sm. boiled potatoes
Chopped parsley
3 tbsp. drained horseradish
1 c. sour cream

Place lamb chops and tomato halves on rack in shallow pan. Broil 4 to 6 inches from source of heat for 8 to 12 minutes or to desired degree of doneness, turning once. Combine butter, salt and pepper; brush chops and tomatoes frequently with butter mixture. Peel potatoes; brown lightly in additional butter in skillet. Arrange chops, tomatoes and potatoes on heated platter; sprinkle tomatoes with parsley. Blend horseradish with sour cream. Season to taste with additional salt. Serve sauce with lamb chop dish. Yield: 6 servings.

Photograph for this recipe on page 18.

GOLDEN CHIFFON CAKE

2 c. sifted flour
1 1/2 c. sugar
3 tsp. baking powder
1 tsp. salt
1/2 c. salad oil
7 eggs, separated
2 tsp. vanilla
2 tsp. grated lemon rind
1 c. (7 or 8) egg whites
1/2 tsp. cream of tartar

Sift flour, sugar, baking powder and salt together into a mixing bowl. Make a well in center of dry ingredients. Add oil, egg yolks, 3/4 cup cold water, vanilla and lemon rind to well. Beat with a spoon until smooth. Combine egg whites and cream of tartar in a large mixer bowl. Beat with electric mixer until stiff peaks form. Do not underbeat. Pour batter over egg whites; fold in gently with a spatula until just blended. Spoon into ungreased 10-inch tube pan. Bake in a preheated 325-degree oven for 55 minutes. Increase oven temperature to 350 degrees; bake for 10 minutes longer or until cake tests done.

Mrs. Lloyd Belden, Lady Asst. Steward
Trowbridge Grange No. 296
Allegan, Michigan

SPICE CHIFFON CAKE

2 1/4 c. sifted cake flour
1 1/2 c. sugar
3 tsp. baking powder
1 tsp. salt
1 tsp. cinnamon
1/2 tsp. each nutmeg, allspice
   and cloves
1/2 c. salad oil
5 unbeaten egg yolks
1 c. egg whites
1/2 tsp. cream of tartar

Sift flour, sugar, baking powder, salt and spices together into a mixing bowl. Add oil, egg yolks and 3/4 cup cold water; beat with spoon until smooth. Combine egg whites and cream of tartar in a large mixer bowl. Beat with electric mixer until stiff peaks form.

Pour egg yolk batter over egg whites; blend in gently with a spatula. Spoon batter into an ungreased 10-inch tube pan. Bake in a preheated 325-degree oven for 55 minutes. Increase oven temperature to 350 degrees; bake for 10 to 15 minutes longer or until cake tests done. Cool.

Mrs. Harold Nihiser, Sr.
Women's Activities Chm.
Antioch Grange No. 2629
Rockbridge, Ohio

CHOCOLATE CAKE AND FROSTING

1 c. milk
2 sq. bitter chocolate
1 c. sugar
1/4 c. margarine or butter
1 egg
1/2 c. milk
1 tsp. soda
1 c. flour

Combine milk and chocolate in double boiler; heat over boiling water until chocolate is melted. Set aside. Cream sugar and margarine until fluffy; beat in egg. Add milk, soda and flour, mixing well. Stir in chocolate mixture until smooth. Spoon batter into greased and floured 8-inch square cake pan. Bake in a preheated 350-degree oven for 30 minutes or until cake tests done.

Frosting

1 c. sugar
1 1/2 tbsp. cornstarch
1 sq. bitter chocolate, grated
Dash of salt
1 1/2 tbsp. butter
1 tsp. vanilla

Combine sugar, cornstarch, 1 cup boiling water, chocolate and salt in saucepan. Cook, stirring, until chocolate is melted and mixture is thickened. Remove from heat; add butter and vanilla. Beat until glossy and smooth; frost cake.

Helen M. Cauxx, Ceres
Putnam Valley Grange No. 841
Peekskill, New York

COKE CAKE

2 c. unsifted flour
2 c. sugar
1 c. margarine
2 tbsp. cocoa
1 c. Coca-Cola
1/2 c. buttermilk
1 tsp. soda
2 eggs
1 tsp. vanilla
1/4 tsp. salt
2 c. miniature marshmallows

Sift flour and sugar together into a large mixing bowl. Combine margarine, cocoa and Coca-Cola in a saucepan; bring to a boil, stirring, until margarine is melted. Pour margarine mixture into flour mixture, blending well. Add buttermilk, soda, eggs, vanilla and salt. Stir in marshmallows. Batter will be thin. Spoon batter into oblong greased and floured pan. Bake in a preheated 350-degree oven for 30 to 35 minutes. Let stand for 10 minutes.

Icing

1/2 c. margarine
2 tbsp. cocoa
6 tbsp. Coca-Cola
1 box confectioners' sugar
1 c. chopped nuts
1 tsp. vanilla

Combine margarine, cocoa and Coca-Cola in saucepan; bring to boiling point. Pour boiling mixture over confectioners' sugar; add nuts and vanilla. Spread Icing on warm cake.

Mrs. Marion Schelleger, Home Ec. Chm.
Ashley Grange
Ashley, Ohio

CHOCOLATE CHIP-DATE CAKE

1 c. chopped dates
1 tsp. soda
1 c. sugar
1 c. shortening
2 eggs, beaten
1 tsp. vanilla
1 3/4 c. flour
1/2 tsp. salt

1 tbsp. cocoa
1/2 c. coarsely ground nuts
1/2 c. chocolate bits

Combine dates, 1 cup boiling water and soda; let stand until cool. Cream sugar and shortening until fluffy; add eggs and vanilla. Sift flour, salt and cocoa together; add to creamed mixture alternately with flour and date mixture. Mix well. Spoon batter into greased 9 x 13-inch pan. Sprinkle with nuts and chocolate bits. Bake in a preheated 350-degree oven for 40 minutes.

Mrs. John N. Newcomer, Past Master's Wife
Lietersburg Grange No. 361
Hagerstown, Maryland

OLD-FASHIONED COCOA CAKE

2/3 c. butter or margarine
1 2/3 c. sugar
3 eggs
2 c. all-purpose flour
2/3 c. cocoa
1 1/4 tsp. soda
1/4 tsp. baking powder
1 tsp. salt
1 1/3 c. milk
1/2 c. crushed peppermint candy

Cream butter, sugar and eggs with electric mixer until fluffy. Beat on high speed for 3 minutes; reduce speed to low. Combine flour, cocoa, soda, baking powder and salt; add to creamed mixture alternately with milk. Blend in crushed candy. Spoon batter into 2 greased and cocoa-dusted 9-inch pans. Bake in a preheated 350-degree oven for 35 minutes. Cool for 10 minutes; remove from pans. Frost as desired.

Carol Crawford, Sec.
Paris Grange No. 1452
Sauquoit, New York

HEAVENLY HASH CAKE

1 c. margarine, softened
2 c. sugar
4 eggs
1 1/2 c. flour
1/4 c. cocoa

Pinch of salt
3 1/2 c. miniature marshmallows

Cream margarine and sugar until fluffy. Add eggs, one at a time, beating well after each addition. Sift flour, cocoa and salt together; add to creamed mixture, blending well. Spoon batter into a greased and floured 9 x 13-inch pan. Bake in a preheated 350-degree oven for 20 to 25 minutes. Sprinkle marshmallows on hot cake; let melt. Cool well.

Icing

1/4 c. cocoa
1/2 c. margarine, softened
4 to 5 tbsp. evaporated milk
1 box confectioners' sugar

Cream cocoa and margarine together well; stir in milk. Add confectioners' sugar gradually to make of spreading consistency. Spread frosting over cake.

Mrs. Graydon Welling, Jr Matron
Lisbon Grange No. 1568
Leetonia, Ohio

COCOA DEVIL'S FOOD CAKE

1 1/2 c. flour
1 1/4 c. sugar
1/2 c. cocoa
3/4 tsp. salt
1 1/4 tsp. soda
2/3 c. shortening, softened
2/3 c. sour milk or buttermilk
2 eggs, unbeaten
1 tsp. vanilla

Sift flour, sugar, cocoa, salt and soda together into a mixer bowl; add shortening. Beat with electric mixer at medium speed for 2 minutes. Add sour milk, eggs and vanilla; beat at medium speed for 2 minutes. Spoon batter into 2 greased and floured layer cake pans. Bake in a preheated 350-degree oven for 30 to 35 minutes or until cake tests done. Remove from pans; cool. Frost as desired.

Mrs. Eugene Merriam, Chaplain, S & H Chm.
Genesee Valley Grange No. 1109
Wellsville, New York

EASY DEVIL'S FOOD CAKE

2 c. sifted cake flour
2 c. sugar
3/4 c. shortening
1 tsp. salt
1/2 c. cocoa
1 1/2 tsp. soda
1 1/4 c. milk
3/4 tsp. baking powder
3 eggs
1 tsp. vanilla

Combine flour, sugar, shortening, salt, cocoa, soda and 3/4 cup milk in mixer bowl. Beat with electric mixer for 2 minutes; add baking powder, remaining milk, eggs and vanilla. Beat for 2 minutes longer. Spoon batter into 2 greased and floured layer cake pans. Bake in a preheated 350-degree oven for 35 to 40 minutes.

Mary Howard
Cox's Chapel Grange No. 954
Mouth of Wilson, Virginia

MOCK CHOCOLATE CAKE

1 pkg. chocolate pudding mix
1 box white cake mix
2 eggs, separated
2 c. milk
1 c. sugar
1 c. evaporated milk
1/4 c. butter
1/2 c. chopped nuts
1 c. shredded coconut

Combine pudding mix, cake mix, stiffly beaten egg whites and milk, blending well. Spoon batter into tube pan. Bake in a preheated 350-degree oven for 35 minutes or until cake tests done. Cool. Beat egg yolks and sugar together for 5 minutes. Combine egg yolk mixture, evaporated milk and butter in a double boiler. Cook, stirring, until smooth and thickened. Cool; beat well. Fold in nuts and coconut. Spread topping over cake. Store cake in a covered container.

Dorothy Wagoner, WA Chm.
Pleasant Grove Grange No. 475
Summerville, Oregon

CALIFORNIA CHOCOLATE CAKE

1 c. butter
2 c. sugar
4 eggs, separated
3 sq. chocolate, melted
1 tsp. vanilla
2 1/4 c. flour
1 tsp. baking powder
1/2 tsp. salt
1 tsp. soda
1 c. buttermilk
1 c. coconut
1 c. nuts

Cream butter and sugar until fluffy; add egg yolks, mixing well. Add melted chocolate and vanilla. Sift flour, baking powder and salt together. Dissolve soda in buttermilk. Add flour mixture and buttermilk mixture to creamed ingredients alternately. Fold in stiffly beaten egg whites, coconut and nuts. Spoon batter into 3 greased and floured 9-inch cake pans. Bake in a preheated 350-degree oven for 30 minutes or until cake tests done.

Mrs. Joe French, Home Ec. Chm.
Lincoln Grange No. 237
Wellsburg, New York

DORIS' CHOCOLATE CAKE

4 sq. chocolate
2 c. sugar
2 c. milk
1/2 c. shortening
2 c. flour
1 1/2 tsp. soda
1 tsp. salt
2 eggs, slightly beaten
1 tsp. vanilla

Combine chocolate, half the sugar, half the milk and shortening in a saucepan; bring just to boiling point, stirring, until chocolate and shortening are melted. Sift flour, soda, remaining sugar and salt together. Add dry ingredients to chocolate mixture, alternately with remaining milk, beaten with eggs and vanilla. Spoon batter into greased and floured 9 x 13-inch pan. Bake in a preheated

350-degree oven for 30 to 35 minutes or until cake tests done. Do not use an electric mixer to make cake.

Mrs. Doris Savage, S&H Chm.
Holland Grange No. 1023
Holland, New York

DEPRESSION CAKE

1/2 c. cocoa
1 c. sugar
1 tbsp. (rounded) shortening
1/2 c. cold coffee
1/2 c. milk
1 tsp. soda
2 c. flour
1 tsp. vanilla

Dissolve cocoa in small amount of hot water. Cream sugar and shortening together; add to cocoa mixture. Blend in coffee, milk, soda, flour and vanilla, beating well. Spoon batter into a 13 x 9-inch cake pan. Bake in a preheated 350-degree oven for 30 minutes or until cake tests done.

Mrs. LeRoy Goodrich
Sherburne Grange
Sherburne, New York

CHOCOLATE YEAST CAKE WITH MOCHA CREAM FILLING

3/4 c. milk
1/4 c. warm water
1 pkg. or cake yeast
Sugar
2 3/4 c. unsifted flour
3/4 c. margarine, softened
2/3 c. cocoa
1/2 c. hot water
3 eggs, beaten
1 tsp. soda
1/2 tsp. salt
1/4 tsp. nutmeg
1/4 tsp. cinnamon
1/2 tsp. vanilla extract
1 c. chopped pecans
Mocha Cream Filling
Confectioners' sugar

Scald milk; cool to lukewarm. Measure warm water into large warm bowl. Sprinkle in yeast; stir until dissolved. Add lukewarm milk, 1 tablespoon sugar and 1 1/2 cups flour; beat until smooth. Cover; let rise in warm place, free from draft for about 45 minutes or until mixture is light and spongy. Cream margarine with 2 cups sugar; set aside. Combine cocoa and hot water; stir until smooth. Let cool. Add cocoa mixture and margarine mixture to yeast mixture. Add eggs, remaining 1 1/4 cups flour, soda, salt, spices and vanilla; beat by hand for 10 minutes or on electric mixer at low speed for about 6 minutes. Stir in pecans; turn into well-greased 10-inch tube pan. Let rise, uncovered, in warm place, free from draft for about 2 hours or until doubled in bulk. Bake in 350-degree oven for about 45 minutes, or until done. Let stand until cold. Split carefully into 3 layers; fill with Mocha Cream Filling. Sprinkle top and side with confectioners' sugar.

Mocha Cream Filling

1 1/2 c. light cream or
   1 c. whipping cream
1/2 c. milk
1 pkg. instant vanilla pudding
1 tbsp. instant coffee

Combine cream and milk in mixing bowl; add pudding and coffee. Beat for about 1 minute or until well blended, using rotary beater. Let stand for 5 minutes before using as filling.

MAHOGANY CHOCOLATE CAKE

1 1/2 c. sugar
2/3 c. butter or margarine
3 eggs, beaten
1 1/4 c. milk
1/2 c. cocoa
1 tsp. soda
2 c. (scant) flour
1 tsp. vanilla

Cream sugar and butter together until fluffy. Add eggs, beating well until blended. Combine half the milk and cocoa in saucepan; heat until cocoa is dissolved. Cool. Add milk mixture to creamed mixture. Dissolve soda in remaining milk; add to cocoa mixture. Stir in flour and vanilla, beating well. Spoon batter into 2 greased and floured layer cake pans. Bake in a preheated 350-degree oven for 30 minutes. Frost as desired.

Mrs. Jesse I. Hawkins, Cookbook Sales Chm.
Alpha Grange No. 154
Chehalis, Washington

NEVER-FAIL CHOCOLATE CAKE

Brown sugar
1/2 c. cocoa
1/3 c. strong coffee
2 tsp. vanilla
Butter
1/2 c. sugar
1 1/2 c. flour
1 tsp. soda
1/2 tsp. baking powder
Pinch of salt
1/2 c. cold coffee
2 eggs, beaten

Mix 1/3 cup firmly packed brown sugar and cocoa, blending well. Combine brown sugar mixture, strong coffee, half the vanilla and 1 teaspoon butter in a saucepan. Cook over moderate heat, stirring, until brown sugar mixture is dissolved and butter is melted. Cool. Cream 1/3 cup butter, 1/2 cup packed brown sugar and sugar together until fluffy. Sift flour, soda, baking powder and salt together. Combine cold coffee, eggs and remaining vanilla. Add egg mixture and flour mixture to creamed ingredients alternately, blending well. Combine cooked mixture and

flour mixture, mixing well. Spoon batter into 9 x 9 x 2-inch pan. Bake in a preheated 350-degree oven until cake tests done.

Mrs. Loren Garverick, Past Deputy
Jugs Corners Grange No. 2680
Mansfield, Ohio

MOTHER'S DAY CAKE

1 1/2 c. flour
2 tbsp. cocoa
1 c. sugar
1 tsp. soda
6 tbsp. cooking oil
1 tbsp. vinegar
1 tsp. vanilla
1/2 c. butter
1 c. (packed) brown sugar
1/4 c. milk
1 3/4 to 2 c. confectioners' sugar

Sift flour, cocoa, sugar and soda together into an oblong cake pan. Punch 3 holes in the dry ingredients. Fill the first hole with oil. Fill the second hole with vinegar and the third with vanilla. Pour 1 cup lukewarm water over mixture in pan; stir well with a fork. Bake in a preheated 325-degree oven for 25 to 30 minutes. Melt butter in a saucepan; add brown sugar. Cook, stirring, for 2 minutes. Add milk; bring to a boil. Remove from heat; cool. Stir in confectioners' sugar gradually to make of spreading consistency. Frost cake; cut into squares to serve.

Mate S. Bradley, Sec.
Floris Grange No. 749
Herndon, Virginia

WACKY CAKE

1 1/2 c. flour
3 tsp. (heaping) cocoa
1 tsp. soda
1 c. sugar
1 tsp. vanilla
1 tbsp. vinegar
5 tbsp. cooking oil

Sift flour, cocoa, soda and sugar together into an ungreased square cake pan. Make a dent in one corner; add vanilla. Make a dent in opposite corner; add vinegar. Draw a line through middle of ingredients; add oil to line. Pour 1 cup warm water over mixture; stir well. Bake in a preheated 350-degree oven for 35 to 45 minutes or until cake tests done. Serve from pan. Cake may be frosted, if desired.

Bonnie Heat, CWA Chm.
Huntsburg Grange No. 2541
Huntsburg, Ohio

RICH CHOCOLATE CAKE

1 c. sour cream
1 egg, slightly beaten
1 c. (packed) brown sugar
1 tsp. vanilla
1 tsp. soda
1 1/2 c. sifted cake flour
1 sq. chocolate, melted

Combine sour cream, egg, brown sugar and vanilla, blending well. Dissolve soda in 1/4 cup boiling water; add to sour cream mixture alternately with cake flour. Stir in chocolate. Spoon batter into greased 10-inch square pan. Bake in a preheated 350-degree oven for 20 minutes or until cake tests done. Ice with mocha frosting, if desired.

Mrs. John Vosburgh
Florida Grange No. 1543
Amsterdam, New York

EASY BOSTON CREAM PIE

3/4 c. boiling water
1/2 c. quick or old-fashioned
   uncooked rolled oats
1/3 c. soft butter or margarine
1/2 c. sugar
1/2 c. (firmly packed) brown sugar
1/2 tsp. vanilla
1 egg
1 sq. unsweetened chocolate, melted
   and cooled
1 c. sifted all-purpose flour
1/2 tsp. soda
1/4 tsp. salt
1 3 1/2-oz. package vanilla
   pudding and pie filling
1 1/2 c. milk
Sifted confectioners' sugar

Preheat oven to 350 degrees. Pour boiling water over oats; let stand for 20 minutes. Cream butter and sugars; blend in vanilla, egg and chocolate. Add oats mixture; mix well. Sift flour, soda and salt together; add to creamed mixture, blending well. Pour into well-greased and floured 9-inch pie plate. Bake for 25 to 30 minutes. Remove from oven; let stand for about 10 minutes. Remove from pie plate; cool on wire rack. Combine pudding and milk. Cook over medium heat, stirring constantly, until mixture comes to a full boil; remove from heat. Place waxed paper directly on pudding; cool completely. Remove paper; stir. Split cake horizontally; spread filling between layers. Sprinkle top with confectioners' sugar.

Photograph for this recipe on page 6.

GOOD NEIGHBOR CAKE

2 c. flour
2 c. sugar
1 c. cocoa
1/2 tsp. baking powder
1/2 tsp. salt
2 eggs
1/2 c. oil
2 tsp. soda
2 tsp. vanilla

Sift flour, sugar, cocoa, baking powder and salt together; add eggs and oil. Dissolve soda in 2 cups boiling water; stir into flour mixture. Add vanilla. Spoon batter into greased and floured 13 x 9-inch pan. Bake in a preheated 350-degree oven for 30 minutes.

Vanilla Frosting

1/2 c. butter or margarine
2 c. confectioners' sugar
1 egg, beaten
1 tsp. vanilla

Cream butter; add confectioners' sugar gradually, beating well. Add egg and vanilla. Spread icing over cake.

Mrs. Laura B. Gillett, Ceres
Central Square Grange No. 583
Central Square, New York

CHOCOLATE CUPCAKES

1 egg
1/2 c. cocoa
1/2 c. shortening
1/2 tsp. salt
1 1/2 c. flour
1/2 c. sour milk
1 tsp. vanilla
1 tsp. soda
1 c. sugar

Place all ingredients in mixing bowl in order given. Beat at medium speed for 2 minutes. Fill greased muffin pans 3/4 full. Bake at 350 degrees for 8 to 10 minutes or until cupcakes test done. Cool; frost as desired. Yield: 18 cupcakes.

Mrs. Velma W. Hensel, CWA
Jolly Grange No. 2656
New Matamoras, Ohio

EVERYDAY CUPCAKES

2 c. flour
2 tsp. baking powder
1/4 tsp. salt
1/4 c. shortening
1 c. sugar
1 egg
3/4 c. milk
1 tsp. vanilla

Sift flour, baking powder and salt together. Cream shortening with sugar; beat in egg well. Add flour mixture alternately with milk, beating well after each addition; stir in vanilla. Pour into greased muffin tins. Bake in preheated 350-degree oven for 15 to 20 minutes or until cakes test done. Frost as desired.

Eugenia V. Smith, LAS, HE Chairman
Contoocook Grange No. 216
Contoocook, New Hampshire

GINGERBREAD GUPPINS

1 egg, well beaten
1/2 c. sugar
1/4 c. molasses
1/4 c. salad oil
1 c. flour

1/8 tsp. salt
1/2 tsp. soda
1/4 tsp. nutmeg
1/2 tsp. ginger
1/4 tsp. cinnamon

Combine egg, sugar and molasses in large mixer bowl; beat thoroughly. Blend in salad oil. Sift flour, salt, soda, nutmeg, ginger and cinnamon together. Add dry ingredients alternately with 1/2 cup boiling water; blend thoroughly. Fill muffin tins 2/3 full. Bake in a preheated 350-degree oven for 25 minutes or until cupcakes test done. Frost as desired.

Mrs. Irene L. Dodge, Sec.
Sandy River Grange No. 339
Phillips, Maine

MAIDS OF HONOR

1 pkg. cake mix
1 tbsp. (rounded) shortening
1 c. flour
1/2 tsp. baking powder
1/4 tsp. salt
Jam or jelly to taste

Prepare cake mix according to package directions. Combine shortening with flour, baking powder and salt; blend thoroughly. Roll out dough paper thin; cut into circles. Line muffin tins with dough; prick surfaces well with a fork. Place 1 heaping teaspoon of desired jam in each pastry-lined cup; top with 1 tablespoon prepared cake batter, covering jelly well. Bake in preheated 350-degree oven until cake topping tests done. May be frosted or served topped with whipped cream, if desired.

Mrs. Irene L. Dodge, Sec.
Sandy River Grange No. 339
Phillips, Maine

DATE LOAF CAKE

1 c. chopped pitted dates
1 tsp. soda
1 c. sugar
1/2 c. butter
1 egg, beaten
1 1/2 c. flour
1 tsp. baking powder
1 c. nuts

Pour 1 cup boiling water over dates; let cool. Add soda to date mixture. Cream sugar and butter until fluffy; add egg, flour and baking powder. Combine date mixture and creamed mixture. Stir in nuts. Spoon batter into greased and floured loaf pan. Bake in preheated 325-degree oven for 1 hour or until cake tests done.

Grace R. Lord, Master
Crooked River Grange No. 32
Harrison, Maine

DATE AND NUT CAKE

1 tsp. soda
1 1-lb. package pitted dates, chopped
1 tbsp. butter
1 c. sugar
1 egg
1/2 tsp. salt
1 c. chopped walnuts
1 1/2 c. flour
1 tsp. vanilla

Sprinkle soda over dates; add 1 cup boiling water. Let stand until cool. Cream butter and sugar together until fluffy; add egg, beating well. Stir in salt, dates and walnuts. Add flour and vanilla, mixing well. Spoon batter into a loaf pan. Bake in a preheated 325-degree oven for 1 hour or until cake tests done.

Ruth Ann Kensinger, Sec.
Lincoln Grange No. 914
Altoona, Pennsylvania

DATE AND PECAN CAKE

2 tsp. soda
1 c. chopped pitted dates
3/4 c. shortening
2 c. sugar
4 eggs
3 c. flour
1 1/2 c. chopped pecans
1 sm. bottle maraschino cherries,
    drained and chopped

Add 2 cups boiling water and soda to dates; let cool. Cream shortening and sugar until fluffy. Beat in eggs, one at a time, beating well after each addition. Add flour and date mixture. Stir in pecans and cherries. Spoon batter into 2 greased and floured layer cake pans. Bake in a preheated 350-degree oven until cake tests done. Cool.

Frosting

1 1/2 c. sugar
3 tbsp. flour
2 tbsp. butter
1 1/2 c. chopped pecans
1 sm. bottle maraschino cherries,
    drained and chopped
1 c. flaked coconut

Combine sugar and flour in saucepan; add 1 1/2 cups water and butter. Cook, stirring, over medium heat until thickened. Stir in pecans, cherries and coconut. Spread icing between layers and over cake.

Lela Hughes, CWA Chm., Dir., Treas.
Porterville Grange No. 718
Porterville, California

RUTH'S DATE CAKE

1/2 lb. pitted dates, chopped
1 tsp. soda
1 c. shortening
1 c. sugar
2 eggs
1 3/4 c. unsifted flour
3 tsp. cocoa
1/2 tsp. salt
1 pkg. chocolate chips
1/2 c. walnuts

Combine dates, 1 cup hot water and soda; let stand until cool. Place shortening in mixer bowl; cream with electric mixer. Add sugar gradually, beating well. Add eggs, one at a time, beating well after each addition. Sift flour, cocoa and salt together; add to creamed mixture alternately with date mixture. Spoon batter into a greased 9 x 13 x 2-inch pan; sprinkle with chocolate chips and walnuts. Bake in a preheated 350-degree oven for 1 hour or until cake tests done.

Ruth Curts, CWA Treas.
Springville Grange No. 713
Porterville, California

EASY SUNSHINE CAKE

4 eggs, separated
1 1/2 c. sugar
1 1/2 c. flour, sifted
1 tsp. baking powder
1/4 tsp. salt
1/2 tsp. almond extract or vanilla
1/2 tsp. cream of tartar

Beat egg yolks with 3 tablespoons water; add sugar gradually, beating until thick and lemony. Add 1/2 cup boiling water gradually; beat until foamy. Sift flour with baking powder and salt; add to egg mixture, beating thoroughly. Stir in almond extract. Beat egg whites with cream of tartar until stiff peaks form; fold into egg mixture. Pour batter into tube pan. Bake at 325 degrees for 1 hour or until cake tests done. Invert to cool. When completely cool, remove from pan; sprinkle with confectioners' sugar, if desired.

Agnes Woike, CWA Chm.
Westfield Grange No. 50
Cromwell, Connecticut

BUSY DAY DARK FRUITCAKE

1 c. raisins
1 c. diced mixed candied fruits
1 c. chopped walnuts
2 1/3 c. all-purpose flour
1 tsp. baking powder
1/4 tsp. soda
1/2 tsp. salt
1/2 tsp. nutmeg
1/2 tsp. cinnamon
1/2 tsp. allspice
1/2 tsp. ground cloves
1/2 c. butter or margarine
1 c. sugar
1 egg, slightly beaten
1/4 c. molasses
2/3 c. applesauce

Combine raisins, candied fruits and walnuts; set aside. Sift flour, baking powder, soda, salt and spices into a mixing bowl. Cream butter and sugar together until fluffy. Add egg and molasses; beat well. Add dry ingredients to creamed mixture alternately with applesauce, beating well after each addition.

Stir in fruit mixture. Spoon batter into a greased 1 1/2-quart glass casserole. Garnish top with additional candied fruit and walnuts, if desired. Cover casserole. Bake in a preheated 325-degree oven for about 1 hour and 45 minutes or until cake tests done. Turn out on rack; cool. May be stored for several weeks if well wrapped. May also be frozen.

Lucy M. Graham, Ceres
Lockport Grange No. 1262
Gasport, New York

COMPANY FRUITCAKE

1 lb. uncooked prunes, chopped
1 lb. seedless raisins
1/2 lb. diced candied citron peels
1/4 lb. chopped nuts
1 c. shortening, softened
1 c. (packed) brown sugar
4 eggs, beaten
1 tbsp. milk
2 c. flour
1/2 tsp. soda
1 tsp. mace
1 tsp. cinnamon

Combine prunes, raisins, citron peels and nutmeats. Cream shortening and brown sugar together until fluffy; add eggs and milk. Sift flour, soda and spices together into creamed mixture, beating well. Stir in fruit mixture. Grease 5 one-pound loaf pans; line with greased brown paper. Spoon batter into prepared pans. Bake in a preheated 250-degree oven for 3 hours or until cakes test done. Cool well; wrap in foil.

Mrs. Ann Cluff, Master
Arundel Grange No. 486
Kennebunkport, Maine

FESTIVE FRUITCAKE

3 c. shelled, whole Brazil nuts
1 8-oz. package shelled walnuts
1 c. whole pitted dates
1 c. golden raisins
1 c. candied red cherries
1/2 c. candied orange peel

1/2 c. candied citron
1 1/4 c. sifted flour
1 1/4 c. sugar
1 tsp. baking powder
1/2 tsp. salt
6 eggs
2 tbsp. brandy flavoring
2 rings candied golden pineapple
2 rings candied green pineapple

Combine Brazil nuts, walnuts, dates, raisins, cherries, orange peel and citron. Grease a large tube pan; line with waxed paper. Sift flour, sugar, baking powder and salt together. Beat eggs with brandy flavoring until light and fluffy. Add flour mixture to fruit mixture alternately with egg mixture; mix well. Spoon batter into pan; arrange pineapple slices over batter. Bake in a preheated 300-degree oven for 2 hours or until cake tests done.

Margaret Thomson, Master
El Camino Grange No. 462
Gerber, California

SPICY FRUITCAKE

2 tbsp. butter
1 c. sugar
1 egg
1 tsp. soda
1 can tomato soup
1 1/2 c. flour
1 tsp. cinnamon
1/2 tsp. cloves
1/2 tsp. allspice
1 c. raisins
2 c. diced candied fruits
1 sm. bottle maraschino cherries,
    drained

Cream butter and sugar together until fluffy; add egg, mixing well. Dissolve soda in soup; stir into creamed mixture. Sift flour and spices together; add to creamed mixture, beating well. Fold in raisins, candied fruits and cherries. Spoon batter into a greased tube pan. Bake in a preheated 350-degree oven for 1 hour or until cake tests done.

Mrs. Dorothy Youngers, Master
Warsaw Grange No. 1088
Warsaw, New York

MOTHER'S SECRET FRUITCAKE

2 lb. mincemeat
2 lb. diced candied fruit
2 c. sugar
1 lb. shelled walnuts
2 c. raisins
1 c. melted margarine
2 tsp. soda
3 eggs, beaten
3 tsp. vanilla
1 lb. diced pitted dates
1 lb. gumdrops
4 c. flour
3 tsp. baking powder
1 tsp. salt

Combine mincemeat, candied fruit, sugar, walnuts, raisins and margarine in large mixing bowl. Dissolve soda in 1/2 cup boiling water; pour over fruit mixture. Add eggs and vanilla. Combine dates and gumdrops, omitting black gumdrops. Add to batter. Sift flour, baking powder and salt together into batter; mix well. Grease 4 layer cake pans; line with greased waxed paper. Spoon batter into prepared pans. Place cake pans in water-filled baking pans. Bake in a preheated 350-degree oven for 1 hour or until cakes test done.

Edith M. Nail, CWA, Vice Chm.
Central Union Grange No. 559
Lemoore, California

UNCOOKED FRUITCAKE

1 lb. graham crackers, crushed
1 1-lb. package pitted dates, chopped
1 1-lb. package miniature
    marshmallows
1 1-lb. package candied orange slices
1 c. whole nuts
1 c. whipped cream

Combine all ingredients, mixing well. Pack into a tube pan; chill for 24 hours. Slice to serve.

Margaret Thomson, Master
El Camino Grange No. 462
Gerber, California

FRUITCAKE DELUXE

1 1/2 c. oatmeal
3 to 4 lb. diced candied fruits
1 lb. yellow raisins
1 lb. shelled pecans
1 1/2 c. sugar
1 1/2 c. (packed) brown sugar
1/2 tsp. salt
2 1/4 c. flour
1 1/2 tsp. baking powder
3/4 c. shortening, softened
3 eggs
1 1/2 tsp. vanilla

Combine oatmeal and 1 7/8 cups boiling water; let stand until cool. Combine candied fruits, raisins and pecans in a large mixing bowl. Sift sugar, brown sugar, salt, flour and baking powder into a separate bowl. Blend in shortening, eggs and vanilla. Beat well. Fold in fruit mixture and oatmeal. Line 3 or 4 loaf pans with greased foil. Spoon batter into prepared pans. Bake in a preheated 325-degree oven for 1 hour or until cake tests done. Store cakes in airtight containers for several days before using. Cakes may be frozen.

Mrs. John O. Smith, WAC
Fairview Grange No. 2177
Goshen, Indiana

HUCKLEBERRY CAKE

1/4 c. shortening
3/4 c. sugar
1 egg
1 1/2 c. flour
2 tsp. baking powder
1/2 c. milk
1 c. huckleberries or blueberries

Cream shortening and sugar until fluffy; add egg, beating well. Sift flour and baking powder together. Add flour mixture to creamed mixture alternately with milk. Stir huckleberries into batter. Pour into greased and floured 8-inch square pan. Bake in a preheated 350-degree oven for about 25 minutes or until cake tests done.

Edrice McLean, CWA Chm., Sec.
Freshwater Grange No. 499
Eureka, California

GRANGE SUGAR CAKE

1 c. sugar
1/2 c. shortening
2 eggs
2 c. flour
1 tsp. cream of tartar
1/2 tsp. soda
1/2 c. milk
1 tsp. lemon extract

Cream sugar and shortening until fluffy. Add eggs, one at a time, beating well after each addition. Sift flour and cream of tartar together. Dissolve soda in milk. Add flour mixture and soda mixture to creamed ingredients, blending well. Stir in lemon extract. Spoon into a cake pan. Bake in a preheated 350-degree oven until cake tests done.

Gladys A. Ridley, WAC Chm.
Mousam Lake Grange
Springvale, Maine

BLUEBERRY GINGERBREAD

1/2 c. butter or margarine
1 c. sugar
3/4 c. molasses
2/3 c. sour milk
1 tsp. soda
1/2 tsp. nutmeg
1/2 tsp. ginger
1 tsp. vanilla
3 c. all-purpose flour
1 egg
2 c. blueberries
Pinch of salt

Cream butter and sugar until fluffy; beat in molasses. Add milk, soda, nutmeg, ginger and vanilla; blend well. Add flour and egg; blend thoroughly. Fold in blueberries and salt; pour into greased 9 x 13 x 2-inch pan. Bake in preheated 350-degree oven for 35 minutes or until gingerbread tests done.

Gladys A. Ridley, WAC Chm.
Mausam Lake Grange
Springvale, Maine

EGGLESS GINGERBREAD

1 c. sugar
1/2 c. butter

1 c. dark molasses
1 c. sour cream
3 3/4 c. flour
1 tbsp. ginger
1 tsp. cinnamon
1/2 tsp. cloves
1/2 tsp. nutmeg
1 1/2 tsp. soda

Cream sugar and butter together. Add molasses and sour cream; blend well. Add flour and spices. Combine soda with 2 tablespoons hot water; add to flour mixture. Beat at high speed for 2 minutes. Pour into greased muffin tins. Bake in preheated 400-degree oven for 15 to 20 minutes or until cupcakes test done. May be baked in 9 x 13 x 2-inch pan, if desired.

Edith Rogers, Master
Floris Grange No. 749
Herndon, Virginia

HEIDELBURG CAKE

1 c. seedless raisins
1 1/2 tsp. soda
2 c. sugar
3 eggs
1 c. cooking oil
1 tsp. vanilla
3 c. flour
1/2 tsp. salt
1 c. chopped walnuts

Bring 1 1/2 cups water and raisins to boil in small saucepan; add soda. Cool. Combine sugar, eggs, oil and vanilla; beat well. Sift flour with salt; add to egg mixture. Stir in raisins and walnuts. Pour mixture into 10-inch greased tube pan. Bake at 375 degrees for 1 hour or until cake tests done.

Isabel Carter, Overseer
Solid Rock Grange No. 502
Freeport, Maine

GUMDROP CAKE

1/2 lb. seedless raisins
1/2 lb. chopped dates
1 tbsp. soda
1 c. lard
1/2 tsp. salt
2 c. sugar

1 tsp. cinnamon
1 tsp. allspice
1 tsp. cloves
1 tsp. baking powder
4 c. flour
1 c. spiced gumdrops
1 c. chopped walnuts

Combine raisins, dates and soda with 2 cups water in saucepan. Bring to a boil; cook over medium heat until liquid is reduced by half. Stir in lard and 1 cup water; remove from heat. Cool to room temperature. Sift salt, sugar, cinnamon, allspice, cloves, baking powder and flour together into large bowl. Stir in date mixture, blending thoroughly. Dredge gumdrops and walnuts in a small amount of flour; fold into batter. Pour into tube pan. Decorate top of cake with additional gumdrops and walnuts, if desired. Bake at 275 degrees for 2 hours and 30 minutes or until cake tests done.

Mrs. Carrie Baumbarger
Providence Grange No. 2572
Grand Rapids, Ohio

HICKORY NUT CAKE

3/4 c. butter
1 1/2 c. shortening
2 c. sugar
4 eggs, separated
1 1/2 tsp. vanilla
1 1/2 tsp. baking powder
2 2/3 c. flour
1/2 tsp. salt
1 c. milk
1 c. finely chopped hickory nuts

Cream butter and shortening with sugar until light and fluffy; add egg yolks, beating well. Stir in vanilla. Sift together baking powder, flour and salt. Add alternately with milk to sugar mixture, blending thoroughly. Fold in hickory nuts. Beat egg whites until stiff peaks form; fold into batter. Pour into 2 large greased and floured layer cake pans. Bake in preheated 350-degree oven for 35 minutes or until cake tests done. Cool on wire racks; frost as desired.

Marie L. Wagner, Eco. Chm.
Eno Grange No. 2080
Bidwell, Ohio

JELLY ROLL

1 c. sugar
5 eggs
1/2 tsp. salt
1 1/2 c. flour
1/2 tsp. baking powder
1 tsp. vanilla

Combine sugar, eggs and salt in mixer bowl. Beat at high speed with electric mixer for 15 minutes. Sift flour and baking powder together; fold into egg mixture. Stir in vanilla. Spread batter evenly in greased and floured 12 x 18 x 1/2-inch cookie sheet. Bake in a preheated 375-degree oven for 12 minutes. Turn out on sugared towel; roll up as for jelly roll. Cool well. Unroll; spread with desired jelly or frosting. Roll up again. May be filled with ice cream and frozen.

Thelma Wilson
Mica Flats Grange No. 436
Coeur d'Alene, Idaho

OLD-FASHIONED JAM CAKE

1 1/3 c. (packed) brown sugar
3/4 c. shortening
3 eggs, well beaten
3 c. flour
1 1/2 tsp. soda
1 1/2 tsp. salt
1 tsp. cinnamon
1 tsp. cloves
1 tsp. allspice
1 c. buttermilk
1 1/2 tsp. vanilla
1 c. jam

Cream brown sugar and shortening in large mixer bowl until fluffy; beat in eggs. Sift flour, soda, salt, cinnamon, cloves and allspice together; add to egg mixture, alternately with buttermilk, beating well after each addition. Stir in vanilla and jam; pour into 3 greased layer cake pans. Bake in preheated 350-degree oven for 30 to 35 minutes or until cake tests done. Cool for 5 minutes; remove from pans. Frost as desired.

Mrs. Opal Trimble, Treas.
Union Grange No. 1505
Beaver, Ohio

STRAWBERRY JAM CAKE

1 1/2 c. sugar
3/4 c. shortening
3 eggs
1/2 tsp. soda
1/2 c. sour milk
2 c. flour
1 tsp. nutmeg
1 tsp. cinnamon
1 tsp. cloves
1 c. strawberry jam

Cream sugar and shortening until light and fluffy; add eggs, one at a time, beating well after each addition. Dissolve soda in sour milk; add to egg mixture. Sift flour, nutmeg, cinnamon and cloves together. Add to egg mixture gradually, beating thoroughly. Stir in jam. Pour into 2 greased and floured 9-inch layer cake pans. Bake in preheated 375-degree oven for 30 minutes or until cake tests done. Cool on wire racks; frost as desired.

Mrs. Nellore Rice, Master
Terre Haute Grange No. 2480
Urbana, Ohio

TEXAS JAM CAKE

1 1/2 c. sugar
1 1/2 c. butter
6 eggs
2 c. jam
Flour
1 tsp. cinnamon
1 tsp. nutmeg
2 tsp. baking powder
1 c. sour milk
1 tsp. soda
2 c. chopped nuts
1 lb. chopped dates
1 c. raisins
1 c. milk

Cream 1 cup sugar with 1 cup butter until light and fluffy. Add eggs, one at a time, beating well after each addition; beat in jam. Sift 4 cups flour with cinnamon, nutmeg and baking powder; add to egg mixture, blending well. Combine sour milk and soda; beat into flour mixture. Mix well. Pour batter into four 8-inch layer cake pans. Bake in preheated 350-degree oven for 25 to 30 minutes or until cake tests done. Cool on wire racks. Combine remaining sugar and butter with 2 tablespoons flour, nuts, dates, raisins and milk in saucepan; mix well. Bring to a boil over medium heat; boil, stirring constantly, until thickened. Beat well until dates are dissolved and mixture is of spreading consistency. Spread between layers and over top and side of cake. Age for 2 days before serving.

James H. Kiles, Texas State Master
Leon Valley Grange No. 1581
San Antonio, Texas

MAPLE-NUT CAKE

1/2 c. shortening
1 c. sugar
2 eggs
1 tsp. vanilla
1/4 tsp. maple flavoring
2 c. sifted flour
1/2 tsp. salt
2 1/2 tsp. baking powder
3/4 c. milk
1/2 c. nuts, chopped

Cream shortening and sugar together until fluffy. Beat in eggs, one at a time, beating well after each addition. Stir in flavorings. Sift flour, salt and baking powder together. Add to creamed mixture alternately with milk. Fold in nuts. Spoon batter into 2 layer cake pans. Bake in a preheated 350-degree oven for 30 to 40 minutes or until cake tests done.

Viola Stanley
Wonder Grange
Medway, Maine

EASY OATMEAL CAKE

1 c. quick-cooking oatmeal
1 c. sugar
1 1/2 c. (firmly packed) brown sugar
1/2 c. shortening
2 eggs
1 1/2 c. flour
1/2 tsp. salt
1 tsp. soda
1 tsp. cinnamon
1 1/2 tsp. vanilla
1 c. chopped nuts
6 tbsp. butter
1/3 c. canned milk
1/2 c. coconut

Pour 1 1/2 cups boiling water over oatmeal; mix well. Cool. Cream sugar, 1 cup brown sugar, shortening and eggs until light and fluffy; stir in oatmeal mixture. Blend thoroughly. Sift flour with salt, soda and cinnamon; add to oatmeal mixture. Stir in 1 teaspoon vanilla and 1/2 cup nuts; mix well. Pour into greased 13 x 9 x 2-inch pan. Bake in preheated 350-degree oven for 35 minutes or until cake tests done. Combine butter, remaining brown sugar, nuts, vanilla, milk and coconut in small saucepan over medium heat. Cook, stirring constantly, for 5 minutes or until thickened. Spread topping over warm cake.

Mrs. Kenneth Livengood, Sec.
Milford Grange No. 1744
Berlin, Pennsylvania

CHOCOLATE-OATMEAL CAKE

1 c. quick-cooking oats
1/2 c. soft butter or margarine
1 c. sugar
1 c. (packed) brown sugar
1 tsp. vanilla
2 eggs
1 1/2 c. all-purpose flour
1 tsp. soda
1/2 tsp. salt
3 tbsp. cocoa

Pour 1 1/3 cups boiling water over oats; stir well. Let stand for 20 minutes. Cream butter, sugar and brown sugar until light and fluffy. Beat in vanilla and eggs; blend thoroughly. Beat in oats mixture. Sift dry ingredients; beat into sugar mixture until well blended. Pour into greased 9-inch square pan. Bake in preheated 350-degree oven for 50 minutes or until cake tests done. Remove from pan; cool on wire rack.

Doris Southard, Sec.
Lysander Grange No. 1391
Cato, New York

RAISIN-OATMEAL CAKE

1 c. quick-cooking oatmeal
1 c. margarine
2 c. sugar
1 c. (packed) brown sugar
3 eggs
1/2 c. raisins
1 c. chopped nuts
1 1/2 c. sifted flour
1 tsp. soda
1/2 tsp. baking powder
1/2 tsp. salt
1/4 c. canned milk
1 c. coconut
1 tsp. vanilla

Pour 1 1/2 cups boiling water over oatmeal and 1/2 cup margarine; cool for 20 minutes. Add 1 cup sugar, brown sugar, 2 well-beaten eggs, raisins and 1/2 cup nuts; blend well. Sift together flour, soda, baking powder and salt; add to oatmeal mixture, blending thoroughly. Pour into 9 x 13 x 2-inch greased pan. Bake in preheated 350-degree oven for 35 minutes or until cake tests done. Combine remaining egg, sugar, nuts and margarine in small saucepan; add milk, coconut and vanilla. Cook over medium heat, stirring constantly, for 2 minutes or until smooth and well blended. Pour over warm cake.

Mrs. Elmer W. Killette, Master's Wife
Tulare Grange No. 198
Tulare, California

LAZY DAISY OATMEAL CAKE

1 c. quick oats
3/4 c. shortening
1 c. sugar
1 1/2 c. (packed) brown sugar
1 tsp. vanilla
2 eggs, well beaten
1 1/2 c. all-purpose flour
1 tsp. soda
3/4 tsp. baking powder
1/2 tsp. salt
1/4 tsp. cinnamon
1/4 tsp. nutmeg
3 tbsp. milk
1/2 c. chopped pecans
3/4 c. coconut

Pour 1 1/4 cups boiling water over oats; cool. Cream 1/2 cup shortening with sugar and 1 cup brown sugar until fluffy; add vanilla and eggs, blending thoroughly. Sift dry ingredients; add with oats mixture to egg mixture. Mix well; pour into greased and floured 13 x 9 x 2-inch pan. Bake in preheated 350-degree oven for 50 minutes or until cake tests done. Combine remaining shortening and brown sugar with milk, pecans and coconut; blend well. Spread over cake. Broil 4 to 6 inches from source of heat for 3 to 4 minutes; watch carefully.

Gertrude Failor, Home Ec. Chm.
Pleasant Run Grange No. 418
Lyndon, Kansas

MANDARIN ORANGE CAKE

1 c. flour
1 c. sugar
1 tsp. soda
1 egg
1   11-oz. can mandarin oranges, drained
Pinch of salt
3/4 c. (packed) brown sugar
2 1/2 tbsp. butter
2 1/2 tbsp. cream

Combine flour, sugar, soda, egg, oranges and salt in large mixing bowl; blend well. Pour into 8 x 11-inch well-greased pan. Bake in preheated 350-degree oven for 30 minutes. Poke holes generously in warm cake with fork. Combine brown sugar, butter and cream in small saucepan; cook, stirring constantly, until sugar is dissolved. Pour over cake. Bake for about 2 minutes longer or until topping is bubbly. Serve with whipped topping, if desired.

Mrs. Sadie E. Fisher, Lady Asst.
Pine Lake Grange No. 1044
La Porte, Indiana

FRESH ORANGE LAYER CAKE

2 1/4 c. sifted flour
1 1/2 c. sugar
2 tsp. baking powder
1/4 tsp. soda
1 tsp. salt

1/2 c. shortening
Grated rind of 1 orange
1/4 c. unstrained orange juice
3/4 c. water or milk
2 eggs

Sift flour, sugar, baking powder, soda and salt together into large bowl. Add shortening and orange rind. Combine orange juice and water; add 2/3 of the mixture to dry ingredients. Beat with electric mixer on medium speed for 2 minutes. Add remaining liquid and eggs. Beat for 2 minutes longer. Pour into 2 greased and floured layer cake pans. Bake in preheated 350-degree oven for 30 minutes or until cake tests done. Remove from pans; cool on wire racks.

Filling and Frosting

2 1/2 tbsp. flour
1/2 c. milk
1/4 c. shortening
1/4 c. butter
1/2 c. sugar
1/4 tsp. salt
1/2 tsp. vanilla
1/2 c. coarsely chopped nuts
Confectioners' sugar, sifted

Blend flour and milk gradually in small saucepan. Cook over medium heat, stirring constantly, for 10 minutes or until thick paste forms; cool to lukewarm. Cream shortening, butter, sugar and salt together; add flour mixture. Beat with rotary beater until fluffy. Fold in vanilla and nuts. Spread 1/3 of the filling between layers. Add about 1 cup confectioners' sugar to remaining filling; blend thoroughly. Frost top and side of cake.

Arline M. Lyman, Overseer
Amherst Grange No. 16
Amherst, Massachusetts

FANCY ORANGE CAKE

1 lg. orange
1 c. seedless raisins
Walnuts
2 c. sifted flour
1 tsp. soda
1 tsp. salt

1 1/3 c. sugar
1/2 c. shortening
1 c. milk
2 eggs
1 tsp. cinnamon

Grind orange, raisins and 1/3 cup walnuts; set aside, reserving juice. Sift flour, soda, salt and sugar together; add shortening and 3/4 cup milk. Beat for 2 minutes or until blended thoroughly. Add eggs, one at a time, beating well after each addition; add remaining milk. Beat for 2 minutes longer; fold in orange mixture. Pour into well greased 13 x 9 x 2-inch pan. Bake in preheated 350-degree oven for 40 to 50 minutes or until cake tests done. Sprinkle reserved juice over warm cake. Combine remaining sugar, cinnamon and 1/4 cup chopped walnuts; sprinkle over cake.

Marion Haggerty, S and H Chm.
Halsey Valley Grange No. 1318
Spencer, New York

THRIFT POUND CAKE

3 c. sifted all-purpose flour
1/2 tsp. soda
1/2 tsp. baking powder
3/4 tsp. salt
1 c. butter or shortening
2 c. sugar
4 eggs
1 tsp. vanilla
1 tsp. lemon juice
1 c. buttermilk

Sift flour, soda, baking powder and salt together. Combine butter and sugar in large mixer bowl; cream with electric mixer until fluffy. Add eggs, one at a time, beating well after each addition. Beat in vanilla and lemon juice. Add dry ingredients to creamed mixture alternately with buttermilk. Beat for about 3 minutes. Spoon batter into large tube pan. Bake in a preheated 350-degree oven for 1 hour and 10 minutes or until cake tests done. One teaspoon grated lemon rind may be substituted for lemon juice.

Mrs. Byron Brumback, Sec.
Middletown Grange No. 761
Middletown, Virginia

POUND CAKE

3 1/2 c. cake flour
1 tsp. baking powder
1/2 tsp. salt
1/4 tsp. mace
1 3/4 c. butter
2 c. superfine sugar
8 eggs
1 tsp. vanilla extract
1/2 tsp. almond extract
1/2 tsp. lemon extract

Sift flour; measure, then sift twice with baking powder, salt and mace. Cream butter until light and fluffy. Add sugar slowly, beating rapidly; beat until butter mixture resembles whipped cream. Add eggs, one at a time, beating well after each addition. Stir in half the flour. Add extracts and remaining flour; mix by hand or at lowest speed on electric mixer. Pour batter into 2 greased 9 x 5 x 4-inch pans or one 10 x 4-inch tube cake pan. Cut through the thick batter several times with a knife to break air bubbles. Bake in preheated oven at 325 degrees for 1 hour to 1 hour 10 minutes. Top may have a rough crack. Remove from pan immediately; let cool on cake rack.

PECAN POUND CAKE

1 c. shortening
1 1/2 c. sugar
2 tbsp. milk
5 eggs
2 c. flour
1/2 tsp. mace
1 tsp. salt
3/4 c. chopped pecans, toasted
2 tsp. lemon juice
1 tsp. grated lemon rind

Cream shortening and sugar together until fluffy; stir in milk, mixing well. Add eggs, one at a time, beating well after each addition. Sift flour, mace and salt together; add to creamed mixture, blending well. Stir 1/2 cup pecans into batter; add lemon juice and rind. Spoon batter into greased 9-inch tube pan; sprinkle with remaining pecans. Bake in a preheated 325-degree oven for 1 hour and 25 minutes or until cake tests done. Cool for 5 minutes; remove from pan.

Pearl Estabrook, Pomona
Bolton Grange No. 142 P of H
Bolton, Massachusetts

NEVER-FAIL POUND CAKE

1 1/2 c. sugar
1 c. butter
4 eggs
Pinch of salt
1/2 c. milk
2 c. flour
2 tsp. baking powder
1 tsp. vanilla

Combine all ingredients in a large mixer bowl; bring to room temperature. Beat with electric mixer at medium speed for 15 minutes. Spoon batter into greased and floured tube pan. Bake in a preheated 325-degree oven for 1 hour or until cake tests done.

Marion Altemus, CWA Chm.
Rocksburgh Grange No. 116
Phillipsburg, New Jersey

COCONUT POUND CAKE

1 c. margarine
2/3 c. shortening
3 c. sugar
5 eggs
3 c. flour
1 tsp. baking powder
1/2 tsp. salt
1 c. milk
1 4-oz. can flaked coconut
1 tsp. coconut flavoring
1/2 tsp. vanilla

Cream margarine, shortening and sugar together until fluffy. Add eggs, one at a time, beating well after each addition. Sift flour, baking powder and salt together. Add dry ingredients to creamed mixture alternately with milk; mix well. Stir in coconut, coconut flavoring and vanilla. Spoon batter into large greased and floured tube pan. Bake in a preheated 325-degree oven for 1 hour and 15 minutes or until cake tests done.

Ann Schaad, Lecturer, WAC
Waterford Grange No. 231
Waterford, Ohio

SPECIAL PRUNE CAKE

1 c. sugar
3/4 c. butter or shortening
3 eggs
3 tbsp. sour cream
1 tsp. salt
2 tsp. soda
2 tsp. cinnamon
1 tsp. allspice
2 c. flour
1 c. prune juice
1 c. cooked chopped prunes

Cream sugar and butter until light and fluffy; add eggs, one at a time, beating well after each addition. Beat in sour cream. Sift dry ingredients; add to egg mixture alternately with prune juice, blending well. Fold in prunes; pour into 9 x 13 x 2-inch pan. Bake at 350 degrees for 45 minutes or until cake tests done.

Filling

2 eggs
2 tbsp. butter
1 c. sugar
1 c. chopped prunes
1/4 tsp. salt
1/2 c. sour cream

Combine eggs, butter, sugar, prunes and salt in medium saucepan; blend well. Cook, stirring constantly, until mixture is heated through and thickened; stir in sour cream. Blend well. Spread between layers of Special Prune Cake. Top with frosting, if desired.

Clarice Johnson, Lecturer
Fairfield Grange No. 720
Salem, Oregon

SOUR CREAM-SPICE CAKE

2 c. flour
1 1/2 c. (packed) brown sugar
1 1/4 tsp. soda
1 tsp. baking powder
1/2 tsp. salt
2 tsp. cinnamon
3/4 tsp. cloves
1/2 tsp. nutmeg
1/4 c. butter or margarine
1/4 c. shortening
2 eggs
1 c. sour cream
1 c. chopped raisins
1/2 c. chopped walnuts

Combine all ingredients with 1/2 cup water in large mixer bowl; blend at low speed for 1 minute. Beat at high speed for 3 minutes. Pour mixture into greased 9 x 13 x 2-inch pan. Bake in preheated 350-degree oven for 40 to 45 minutes or until cake tests done. May be baked in 2 layer cake pans for 30 to 35 minutes.

Mrs. Diane Doyle
Holland Grange No. 1023
Holland, New York

WONDER SPICE CAKE

1 1/2 c. flour
1 c. sugar
1 tsp. soda
1/2 tsp. salt
1 tsp. cinnamon
1 tsp. nutmeg
1/2 tsp. cloves
6 tbsp. oil
1 tbsp. vinegar
1 tsp. lemon extract

Sift dry ingredients together into large mixing bowl. Stir in oil, vinegar, lemon extract and 1 cup water; blend well. Pour into greased 9 x 13 x 2-inch pan. Bake at 350 degrees for 45 to 55 minutes or until cake tests done.

Mary Avery, Master
South Barre Grange No. 467
Barre, Vermont

NEW MAGIC SPICE CAKE

2 1/4 c. sifted flour
1 c. sugar
1 tsp. baking powder
3/4 tsp. soda
1 tsp. salt
3/4 tsp. cloves
3/4 tsp. cinnamon
3/4 c. (packed) brown sugar
3/4 c. shortening
1 c. buttermilk or sour milk
3 eggs

Sift flour, sugar, baking powder, soda, salt, cloves and cinnamon together into large mixer bowl. Add brown sugar, shortening, and buttermilk; beat at medium speed for 2 minutes. Add eggs; beat 2 minutes longer. Pour batter into 2 greased layer cake pans. Bake at 350 degrees for 30 to 35 minutes or until cake tests done. Cool; frost as desired.

Arline M. Lyman, Overseer
Amherst Grange No. 16
Amherst, Massachusetts

FOUR-EGG SPONGE CAKE

4 eggs, separated
1/2 tsp. salt
1 1/2 c. sugar
1 tsp. vanilla
1 1/2 c. sifted flour
1/2 tsp. cream of tartar

Beat egg yolks with 1/4 teaspoon salt in large mixer bowl until light and lemony. Add 2 tablespoons cold water; beat for 1 minute longer. Add 1/2 cup hot water; beat for 5 minutes longer. Beat in sugar gradually; stir in vanilla. Beat until light and fluffy; blend in flour gently. Beat egg whites until frothy; add cream of tartar and remaining salt. Beat until stiff peaks form; fold into flour mixture. Pour into large tube pan. Bake in preheated 325-degree oven for 1 hour or until cake tests done. Invert pan; cool for 20 minutes. Remove cake from pan; cool completely. Yield: 10 to 12 servings.

Mate L. Bradley, Sec.
Floris Grange No. 749
Herndon, Virginia

NEVER-FAIL SPONGE CAKE

4 eggs, separated
1/2 tsp. lemon extract
Pinch of salt
1 c. sugar
3/4 c. flour
1 1/2 tbsp. cornstarch
1/2 tsp. baking powder

Beat egg yolks with 3 tablespoons cold water; add lemon extract and salt. Beat until thick and lemony. Add 1/2 cup sugar gradually, beating for 2 minutes longer. Add flour, cornstarch and baking powder; blend thoroughly. Beat egg whites until frothy; add remaining sugar, beating until stiff peaks form. Fold egg whites into batter gently; pour into large tube pan. Bake in preheated 350-degree oven for 30 to 40 minutes or until cake tests done.

Nellie M. Hill, Master
Kezar Lake Grange No. 440
North Lovell, Maine

REFRIGERATOR SPONGE CAKE

4 eggs, separated
1 1/2 c. sugar
1 tsp. vanilla
1 1/2 c. sifted flour
1 1/2 tsp. baking powder

Beat egg yolks, adding sugar gradually, until light and fluffy. Add vanilla and 1/2 cup water; beat until mixed thoroughly. Sift flour with baking powder; add to egg mixture gradually, beating well after each addition. Beat egg whites until stiff peaks form; fold into batter. Grease bottoms of two 8-inch layer cake pans; pour batter into pans. Bake in preheated 375-degree oven for 25 minutes. Remove from pans; cool on wire racks.

French Chocolate Filling

3/4 c. butter
1 c. confectioners' sugar, sifted
3 eggs, separated
4 oz. bitter chocolate, melted
1 tsp. vanilla

Cream butter with confectioners' sugar until light and fluffy; add egg yolks, one at a time, beating well after each addition. Beat in chocolate and vanilla. Beat egg whites until stiff peaks form. Fold into chocolate mixture until well blended. Split cooled cake layers; spread filling between layers. Chill for several hours before serving.

Mrs. D. Vincent Andrews, Sec.
Florida State Grange
Sarasota, Florida

TRIPLE DELIGHT CAKE

1 3/4 c. sugar
3/4 c. shortening
3 eggs
3 c. flour
4 tsp. baking powder
1 tsp. salt
1 1/4 c. milk
1 tsp. vanilla
1 tbsp. strawberry jam
1/4 tsp. cinnamon
1/8 tsp. ground cloves
1/8 tsp. allspice
1 sq. bitter chocolate, melted
1/4 tsp. soda

Cream sugar and shortening together until fluffy. Add eggs, one at a time, beating well after each addition. Sift flour, baking powder and salt together 3 times. Add flour mixture to creamed mixture alternately with milk. Stir in vanilla. Spoon 1/3 of the batter into a greased and floured 9-inch cake pan. Divide remaining batter into separate bowls. Add jam, cinnamon, cloves and allspice to batter in one bowl. Spoon spiced batter into another greased and floured 9-inch cake pan. Add melted chocolate, 1 tablespoon additional sugar, soda and 1 tablespoon hot water to remaining batter. Mix well. Spoon chocolate mixture into third greased and floured 9-inch cake pan. Bake in a preheated 350-degree oven for 30 to 35 minutes or until cake tests done. Assemble cake with chocolate layer on bottom, spice layer over chocolate layer and plain layer on top. Frost as desired.

Mrs. Eugenia V. Smith, LAS HE Chm.
Contoocook Grange No. 216
Contoocook, New Hampshire

STRAWBERRY MERINGUE COMPANY CAKE

1 10-oz. package frozen strawberries
1/2 c. butter
1 1/2 c. sugar
4 eggs, separated
1 tsp. vanilla
3/4 c. flour
1 tsp. (heaping) baking powder
1/4 c. milk
1 c. whipped cream

Drain strawberries well and set aside. Cream butter and 1/2 cup sugar until fluffy; add beaten egg yolks and vanilla, mixing well. Sift flour and baking powder together; add to creamed mixture alternately with milk. Batter will be thin. Spoon batter into 2 layer cake pans. Beat egg whites until soft peaks form. Add remaining sugar gradually, beating until stiff peaks form. Spoon meringue over cake batter in pans. Bake in 350-degree oven for 30 minutes. Place 1 cake layer, meringue side down, on serving platter. Cover with whipped cream and strawberries. Place remaining cake layer, meringue side up, over whipped cream layer. Chill well before serving.

Mrs. Elizabeth P. Coleman
Chm., Home and Comm. Serv. Com.
Chesterfield Grange No. 83
Chesterfield, Massachusetts

WHITE CAKE DELIGHT

2 1/2 c. sugar
1/2 c. shortening
2 1/2 c. flour
4 eggs, separated
1/2 tsp. salt
1 tsp. vanilla
2 tsp. baking powder
Grated rind and juice of 1 lemon
2 1/2 tbsp. cornstarch
1 No. 2 can crushed pineapple
1/2 c. lime juice
1 c. sweetened condensed milk

Cream 1 1/2 cups sugar and shortening until light and fluffy. Sift flour 3 times; reserve 1/2 cup flour. Add flour alternately with 1 1/3 cups water, beating well after each addition. Stir in salt and vanilla. Combine reserved flour with baking powder. Beat into sugar mixture. Beat egg whites until stiff peaks form; fold into batter. Line bottom of two 9-inch layer cake pans with heavy brown paper. Pour batter into prepared pans. Bake in preheated 350-degree oven for 30 minutes or until cake tests done. Remove from pans; cool on wire racks. Combine lemon rind, remaining sugar and cornstarch with 1/2 cup cold water; blend well. Beat egg yolks until thick and lemony. Combine egg yolks and cornstarch mixture in large heavy saucepan; blend in 2 cups water and lemon juice. Cook, stirring constantly, over medium heat, until smooth and thickened and mixture coats spoon; remove from heat. Cool to room temperature. Spread filling between layers. Drain pineapple thoroughly; combine with lime juice and condensed milk in small bowl, stirring until mixture is thickened. Spread over top and side of cake.

Mrs. Nedra Shepard
Sec., Colorado State Grange
Maple Grove Grange No. 154
Wheat Ridge, Colorado

WHIPPED CREAM CAKE

2 c. cake flour, sifted
1 1/2 c. sugar
2 tsp. baking powder
1/2 tsp. salt
1 c. heavy cream
3 egg whites
1/4 tsp. salt
1 tsp. vanilla or almond extract

Sift flour with sugar, baking powder and salt. Whip cream until soft peaks form. Beat egg whites and salt until stiff peaks form; fold cream into eggs. Fold in 1/2 cup water and vanilla. Fold dry ingredients into whipped cream mixture gradually. Pour batter into greased 9-inch tube pan. Bake at 375 degrees for 45 minutes or until cake tests done. Frost as desired.

Jeanne R. Sabin
Sherburne Grange No. 1400
Sherburne, New York

ANGEL FOOD CAKE WITH LEMON SAUCE

1 pkg. angel food cake mix
2 pkg. instant lemon pudding mix
1 pt. whipping cream, whipped

Prepare angel food cake according to package directions; let cool. Prepare lemon pudding according to package directions. Fold lemon pudding and whipped cream gently together. Slice cake; serve with Lemon Sauce.

Virginia Smith
Amherst Grange No. 16, Inc.
Westhampton, Massachusetts

BANANA-NUT LOAF

1 pkg. yellow cake mix
1/8 tsp. soda
2 eggs
1/3 c. water
1 c. mashed banana
1/3 c. nuts

Combine cake mix and soda in a mixing bowl. Beat eggs and water together well; add egg mixture to cake mix. Add banana and nuts, blending well. Spoon batter into 2 greased layer cake pans. Bake in a preheated 350-degree oven until cake tests done.

Lila M. Byerley, Rec. Sec.
Berryton Grange No. 1430
Berryton, Kansas

CHERRY DESSERT

2 cans cherry pie filling
1 pkg. white or yellow cake mix
1/2 c. chopped nuts
1/2 c. coconut
1/2 c. melted butter or margarine

Arrange pie filling in greased 8 x 14-inch baking dish. Sprinkle cake mix over filling. Sprinkle nuts, and coconut over cake mix. Pour butter over all. Bake at 350 degrees for 45 minutes. Apples, berries or other fruit may be used instead of cherries.

Ethel Diediker, Steward
Reseda Grange No. 703
Sepulveda, California

LEMON TUBE CAKE

1 pkg. lemon supreme cake mix
1 pkg. instant lemon pudding mix
4 eggs, slightly beaten
1 c. milk
1/2 c. salad oil

Combine cake mix and pudding mix in a mixing bowl. Blend eggs, milk and oil together, beating well. Pour egg mixture into cake mix mixture, blending well. Spoon batter into greased and floured tube pan. Bake in a preheated 350-degree oven for 45 minutes or until cake tests done. May glaze with confectioners' sugar and lemon juice icing, if desired.

Mrs. Vernon Merriman, Treas.
Paw Paw Grange No. 1884
Paw Paw, Illinois

SALLY'S HONEYMOON BEER CAKE

1 pkg. white cake mix
1 pkg. chocolate instant pudding mix
1/3 c. cooking oil
3 eggs
1 c. beer, at room temperature

Combine all ingredients in a large mixing bowl; beat at medium speed on electric mixer for 10 minutes. Pour into a 10-inch greased and floured tube pan. Bake at 350 degrees for 1 hour.

Wine Cream Frosting

1/4 c. butter
3 c. confectioners' sugar
1 egg
2 tsp. red wine
1/8 tsp. salt
2 tbsp. cream or milk

Cream butter until light; add 1 cup sugar, beating well. Add egg, wine, salt and cream. Beat until smooth. Add remaining sugar; beat until smooth and of spreading consistency. Cake may be served plain, if desired.

Viola Blake, Home Ec. Chm.
New Hampton Grange No. 123
New Hampton, New Hampshire

QUICKIE DESSERT

1 can pie filling
1 sm. package cake mix
1/2 c. melted butter or margarine
1/2 c. walnuts or pecans

Spread pie filling in greased 9-inch square pan. Sprinkle dry cake mix over filling. Drizzle butter over cake mix. Sprinkle walnuts on top. Bake at 350 degrees for 30 to 35 minutes. May be served with whipped cream.

Mrs. Wanda Honn
Exec. Com., Sec. & Treas. of CWA
Winchester Bay Grange No. 906
North Bend, Oregon

RHUBARB DESSERT CAKE

1 c. fresh sliced rhubarb
1 pkg. white cake mix
2 c. sugar
Dessert topping

Cut rhubarb into pieces; line the bottom of a loaf pan. Prepare cake mix according to package directions. Spoon batter over rhubarb. Combine 2 cups water and sugar in a saucepan; bring to a boil. Cook, stirring, until sugar is dissolved. Pour boiling mixture over cake batter. Do not stir. Bake in a preheated 350-degree oven for 35 to 40 minutes or until cake tests done. Cool; cut into squares. Serve with dessert topping.

Mrs. Vernon Merriman, Treas.
Paw Paw Grange No. 1884
Paw Paw, Illinois

TUTTI-FRUTTI CAKE

1 pkg. white or yellow cake mix
2 c. pineapple juice
1 pkg. vanilla pudding mix
2 bananas, chopped
1 c. miniature marshmallows
Maraschino cherries

Prepare cake mix according to package directions; pour into 2 large pans to about 1/2-inch depth. Bake according to directions. Layers will be thin. Pour 1 1/2 cups juice in saucepan; bring to a boil. Mix remaining juice with dry vanilla pudding; stir into hot juice. Cook, stirring, until blended. Remove from heat; cool. Add bananas and marshmallows. Cut cake into bars or squares. Serve with pudding mixture. Top with cherry. Equal portions of orange and pineapple juice may be used.

Agnes Stewart, Wife of State Sec.
Cadmus Grange
Meriden, Kansas

EASY BUTTER ICING

1/2 c. butter
1/2 c. vegetable shortening
2 2/3 c. confectioners' sugar
1 tsp. vanilla
1/4 c. evaporated milk

Combine all ingredients in mixer bowl. Beat at medium speed for 15 minutes or until smooth and of spreading consistency. May be refrigerated or frozen and rewhipped when ready to use.

Mrs. Doris Koenig, Past Lady Asst.
Steward, Pennsylvania State Grange
Central Grange No. 1650
Slatington, Pennsylvania

EASY FUDGE FROSTING

4 tbsp. butter
2 oz. bitter chocolate
1 c. sugar
1/4 tsp. salt
1/4 c. milk
1 tsp. vanilla

Melt butter and chocolate over low heat. Remove from heat; add sugar, salt and milk. Bring to a boil over high heat; boil for 1 minute. Remove from heat; add vanilla. Beat until of spreading consistency.

Helen Saunders, Master
Pleasant Valley Grange No. 136
West Bethel, Maine

MINUTE FUDGE FROSTING

1 1/2 c. sugar
2 tbsp. butter or margarine

2 tbsp. vegetable shortening
1 tbsp. light corn syrup
2 tbsp. milk
Pinch of salt
2 oz. bitter chocolate, melted
1 tsp. vanilla

Combine sugar, butter, shortening, corn syrup, milk, salt and chocolate in saucepan. Bring to a rolling boil; boil for 1 minute. Cool; add vanilla. Beat until of spreading consistency.

Katheryn Robinson, Sec.
Acorn Grange No. 418, Cushing, Maine
Thomaston, Maine

STRAWBERRY SWIRL FROSTING

2 egg whites
1 c. strawberry preserves
1 tsp. lemon juice
1 tbsp. strawberry gelatin

Beat egg whites until stiff peaks form. Heat preserves over low heat until bubbly; add lemon juice and gelatin. Pour gelatin mixture over beaten egg whites gradually, beating constantly, until mixture stands in peaks. Spread between layers and over sides and top of cake.

Mrs. Mildred E. Jones, CWA Sec.
Glen Avon Grange No. 591
Riverside, California

VANILLA FROSTING AND FILLING

1 pkg. instant vanilla pudding mix
1 c. milk
1/2 c. butter
1/2 c. shortening
1 c. powdered sugar
1/2 tsp. vanilla

Combine pudding mix and milk; let stand for 5 minutes. Cream butter, shortening and sugar until fluffy; stir in vanilla. Blend creamed mixture and pudding together; beat until light and fluffy. May be frozen.

Mrs. Stanley Michalek, Sec.
Fairfield Grange No. 720
Gervais, Oregon

MAPLE SYRUP FROSTING

1 1/2 c. maple syrup
2 egg whites
1/8 tsp. cream of tartar

Boil syrup until a thread forms when dropped from a spoon. Beat egg whites until stiff; add cream of tartar. Add syrup to beaten egg whites gradually, beating constantly until of spreading consistency. Spread on cake.

Mrs. Doris Sawyer, Home Ec. Aux. Member
White Mt. Grange
Littleton, New Hampshire

TOFFEE TOPPING

1/2 c. butter
2 c. confectioners' sugar
4 egg yolks
1 c. heavy cream, whipped
3 1/2 lg. toffee bars, crushed
1/4 c. ground nuts

Cream butter and confectioners' sugar until light and fluffy. Add egg yolks, one at a time, beating well after each addition. Fold in whipped cream until well blended; fold in toffee bars and nuts. Serve over cake.

Ruth Olson
Zimmerman, Minnesota

WHIPPED FROSTING

3 tbsp. flour
1/2 c. milk
3 tbsp. shortening
3 tbsp. butter
1/2 c. sugar

Blend flour in small amount of water until smooth. Combine flour mixture and milk in a double boiler. Cook, stirring constantly, until thickened. Cool. Cream shortening, butter and sugar until fluffy. Stir into cooled frosting, blending well. Beat until of spreading consistency.

Carol Crawford, Sec.
Paris Grange No. 1452
Sauquoit, New York

Puddings

Creamy, soft puddings — warm for a winter's evening or chilled for
a refreshing summer treat; quick and simple or festively elegant.
This chapter is filled with dreamy baked, boiled and steamed puddings
that may be tailored for any occasion or any season. They are delicious
plain; or you may add fruit, nuts, and a mound of whipped cream
to top them off.

Puddings are especially popular with children. Each soft, flavorful
mouthful feels so nice on the tongue and goes down so easily.
Why not stir up one of the luscious puddings in this chapter
to highlight your family's dinner tonight?

DEEP-DISH APPLE PUDDING

4 to 6 c. sliced apples
1/2 c. sugar
Cinnamon to taste
1/2 c. (firmly packed) brown sugar
1/2 c. melted butter
1 c. flour

Combine apples, sugar and cinnamon. Pour into buttered baking dish. Combine brown sugar, butter and flour; mix until crumbly. Spread over apples. Bake in 350-degree oven until apples are tender. Serve warm with cream.

Mrs. Clifford L. Smart
Women's Activity Com.
Bee Hive Grange No. 385
Wenatchee, Washington

JIFFY APPLE-LEMON PUDDING

1 pkg. lemon instant pudding mix
1 c. cold milk
1 c. canned applesauce
1/4 c. grated lemon rind

Combine pudding mix and milk in small bowl; beat for about 2 minutes. Add applesauce and lemon rind; beat until combined. Spoon into dessert glasses. Chill for about 5 minutes or until set. Garnish with whipped cream and maraschino cherries, if desired. Yield: 4 servings.

Mrs. Marion Judd, Master
Lake Harbor Grange No. 1185
Muskegon, Michigan

HOME-STYLE BLUEBERRY TAPIOCA PUDDING

3 tbsp. quick-cooking tapioca
1/3 c. (firmly packed) brown sugar
1/4 tsp. salt
2 eggs, separated
2 1/2 c. milk
1 tsp. vanilla
1/2 tsp. grated orange rind
4 tbsp. sugar
2 c. fresh blueberries, washed and
   drained

Combine tapioca, brown sugar and salt in saucepan. Beat egg yolks with milk; stir into tapioca mixture gradually. Cook, stirring constantly, until tapioca mixture starts to boil. Remove from heat; let cool. Stir in vanilla and grated orange rind. Beat egg whites until stiff; beat in sugar gradually. Reserve 1/2 cup egg whites; fold remaining egg whites into tapioca mixture. Fold in blueberries. Chill thoroughly before serving. Garnish with reserved egg whites and additional blueberries. Yield: 6 servings.

Photograph for this recipe on page 46.

BLUEBERRY PUDDING

2 c. blueberries
Juice of 1/2 lemon
1/2 tsp. cinnamon
1 3/4 c. sugar
3 tbsp. butter
1/2 c. milk
1 c. flour
1 tsp. baking powder
1/4 tsp. salt
1 tbsp. cornstarch

Line an 8-inch pan with blueberries. Combine lemon juice and cinnamon; sprinkle over berries. Mix 3/4 cup sugar and butter together. Add milk, flour, baking powder and salt. Spread over berries. Mix remaining sugar and cornstarch together; spread over batter. Pour 1 cup boiling water over mixture. Bake in a preheated 375-degree oven for 1 hour.

Nanci Allard, Ec. Com.
Elmwood Grange No. 314
Conway, New Hampshire

APPLE BREAD PUDDING

4 slices lightly toasted bread
1 1/2 c. skim milk, scalded
4 eggs
1 tsp. apple pie spice
Pinch of salt
5 tbsp. sugar
2 apples

Cut bread into small cubes; place in greased casserole. Add milk; let stand for 10 to 15 minutes. Beat eggs, spice, salt and sugar together; add to bread mixture. Peel apples; cut into cubes or thin slices. Stir into bread mixture. Bake in preheated 325-degree oven for 35 minutes or until mixture is set. Chill before serving.

Lucy M. Graham, Ceres
Lockport Grange No. 1262
Gasport, New York

LEMON BREAD PUDDING

2 c. stale bread crumbs
4 c. scalded milk
1/4 tsp. salt
1 c. sugar
1 tbsp. melted butter
Grated rind and juice of l lemon
3 eggs, separated
1 c. confectioners' sugar

Soak bread crumbs in milk until cool; add salt, sugar, butter and lemon rind. Beat egg yolks slightly; stir into bread crumb mixture. Pour into greased 12 x 8 x 2-inch baking dish. Bake at 325 degrees for 50 minutes or until set. Remove from oven; cool slightly. Beat egg whites until soft peaks form; add lemon juice and confectioners' sugar gradually, beating until stiff peaks form. Spread meringue over pudding, sealing edges; return to oven. Bake at 300 degrees for 20 minutes. Cool thoroughly before serving.

Mrs. Velma W. Hensel, CWA Com.
Jolly Grange No. 2656
New Matamoras, Ohio

EASY CHOCOLATE BREAD PUDDING

2 c. sugar
1 c. milk
2 c. bread cubes
1 c. raisins
1 beaten egg
1 tbsp. cocoa
1 tsp. cinnamon
1 tsp. soda
1/4 tsp. salt
Butter
1 c. cream
1 tsp. vanilla

Combine 1 cup sugar, milk, bread cubes, raisins, egg, cocoa, cinnamon, soda and salt in bowl; blend well. Turn into well-greased top of double boiler; dot with 1 tablespoon butter. Place over boiling water; steam, covered, for 1 hour and 30 minutes. Combine remaining sugar, 1/2 cup butter and cream in small saucepan; bring to a boil, stirring until smooth and blended. Stir in vanilla. Serve warm over pudding.

Mrs. George J. Lee, WAC, Sec.
Priest Lake Grange No. 447
Priest River, Idaho

QUICK CHOCOLATE BREAD PUDDING

1 1/2 slices lightly toasted bread, cubed
2 c. chocolate milk
3 eggs, beaten
Sugar to taste
1/4 tsp. cinnamon

Combine all ingredients in bowl; blend well. Pour into greased baking dish; set in pan of water. Bake at 350 degrees until knife inserted in center comes out clean.

Mary T. Hironymous
American River Grange No. 172
Sacramento, California

CARAMEL PUDDING

1 c. (packed) brown sugar
4 slices buttered bread, cubed
2 eggs, beaten
2 c. milk
1/2 tsp. salt
1/2 tsp. vanilla

Place brown sugar in double boiler. Add bread cubes; do not stir. Add eggs, milk, salt and vanilla. Pour over bread; do not stir. Cover; cook over low heat for 1 hour. Loosen edges with knife. Turn out into serving dish; sugar will be on top. Serve with whipped cream, if desired.

Pearl L. Briggs, CWA Chm.
Manteca Grange No. 507
Manteca, California

DELICIOUS DATE PUDDING

2 c. chopped dates
1 tsp. soda
1 tbsp. butter
1 1/2 c. sugar
1 egg
1 1/2 c. flour

Combine 1 cup dates and soda in small bowl; cover with 1 cup boiling water. Let stand for several minutes. Cream butter and 1 cup sugar; add egg. Beat until smooth; stir in date mixture. Beat in flour; mix well. Pour into 8-inch square pan. Bake at 350 degrees for 30 to 35 minutes. Combine remaining dates and sugar with 3/4 cup boiling water. Bring to a boil; cook, stirring constantly, until smooth. Pour over pudding. Whipped cream may be used for topping, if desired.

Mrs. Wanda Honn, Exec. Com., CWA Sec., Treas.
Winchester Bay Grange No. 906
North Bend, Oregon

MARY'S DATE PUDDING

1 c. (packed) brown sugar
2 c. sugar
Butter
1 c. flour
1 c. milk
1/3 tsp. salt
3 tsp. baking powder
1 tsp. vanilla
3/4 tsp. cinnamon
3/4 tsp. cocoa
1 c. chopped dates
1 c. chopped pecans

Combine brown sugar, 1 cup sugar and 2 cups water in small saucepan; bring to a boil, stirring until sugars are dissolved. Pour into greased 12 x 9 x 2-inch baking dish; dot generously with butter. Combine remaining ingredients in bowl; blend thoroughly. Pour over mixture in baking dish. Bake at 375 degrees for 35 minutes. Batter will rise to form crust. Serve with whipped cream, if desired.

Mrs. Howard H. Huck, Sec.
Hall of Fame Grange No. 2003
Kansas City, Kansas

RANCH PUDDING

2 c. (packed) brown sugar
2 tbsp. butter
1/2 c. milk
1 1/4 c. packaged biscuit mix
1 c. chopped dates or raisins
1/2 to 1 c. chopped nuts
1 tsp. vanilla

Combine 1 cup brown sugar, 2 1/2 cups water and butter in saucepan; boil for 5 minutes. Pour boiled mixture into 8-inch square pan. Combine remaining ingredients; spoon over boiled mixture. Bake in a preheated 350-degree oven for 30 to 45 minutes. Serve warm with whipped cream.

Mrs. Dale Wimp, Master's Wife, Treas.
Elbow Creek Grange No. 733
Visalia, California

CARAMEL DUMPLINGS

2 tbsp. butter
1 1/2 c. boiling water
1 1/2 c. (packed) brown sugar
1/8 tsp. salt

Combine all ingredients in 1 1/2-quart glass saucepan; boil for about 5 minutes.

Dough

1 1/4 c. flour
1 1/2 tsp. baking powder
1/3 c. sugar
1/8 tsp. salt
2 tbsp. butter
1/3 c. milk
1/2 tsp. vanilla

Sift flour, baking powder, sugar and salt together into large bowl; cut in butter. Add milk and vanilla; mix thoroughly. Drop by teaspoonfuls into boiling caramel sauce; cover tightly. Boil over low heat for 20 minutes. Serve immediately from saucepan. Yield: 5-6 servings.

Mate L. Bradley, Sec.
Floris Grange No. 749
Herndon, Virginia

ROAST PORK
WITH SAUERKRAUT AND APPLE

1 3 1/2-lb. pork loin roast
Onion salt to taste
Marjoram to taste
Pepper to taste
1 qt. drained sauerkraut
2 red apples, thinly sliced
1/2 c. apple brandy
1 tbsp. light brown sugar
2 tbsp. butter

Sprinkle pork with onion salt, marjoram and pepper; score fatty side. Secure on spit. Insert meat thermometer. Adjust spit about 8 inches from prepared coals, placing foil pan under pork to catch drippings. Roast for 15 to 20 minutes per pound or until meat thermometer registers 185 degrees. Place on heated serving platter; keep warm. Combine sauerkraut, apple slices, brandy, brown sugar and butter in skillet. Simmer, covered, for 5 minutes or until apples are tender. Spoon into serving dish. Garnish with additional apple slices and parsley. Serve with pork.

Photograph for this recipe on page 51.

FILBERT TORTE
WITH STRAWBERRY WHIPPED CREAM

Graham cracker crumbs
2 c. sugar
1/2 tsp. ground allspice
1 lb. filberts, ground
1 tsp. grated lemon peel
6 eggs, separated
1/4 tsp. salt
1 tbsp. light corn syrup
1 tsp. water
1 egg white, slightly beaten

Grease 9-inch 6 1/2-cup ring pan; sprinkle with graham cracker crumbs. Set aside. Mix sugar and allspice together; mix in filberts and lemon peel with tossing motion. Beat egg yolks until thick and lemon colored; blend into filbert mixture, working in well with hands. Beat egg whites until frothy; add salt. Beat until stiff but not dry; fold into filbert mixture. Turn into prepared ring pan. Bake at 350 degrees for 35 to 40 minutes or until cake tests done. Cool for 5 minutes. Loosen cake with spatula; turn out onto ungreased baking sheet. Blend corn syrup and water; brush over top of torte. Brush entire torte with egg white. Bake for 5 minutes longer. Cool; place torte on serving plate.

Strawberry Whipped Cream

2 pt. fresh strawberries
1 1/2 c. heavy cream
3 tbsp. kirsch

Slice strawberries, reserving 1 cup for garnish. Whip cream until stiff, adding kirsch gradually. Fold in sliced strawberries. Mound in center of torte; garnish with reserved strawberries.

Photograph for this recipe on page 51.

HOT POTATO SALAD WITH BACON

4 lb. pared potatoes, sliced
1/2 c. chopped onion
2/3 c. bacon drippings
1/2 c. vinegar
2 tbsp. chopped parsley
2 tsp. sugar
1 tsp. paprika
1/2 tsp. salt
1/4 tsp. pepper
12 slices fried bacon, crumbled

Cook potatoes in saucepan in 2 inches salted water until tender; drain. Saute onion in bacon drippings until tender; stir in vinegar, parsley, sugar, paprika, salt and pepper. Combine potatoes, bacon and onion mixture. Toss gently. Serve warm with pork roast and sauerkraut.

Photograph for this recipe on page 51.

GRILLED CHICKEN
WITH KRAUT RELISH

6 c. sauerkraut
1   4-oz. jar pimento
2 med. green peppers, chopped
2 med. onions, chopped
1/4 tsp. paprika
Freshly ground pepper to taste
1 clove of garlic, minced
1/2 c. melted butter
1/4 c. wine vinegar
1/2 c. (firmly packed) dark brown sugar
2 tbsp. Worcestershire sauce
2 tbsp. cornstarch
1/4 c. water
12 chicken legs with thighs

Drain the sauerkraut and reserve liquid. Drain the pimento and chop. Toss sauerkraut with green peppers, pimento, half the onions, paprika and pepper in a bowl and chill. Saute remaining onion and the garlic in butter in a saucepan until golden. Add the vinegar, sugar, Worcestershire sauce, pepper and reserved sauerkraut liquid and stir until sugar is melted. Bring to a boil over medium heat. Blend the cornstarch with water and stir into onion mixture. Boil for 30 seconds, stirring constantly, then remove from heat. Place chicken on grill 7 to 8 inches from source of heat; cook for 10 minutes. Brush with sauce and continue grilling for 10 minutes. Turn chicken and grill an additional 10 minutes or until done, brushing frequently with sauce to glaze. Serve kraut relish with grilled chicken.

Photograph for this recipe on page 52.

OLD-FASHIONED
STRAWBERRY SHORTCAKE

2 c. sifted all-purpose flour
4 tsp. baking powder
1/2 tsp. salt
1/2 tsp. cream of tartar
1/4 c. sugar
1/2 c. vegetable shortening
1/3 c. milk
1 egg
Butter
3 pt. fresh California strawberries,
    sliced and sweetened
Whipped cream

Sift flour, baking powder, salt, cream of tartar and sugar together. Cut in shortening until mixture resembles coarse meal. Combine milk with egg; stir into flour mixture with a fork until soft dough is formed. Turn out onto lightly floured board and pat or roll into 8-inch circle, 1/2 inch thick. Place on ungreased baking sheet. Bake in preheated 425-degree oven for 10 to 12 minutes or until golden brown. Split and spread butter on both halves. Pile strawberries and whipped cream between layers and on top. Yield: 8 servings.

Photograph for this recipe on page 52.

BROWN SUGAR DUMPLINGS

6 tbsp. butter
1/2 c. sugar
2 c. (heaping) flour
2 tsp. baking powder
1/2 c. milk
1 c. raisins
1 c. (packed) brown sugar
1 tbsp. vanilla

Cream 2 tablespoons butter with sugar until fluffy. Sift flour and baking powder together. Add flour mixture to creamed mixture alternately with milk. Stir in raisins. Combine 3 cups hot water, brown sugar, vanilla and remaining butter in saucepan. Bring to a boil. Drop dumpling mixture by spoonfuls into boiling sauce. Transfer dumplings and sauce to casserole. Bake in a preheated 400-degree oven for 15 to 20 minutes.

Beryl Hines, CWA
Rockemeka Grange No. 109
East Peru, Maine

LINCOLN'S AND LEE'S DUMPLINGS

1 c. (packed) brown sugar
1/2 c. butter
1 c. flour
1/2 c. sugar
1/2 c. chopped nuts
1/2 c. raisins
1/2 c. milk
1/2 tsp. baking powder
1/4 tsp. salt

Combine brown sugar, butter and 2 cups water in saucepan; bring to a boil. Cook, stirring constantly, until sugar is dissolved and sauce is blended. Combine flour, sugar, nuts, raisins, milk, baking powder and salt in bowl; blend well. Pour hot syrup into shallow baking dish. Drop batter by spoonfuls into hot syrup. Bake at 350 degrees for 20 to 30 minutes. Spoon syrup over dumplings. Serve with whipped cream or topping.

Mrs. Frank Conrad, Lecturer
University Grange No. 335
Lebanon, New Hampshire

MOLASSES-NUT PUDDING

1 pkg. yellow cake mix
1/2 c. butter or margarine, melted
4 eggs
1/2 c. molasses
1 c. light corn syrup
1 tsp. vanilla
1 c. chopped pecans

Reserve 2/3 cup cake mix. Combine remaining cake mix, butter and 1 slightly beaten egg, mixing well. Spread in 13 x 9-inch pan. Bake in a preheated 350-degree oven for 15 minutes. Combine molasses, syrup, vanilla, remaining beaten eggs and reserved cake mix; mix well. Spoon filling into baked crust; sprinkle with pecans. Bake for 30 minutes longer.

Frances Hirsch, CWA
Quillisascut Grange No. 372
Rice, Washington

ORANGE-RHUBARB PUDDING

4 c. diced rhubarb
1 c. sugar
Flour
1/4 c. orange juice
1 tsp. baking powder
1/4 tsp. salt
1 tbsp. grated orange rind
1/4 c. shortening
1 egg, well beaten
1/3 c. milk

Cover rhubarb with boiling water; let stand for 5 minutes. Drain rhubarb thoroughly; place in greased 8-inch square glass baking dish. Combine sugar with 1 tablespoon flour; sprinkle over rhubarb. Pour orange juice evenly over all. Sift 1 1/4 cups flour with baking powder and salt into medium bowl; stir in orange rind. Cut in shortening. Combine egg with milk; mix well. Add egg mixture to dry ingredients, stirring just to moisten. Spread evenly over rhubarb mixture. Bake at 375 degrees for 35 minutes or until top is golden. Yield: 5-6 servings.

Mrs. Floyd Milburn, Women's Act. Chm.
Clear Creek Grange No. 233
DeSoto, Kansas

FRESH RHUBARB PUDDING

2 c. diced rhubarb
2 c. bread cubes
1 1/2 c. sugar
2 eggs, well beaten
2 c. milk

Combine all ingredients in bowl; blend well. Pour into buttered baking dish. Bake at 350 degrees for 45 minutes. Top may be sprinkled with mixture of cinnamon and sugar before baking, if desired.

Guynetha Alexander, WAC Chm.
Hopewell Grange No. 518
Everson, Washington

PUMPKIN-BUTTERSCOTCH PUDDING

1/3 c. butter
1 1/2 c. graham cracker crumbs
1   4-oz. package butterscotch
     pudding mix
1/4 c. (packed) brown sugar
1 c. milk
1 c. cooked pumpkin
3/4 tsp. cinnamon
1/4 tsp. ginger
1/4 tsp. nutmeg
1 tsp. vanilla
1 pkg. dessert topping mix
1 c. miniature marshmallows
2 tbsp. powdered sugar

Combine butter and cracker crumbs, mixing well. Reserve some of the crumb mixture for topping. Press remaining crumb mixture into bottom of 9 x 13-inch pan. Combine pudding mix, brown sugar, milk, pumpkin, spices and vanilla in saucepan. Bring to a boil. Remove from heat; cool. Pour pumpkin mixture over prepared crust. Prepare dessert topping mix according to package directions. Combine topping, marshmallows and powdered sugar, spoon over pumpkin filling. Sprinkle with reserved crumbs. Chill for 24 hours.

Mrs. John E. Jones, WA Chm.
Amity Grange No. 1540
Washington, Pennsylvania

OLD-FASHIONED CREAMY RICE PUDDING

4 tbsp. uncooked rice
3 pt. milk
6 tbsp. sugar

Pour rice into lightly buttered casserole. Add milk and sugar; stir to mix well. Bake at 350 degrees for 10 minutes. Reduce temperature to 275 degrees; bake for 2 hours longer. Fold skim back into pudding as it forms. Add hot milk, if needed. Sprinkle with nutmeg, if desired.

Edrice McLean, CWA Chm., Sec.
Freshwater Grange No. 499
Eureka, California

QUICK AND EASY LEMON PUDDING

1 pkg. lemon pudding and pie filling mix
2 egg whites

Prepare pudding according to package directions; cool. Beat egg whites until stiff peaks form. Fold meringue into pudding; spoon into serving dishes. Yield: 5-6 servings.

Mrs. Mainard Saxton, CWA Chm.
Scholls Grange No. 338
Sherwood, Oregon

CARAMEL CUSTARD

3 c. milk
3/4 c. sugar
6 egg yolks, beaten
1/4 tsp. salt
1 tsp. vanilla

Scald milk. Melt sugar in small heavy pan over low heat. Stir sugar slowly into hot milk; cook, stirring, until sugar melts. Pour slowly over eggs in baking dish; add salt and vanilla. Set in shallow pan on paper towel. Pour hot water into pan about 1-inch deep. Bake at 350 degrees for about 45 minutes or until knife inserted in center comes out clean. Yield: 6 servings.

Mrs. McKee Speer, Master
North Washington Grange No. 1826
Apollo, Pennsylvania

BEST-EVER BAKED CUSTARD

4 eggs
1 can sweetened condensed milk
1 tsp. vanilla
Nutmeg (opt.)

Beat eggs until thick and lemony; add condensed milk, mixing thoroughly. Beat in 3 cups water, vanilla and nutmeg. Pour into baking dish; set dish in pan of water. Bake at 350 degrees until knife inserted in center comes out clean.

Mrs. Hannah E. Williams, Sec.
Wapping Grange No. 30
Manchester, Connecticut

BROWNIE CUSTARD

1 qt. milk
4 eggs, beaten
1/2 c. sugar
1/2 tsp. vanilla
4 brownies with nuts

Combine milk, eggs, sugar and vanilla; beat until well mixed. Pour into casserole. Crumble brownies; sprinkle on top. Bake at 350 degrees for about 1 hour.

Nellie M. Hill, Master
Kezar Lake Grange No. 440
North Lovell, Maine

GRAPE NUTS CUSTARD

4 eggs
4 c. milk
3/4 c. crunchy nut-like cereal nuggets
3/4 c. sugar
1/2 tsp. vanilla

Beat eggs until thick and lemony; beat in milk, cereal nuggets, sugar and vanilla. Pour into greased baking dish. Bake at 325 degrees or until knife inserted in center comes out clean. This recipe won a prize at Slocum Grange dairy contest and at Pomona Grange.

Mrs. Inez Freebora
Slocum Grange No. 36
North Kingston, Rhode Island

INDIVIDUAL BAKED CUSTARDS

3 or 4 eggs
6 tbsp. sugar
1/4 tsp. salt
3 c. whole or skim milk, hot
1 tsp. vanilla
Nutmeg

Preheat oven to 325 degrees. Beat eggs slightly. Add sugar and salt. Stir milk in gradually; add vanilla. Pour into custard cups; sprinkle with nutmeg. Set cups in pan of hot water. Bake for 30 to 40 minutes or until custard is set. Yield: 6 servings.

Evelyn G. Lear, Sec.
Cornish Grange No. 25
Cornish, New Hampshire

MARY'S CUSTARD

1 slice bread
1 qt. milk
4 eggs, well beaten
3 tbsp. sugar
1 tbsp. vanilla

Soak bread in small amount of water in large bowl; add milk, eggs, sugar and vanilla. Beat thoroughly. Pour into baking dish; set dish in pan of water. Bake at 350 degrees until knife inserted in center comes out clean.

Marie L. Wayner, Eco. Chm.
Eno Grange No. 2080
Bidwell, Ohio

SIMPLE BAKED CUSTARD

2 eggs
4 tbsp. sugar
2 c. scalded milk
1/4 tsp. nutmeg or vanilla

Beat eggs until thick and lemony, adding sugar gradually; blend well. Add milk gradually; stir in nutmeg. Pour into baking dish; set baking dish in pan of water. Bake at 325 degrees until knife inserted in center comes out clean.

Mrs. Charles Lewis, HEC
New York Valley Grange
Yates Center, Kansas

Fruit Desserts

Fruit has been a source of sustenance and enjoyment since long before recorded history. It is as much a favorite today as ever. Nature's eye-appealing fruits add color and versatility to a dessert course. Fresh, frozen, canned or dried, fruit is available year round for healthful and delicious concoctions.

Fruit is a naturally sweet dessert in itself *but* . . . don't stop there! There are so many ways to enhance its flavor. Mold it in a gelatin . . . wedge it in ice cream . . . bake it in a cake . . . mix it in a cocktail. If you're looking for new ways with fruit, you'll enjoy the exciting recipes on the pages that follow.

APPLE CRISP

1 c. sugar
1/2 c. shortening
1 egg, well beaten
4 med. apples, peeled and diced
1 tsp. vanilla
1 1/2 c. flour
1/2 tsp. baking powder
1/4 tsp. salt
1 tsp. soda
Raisins (opt.)
Chopped nuts (opt.)

Combine sugar and shortening in large bowl; mix well. Add egg; blend thoroughly. Add remaining ingredients; stir until dry ingredients are moistened. Turn into greased and floured pan.

Topping

1/2 c. (packed) brown sugar
2 tbsp. flour
2 tsp. cinnamon
3 tbsp. butter or margarine

Combine all ingredients; sprinkle over apple mixture. Bake at 350 degrees for 45 minutes.

Mrs. Thomas Goshe
Home Ec. Chm., Women's Activities
McCutchen Grange No. 2360
New Riegel, Ohio

APPLE-OAT CRUNCH

Sliced apples
3/4 c. rolled oats
3/4 c. (packed) brown sugar
1/2 c. flour
1/2 c. margarine

Arrange apples in greased 8-inch square pan. Combine oats, brown sugar and flour; add margarine, mixing until mixture is crumbly. Sprinkle over apples. Bake at 350 degrees for 40 to 45 minutes or until brown.

Mrs. Mark W. Cheesebrough
Mountour Valley Grange No. 2005
Oakdale, Pennsylvania

APPLE-DATE SQUARES

1/2 c. shortening
3/4 c. sugar
1 egg
1 1/3 c. sifted all-purpose flour
1 tsp. soda
1 tsp. salt
2 c. finely chopped tart apples
1   8-oz. package chopped dates
1/4 c. (packed) brown sugar
1 tsp. cinnamon
1/2 c. chopped walnuts

Cream shortening with sugar; add egg, beating well. Sift flour with soda and salt; add to egg mixture. Stir in apples and dates; spread in greased 12 x 8 x 2-inch pan. Combine brown sugar, cinnamon and walnuts; sprinkle over top. Bake at 350 degrees for 30 to 35 minutes. Cut into squares; serve with whipped cream or ice cream.

Marion K. Houston
Nutfield Grange No. 37
Derry, New Hampshire

APPLE STRUDEL

1 c. sugar
1/2 c. margarine
1 c. flour
1 tsp. baking powder
1 tsp. cinnamon
1/4 tsp. nutmeg
1/4 tsp. cloves
2 eggs, well beaten
3 c. sliced apples

Combine sugar and margarine; beat until light and fluffy. Sift flour with baking powder, cinnamon, nutmeg and cloves. Combine sugar mixture, dry ingredients and eggs; blend thoroughly. Arrange apples in 12 x 8 x 2-inch greased pan; pour batter over apples. Bake at 350 degrees for 30 to 35 minutes or until apples are tender and top is golden. May be served with whipped cream or ice cream, if desired.

Mrs. Frank Conrad, Lecturer
University Grange No. 335
Lebanon, New Hampshire

APPLE TORTE

1 egg
1 1/2 c. sugar
Flour
1 tsp. baking powder
Salt
1 c. finely chopped apples
1/2 tsp. almond extract
1/2 c. chopped nuts
1 tsp. butter

Beat egg until thick and lemony, adding 3/4 cup sugar gradually. Sift 1/2 cup flour with baking powder and 1/4 teaspoon salt. Add to flour mixture; blend well. Stir in apples and almond extract; fold in nuts. Pour into greased 8-inch square pan. Bake at 350 degrees for 30 minutes. Combine remaining sugar, 1 tablespoon flour, butter, additional salt to taste with 1 cup boiling water in small saucepan. Cook, stirring constantly, over medium heat until sauce is smooth and thickened. Serve over torte.

Edna I. Everingham, Lecturer
La Fayette Grange No. 1330
La Fayette, New York

SOUR CREAM-APPLE PIE DISH

1 pkg. pie crust mix
1 1/2 lb. crisp apples
1/2 c. sugar
1/2 tsp. cinnamon
3 tbsp. all-purpose flour
1 c. sour cream

Prepare pie crust according to package directions. Roll out on lightly floured surface into rectangle. Line 12 x 8 x 2-inch baking pan with pastry. Wash, core and pare apples; cut into wedges. Place apples over pie crust. Combine sugar, cinnamon, flour, and sour cream in small bowl; blend well. Spoon over apples. Bake in preheated 400-degree oven for 1 hour or until apples are tender. Cool; cut into squares. May be served with whipped cream, if desired. Yield: 8-10 servings.

Mrs. Walter L. Grace
Wilbraham Grange No. 153
Wilbraham, Massachusetts

CARAMELIZED APPLE HALVES WITH ZABAGLIONE SAUCE

1/2 c. sugar
1/2 c. (packed) brown sugar
1 c. dry California sherry
2 tsp. shredded lemon peel
6 Washington Winesap apples
Zabaglione Sauce

Combine sugars, sherry and lemon peel in saucepan; cook over low heat until sugars are dissolved, stirring constantly. Halve, core, and peel apples. Simmer apples in syrup until just tender, basting frequently. Chill; serve with Zabaglione Sauce. Yield: 6 servings.

Zabaglione Sauce

1 c. milk
1 1/2 c. light cream
1 pkg. instant vanilla pudding
1 egg white
2 tbsp. sugar
4 tbsp. dry California sherry

Pour milk and cream into mixing bowl. Add pudding; beat with a rotary beater for about 1 minute or until well mixed. Do not overbeat. Beat egg white until stiff. Add sugar gradually; beat until sugar is dissolved. Fold into pudding; chill thoroughly. Stir in sherry just before serving.

GRANDMA'S APPLE DUMPLINGS

2 c. packaged biscuit mix
4 lg. apples
1/2 c. flour
1/2 c. molasses
1/4 c. sugar
1/2 tsp. lemon juice (opt.)
Nutmeg to taste

Prepare biscuit mix according to package directions; roll dough out thin on lightly floured surface. Cut 8 medium circles. Pare, core and quarter apples; place 1 quarter apple on each circle. Cover apple quarter completely with dough; press edges to seal. Bake at 425 degrees for 10 minutes or until golden. Combine flour, molasses, sugar and 1 cup water in small saucepan; bring to a boil, stirring constantly, until sugar is dissolved and sauce is smooth. Stir in lemon juice. Serve sauce over hot dumplings; sprinkle with nutmeg.

Gladys A. Ridley, WAC Chm.
Mousam Lake Grange
Springvale, Maine

TART APPLE CRUNCH

8 tart apples
1 tsp. cinnamon
1 c. (packed) brown sugar
1 c. sugar
1 c. flour
1/2 tsp. salt
1 tsp. baking powder
1 egg
1/2 c. melted margarine

Peel, core and slice apples. Arrange in greased baking dish. Combine cinnamon with brown sugar; sprinkle half the mixture over apples. Combine sugar, flour, salt and baking powder with egg; blend to consistency of coarse cornmeal. Sprinkle over apples; top with remaining cinnamon mixture. Pour margarine over top evenly. Bake at 350 degrees for 45 minutes or until browned and bubbly. May be served hot or cold. Top with whipped cream or ice cream.

Mrs. Hazel Murray, Sec.
Pennfield Grange No. 85
Battle Creek, Michigan

APPLE DESSERT

1 egg
1/2 c. (packed) brown sugar
1/2 c. sugar
1/2 c. flour
1 tsp. vanilla
Pinch of salt
1 c. chopped nuts
1 c. chopped apples

Beat egg well; add sugars gradually, beating until light and fluffy. Beat in flour, vanilla and salt; blend well. Stir in nuts and apples. Pour mixture into greased 9-inch pie pan. Bake at 350 degrees for 35 minutes. Serve with whipped cream or ice cream.

Hazel Haier, WAC
Kirtland Grange No. 1245
Kirtland, Ohio

BLUEBERRY BUCKLE

1 1/4 c. sugar
1/4 c. shortening
1 egg
2 1/3 c. flour
2 tsp. baking powder
1/2 tsp. salt
1/2 c. milk
2 c. blueberries
1/2 tsp. cinnamon
1/4 c. soft butter

Cream 3/4 cup sugar and shortening until fluffy; beat in egg. Sift 2 cups flour, baking powder and salt together. Add dry ingredients to creamed mixture alternately with milk. Fold in blueberries. Spoon batter into 9-inch square pan. Combine remaining sugar, remaining flour, cinnamon and butter. Sprinkle topping over batter. Bake in a preheated 375-degree oven for 45 to 50 minutes.

Mrs. Albert J. Halsey
Sub. Sec., Pomona Lecturer
Southampton Grange No. 1281
Southampton, New York

BLUEBERRY SALLY LUNN

2 c. sifted flour
3 tsp. baking powder

1/2 tsp. salt
1/2 c. soft butter
1/2 c. sugar
2 eggs
3/4 c. milk
1 c. blueberries
2 tbsp. (packed) brown sugar
1/2 tsp. cinnamon

Sift flour, baking powder and salt together. Combine butter, sugar and eggs in large bowl of electric mixer; beat at high speed until fluffy. Add dry ingredients alternately with milk, beating at low speed. Fold in blueberries. Turn into greased 8-inch square pan. Combine brown sugar and cinnamon; sprinkle over batter. Bake in a preheated 375-degree oven for about 35 minutes. Serve warm. Yield: 9 servings.

Mrs. Glenn Silvernail
North Urbana Grange
Hammondsport, New York

CHERRY CRUNCH

2 tbsp. melted butter
1 qt. frozen cherries
1 c. sugar
3 tbsp. butter
1/2 c. flour
1/2 c. rolled oats

Place melted butter in bottom of glass baking dish; add cherries. Combine sugar, butter, flour and oats; spread over cherries. Bake at 350 degrees for 30 to 35 minutes. Serve with whipped cream or ice cream.

Mrs. John O. Smith, WAC
Fairview Grange No. 2177
Goshen, Indiana

RED CHERRY ROLL

1 c. sugar
Flour
2 tbsp. cherry juice
1 tbsp. butter
2 tsp. baking powder
1/4 tsp. salt
2 tbsp. shortening
1/2 c. milk
2 c. canned red cherries, drained

Combine sugar, 1 tablespoon flour and juice in saucepan; cook for 1 minute. Add butter; let stand to cool. Sift 1 1/2 cups flour, baking powder and salt. Cut in shortening. Add milk; mix well. Turn out on floured board; knead lightly. Roll out to 1/4-inch thickness; spread with cherries. Roll like jelly roll; press edges together. Cut into 1 1/2-inch slices. Place slices in greased pan. Pour cherry juice sauce over top. Bake at 425 degrees for 25 to 30 minutes.

Mrs. Jo Ann Berg, Flora
White Pigeon Grange No. 1732
Blaine, Kansas

DESSERT DUMPLINGS

2/3 c. sifted flour
2 tbsp. sugar
1/4 tsp. baking powder
1/8 tsp. salt
1 tbsp. butter
1 egg, beaten
1 tbsp. milk
1/4 tsp. vanilla
Cherry Sauce

Sift flour, sugar, baking powder and salt together. Cut in butter. Add egg, milk and vanilla; mix until moistened. Drop into boiling Cherry Sauce mixture, making 8 dumplings; cover. Reduce heat to low; cook for 20 minutes.

Cherry Sauce

1 8-oz. jar maraschino cherries
1/2 c. sugar
3 tbsp. cornstarch
1/4 tsp. salt
1/4 c. butter
3 drops of red food coloring

Drain cherries, reserving 1/2 cup juice. Chop cherries; set aside. Combine sugar, cornstarch and salt in 10-inch skillet; stir in reserved juice and 1 1/2 cups water. Add cherries, butter and food coloring. Bring to a boil, stirring constantly; reduce heat.

Mary Grafton, Matron
Pleasant Hill Grange No. 1757
Steubenville, Ohio

CHERRY-PEACH OMELET

6 eggs, separated, at room temperature
1/3 c. light cream
2 tbsp. sugar
1/4 tsp. salt
2 tbsp. butter or margarine
1 tsp. grated lemon peel
Cherry-Peach Sauce

Beat egg yolks until light and fluffy; stir in cream, 1 tablespoon sugar and salt. Whip egg whites until stiff but not dry; fold into egg yolk mixture. Melt butter in omelet skillet. Pour in egg mixture; cook over medium heat for 3 to 5 minutes or until bottom is golden brown. Place in 350-degree oven for 15 minutes or until knife inserted in center comes out clean. Turn out on heatproof platter. Combine lemon peel and remaining sugar; sprinkle over omelet. Place in broiler for about 1 minute or until sugar is slightly melted. Serve with Cherry-Peach Sauce. Garnish with whole cherries, if desired. Yield: 4-6 servings.

Cherry-Peach Sauce

1   12-oz. package frozen sliced
    peaches, thawed
1   8-oz. jar red maraschino cherries
2 tbsp. sugar
1 tbsp. cornstarch
Dash of salt
Dash of ground cardamom
1 tbsp. lemon juice

Drain peaches; reserve syrup. Drain cherries; reserve syrup. Cut peach slices in half; sliver cherries. Combine reserved syrups; add enough water to measure 1 cup liquid. Combine sugar, cornstarch, salt and cardamom in heavy saucepan; add cherry syrup mixture gradually, stirring constantly. Add lemon juice. Bring to a boil; simmer for 30 seconds, stirring constantly. Stir in peaches and cherries; heat through. Yield: 2 1/3 cups sauce.

CHANTILLY CHERRY CUPS

1   8-oz. package cream cheese
1/3 c. sifted confectioners' sugar
1 tsp. vanilla
10 packaged dessert shells
1 c. flaked coconut
1/8 tsp. almond extract
1 can cherry pie filling

Combine cream cheese, confectioners' sugar and vanilla in a medium bowl; beat until smooth. Spread about 2 tablespoons cream cheese mixture around sides of dessert shells. Roll shells in coconut on waxed paper; place on a tray or large flat plate. Stir almond extract into cherry pie filling; spoon into shells. Chill. Yield: 10 servings.

Mrs. Kenneth Livengood, Sec.
Milford Grange No. 1744
Berlin, Pennsylvania

CHERRY BLOSSOM COBBLER

1 c. sugar
3 tbsp. cornstarch
3 c. pitted tart cherries
1 1/2 c. packaged biscuit mix
3 tbsp. cinnamon sugar
1/2 c. cream
4 tbsp. butter or margarine, melted
1/4 c. finely chopped walnuts

Combine sugar and cornstarch in medium saucepan; stir in cherries. Cook, stirring constantly, over low heat until mixture thickens. Boil for 3 minutes. Spoon into deep 6-cup baking dish. Combine biscuit mix, 1 tablespoon cinnamon sugar, cream and 2 tablespoons melted butter in medium bowl; stir just enough to moisten. Roll dough out to about a 12 x 6-inch rectangle. Brush with remaining butter; sprinkle with remaining cinnamon sugar and walnuts. Roll as for jelly roll; cut into slices. Arrange over cherries. Bake at 400 degrees for 20 minutes or until brown. Serve warm with cream.

Stella Brimhall
Mt. Allison Grange No. 308
Arboles, Colorado

FRUIT SQUARES

3 c. flour
2 tsp. baking powder
1 c. soft margarine
2 eggs, beaten
1 1/2 c. sugar
1 tsp. vanilla
1 can cherry pie filling

Combine flour, baking powder and margarine; mix thoroughly. Add eggs, sugar and vanilla to flour mixture; mix until dough is firm. Divide into 2 parts. Pat half into 10 x 13-inch pan. Spread pie filling over dough; cover with remaining dough. Bake at 375 degrees for 30 to 35 minutes.

Mrs. Elva Oldham, Pomona
Rockemeka Grange No. 109
East Peru, Maine

CALIFORNIA FRUIT CRUNCH

1 No. 2 1/2 can fruit cocktail
1 egg
1 c. sugar
1 c. sifted flour
1 tsp. soda
1/2 tsp. salt
2/3 c. (packed) light brown sugar
1/2 c. chopped nuts
Whipped cream or topping

Drain fruit cocktail thoroughly. Beat egg with sugar until fluffy. Reserve 1/3 of the fruit cocktail; add remaining to egg mixture. Sift flour, soda and salt; stir into fruit mixture, blending well. Spread into greased 8 x 8 x 2-inch pan. Sprinkle with brown sugar and nuts. Bake in 350-degree oven for 45 to 50 minutes or until cake tests done. Cool in

pan. Cut into squares. Serve topped with whipped cream or topping and remaining fruit.

Mrs. Marion Judd, Master
Lake Harbor Grange No. 1185
Muskegon, Michigan

FRUIT CHOCOLATE BONBONS

1 6-oz. package chocolate chips
6 tbsp. chopped candied fruits
Stale pound cake pieces
Rum
Whipped cream
Fresh strawberries

Melt chocolate in double boiler over hot water. Spread with spatula into 6 paper baking cups. Place in refrigerator until firm. Peel off paper cups carefully. Soak candied fruits and cake in rum; fill chocolate cups with fruit mixture and cake. Decorate with rosettes of whipped cream; top with strawberries. Yield: 6 servings.

Edith Rogers, Master
Floris Grange No. 749
Herndon, Virginia

FRUIT COCKTAIL CAKE

1 No. 2 1/2 can fruit cocktail
1 1/2 c. sugar
1 1/2 c. flour
1 tsp. soda
Pinch of salt
2 eggs, well beaten
3/4 c. (packed) brown sugar
1/2 c. chopped nuts

Drain fruit cocktail thoroughly. Combine sugar, flour, soda, salt and eggs; mix well. Add drained fruit cocktail; blend thoroughly. Pour into greased 8 x 12-inch pan. Mix brown sugar and nuts; sprinkle over top of batter. Bake at 350 degrees for 35 minutes or until cake tests done. Serve plain or with whipped cream. Yield: 10 servings.

Edward Andersen, Master
Nebraska State Grange
Waterloo, Nebraska

MYSTERY PUDDING

1 1/8 c. flour
1 c. sugar
1 tsp. soda
1/2 tsp. salt
1 beaten egg
1 tsp. vanilla
1 No. 2 1/2 can fruit cocktail
1 c. (packed) brown sugar
1 c. chopped nuts

Sift together dry ingredients; add egg, vanilla and fruit cocktail. Blend well. Pour into greased 9 x 11-inch pan. Combine brown sugar with nuts; sprinkle over batter. Bake at 300 degrees for 1 hour. Serve with whipped cream or ice cream, if desired.

Mrs. Jesse I. Hawkins, Chm., Cookbook Sales
Alpha Grange No. 154
Chehalis, Washington

PINEAPPLE CAKE DESSERT

1 sm. package yellow cake mix
1 8-oz. package cream cheese,
   softened
2 c. milk
1 pkg. instant pineapple pudding
1 lg. can crushed pineapple,
   drained
Whipped cream

Prepare cake mix according to package directions. Spoon into greased and floured 9 x 13-inch pan. Bake in a preheated 350-degree oven for 10 to 12 minutes. Blend cream cheese, milk, pineapple pudding and crushed pineapple together. Mix well; pour over cake. Top with whipped cream. One-half box yellow cake mix may be used.

Minnie Lampard, Flora
Ney Grange No. 1845
Genoa, Illinois

PARTY CAKE

1 pkg. yellow cake mix
1 can sliced peaches
1 can pear halves
1 can pineapple chunks
1 jar apricot preserves
Grated coconut
Maraschino cherries
Whipped cream

Prepare cake according to package directions, using 8 x 11-inch pan. Cool cake; remove to serving platter. Cut out center of cake, leaving 3/4-inch shell. Drain fruits well; arrange in cake shell. Melt preserves; spoon over fruits and sides of cake. Press coconut around sides of cake. Garnish with cherries and whipped cream.

Mary T. Hironymous
American River Grange No. 172
Sacramento, California

RASPBERRY SLICE

1 c. flour
1 tsp. baking powder
Butter
2 eggs
3/4 c. raspberry jam
3/4 c. sugar
2 c. flaked coconut

Mix flour, baking powder, 1/2 cup butter and 1 beaten egg together; spread in bottom of greased 8-inch square pan. Spoon raspberry jam over flour mixture. Combine sugar, remaining beaten egg, 1 teaspoon melted butter and coconut; mix well. Spread coconut mixture over jam layer. Bake in a preheated 350-degree oven for 30 minutes.

Mrs. Olga Fleury
Chm., Service and Hospitality
Westville Grange No. 1047
Constable, New York

DELIGHTFUL RHUBARB CRUNCH

1 c. (packed) brown sugar
3/4 c. quick-cooking oats
1 c. flour
1 tsp. cinnamon
1/2 c. melted butter
4 c. diced rhubarb
1 c. sugar
1 tbsp. cornstarch
1 c. water
1 tsp. vanilla

Mix brown sugar, oats, flour, cinnamon and butter until crumbly. Press 1/2 of the crumbs in 9-inch square pan. Place rhubarb on top of crumbs; add remaining crumbs. Mix sugar, cornstarch, water and vanilla in saucepan; cook until thick. Pour over rhubarb mixture. Bake at 350 degrees for 1 hour.

Mrs. Clarence Solomon, WA Com.
Jackson Grange No. 228
Hancock Co., Findlay, Ohio
Florence E. Lentz, CWA
Bethel Grange No. 404
Port Orchard, Washington

EASY RHUBARB DESSERT

1 1/4 c. flour
1/3 c. confectioners' sugar
3/4 tbsp. baking powder
Dash of salt
1/2 c. shortening
2 eggs, well beaten
1 1/2 c. sugar
2 c. rhubarb, chopped

Combine flour, confectioners' sugar, baking powder, salt and shortening in bowl; form into dough. Pat into 8-inch square pan. Bake at 350 degrees for 15 minutes. Combine eggs, sugar and rhubarb; pour over crust. Bake for 35 minutes longer or until topping is set. May be served with whipped cream, if desired.

Mrs. John Larson
Lady Asst. Steward, Home Ec Chm.
Big Lake Grange
Big Lake, Minnesota

NEW HAMPSHIRE RHUBARB COBBLER

Flour
1 3/4 c. sugar
2 eggs, slightly beaten
3 c. diced rhubarb
2 tbsp. soft butter
1/2 tsp. baking powder
1/4 tsp. salt

Combine 3 tablespoons flour, 1 1/4 cups sugar and 1 egg, mixing well. Coat rhubarb

with flour mixture; place in greased 8-inch square pan. Combine 1/2 cup flour, remaining sugar, butter, baking powder, salt and remaining egg. Beat with wooden spoon until smooth. Drop batter evenly over rhubarb mixture with spoon. Bake in 350-degree oven for 35 to 40 minutes. Serve warm with cream, if desired.

Mrs. Paul Pennock, Chaplain
Mt. Belknap Grange No. 52
Laconia, New Hampshire

RHUBARB DELIGHT

2 c. graham cracker crumbs
1/2 c. butter
1/4 c. sugar
1 c. miniature marshmallows
1   6-oz. package strawberry gelatin
1 qt. sweetened rhubarb sauce
Whipped cream

Combine crumbs, butter and sugar until well mixed; reserve 3/4 cup crumb mixture. Pat remaining crumb mixture in 9 x 13-inch pan. Spread marshmallows over crumb mixture. Combine gelatin and hot rhubarb sauce; cool until partially congealed. Pour over marshmallows; chill until firm. Cover with whipped cream; sprinkle reserved crumbs on top.

Minnie Lampard, Flora
Ney Grange No. 1845
Genoa, Illinois

RHUBARB-GELATIN COBBLER

3 c. rhubarb, cut up
1 c. sugar
1 pkg. strawberry gelatin
1 sm. package cake mix
Butter

Arrange rhubarb in flat baking dish. Combine sugar, gelatin and cake mix; mix well. Sprinkle over rhubarb; dot with butter. Pour 1 cup water over all. Bake at 350 degrees for 20 to 25 minutes.

Mrs. Ruth E. Nelson
Hopewell Grange No. 518
Everson, Washington

OATMEAL-RHUBARB CRUMBLE

1 c. sifted flour
1/2 tsp. salt
1 c. sugar
1 c. rolled oats
1/2 c. melted butter or margarine
3 c. diced rhubarb
1/2 tsp. cinnamon
1 tbsp. water

Reserve 1 tablespoon flour for rhubarb filling. Sift remaining flour, salt and 1/2 cup sugar together; stir in oats. Stir in melted butter until mixture is crumbly. Press 1/2 of the oat mixture evenly over bottom and side of 9-inch pie pan. Combine rhubarb, remaining sugar, reserved flour, cinnamon and water. Pour into crust. Sprinkle remaining oat mixture over fruit. Bake at 350 degrees for about 45 minutes or until rhubarb is tender and crust is lightly browned. Yield: 6-8 servings.

Frances Hirsch, CWA
Quillisascut Grange No. 372
Rice, Washington

RHUBARB-STRAWBERRY COBBLER

1 c. sugar
3 tbsp. cornstarch
1/8 tsp. salt
1 pt. fresh strawberries, sliced
2 c. fresh rhubarb, diced
1 tbsp. lemon juice
1 tbsp. butter or margarine
1   10-count can butter flake
    refrigerator biscuits
Cinnamon sugar

Combine sugar, cornstarch and salt in large saucepan. Stir in strawberries, rhubarb, lemon juice and butter. Cook over medium heat, stirring frequently, until bubbly and slightly thickened. Pour into 2-quart casserole or baking dish. Separate biscuit dough into 10 biscuits; cut each biscuit in half. Arrange, cut side down, on hot fruit in circle around edge of casserole. Sprinkle biscuits with cinnamon sugar. Bake in a preheated 400-degree oven for 15 to 20 minutes or

until biscuits are golden brown. Serve warm with cream. One 16-ounce package frozen rhubarb, thawed and undrained, may be substituted for fresh rhubarb. Decrease sugar to 3/4 cup. Yield: 6 servings.

Mrs. Josephine E. Shorey, Sec.
Branch Mills Grange No. 336
Palermo, Maine

RHUBARB SHORTCAKE

3 c. diced rhubarb
1 1/2 c. sugar
1 1/2 tbsp. flour
Dash of salt
3 tbsp. butter
1 recipe baking powder biscuits

Combine rhubarb, 6 tablespoons water, sugar, flour, salt and butter in saucepan. Cook over medium heat for 5 minutes; cool. Split biscuits; spread with rhubarb. Replace biscuit tops; spoon rhubarb mixture over each biscuit. Top with whipped cream.

Mrs. Helen Morehouse, Lecturer
Belle Valley Grange No. 1294
Erie, Pennsylvania

LEMON SPONGE SHORTCAKE

5 eggs, separated
1 c. sugar
1 1/2 tsp. grated lemon peel
1/4 tsp. salt
1/4 c. lemon juice
2 tbsp. water
1 c. sifted cake flour
1/4 tsp. cream of tartar

Beat egg yolks with 1/2 cup sugar, lemon peel and salt. Add lemon juice and water; beat until light and fluffy. Blend in cake flour. Beat egg whites with cream of tartar until soft peaks form. Add remaining sugar gradually; beat until stiff but not dry. Fold in egg yolk mixture; pour into 2 ungreased 9-inch layer cake pans. Bake in 350-degree oven for 25 minutes or until cake tests done. Cool layers on racks.

Strawberry Cream

2 pt. fresh California strawberries
Sugar
2 c. whipping cream
1 tbsp. lemon juice

Set aside several strawberries for garnish. Slice remaining strawberries; mix with 1/3 cup sugar. Chill for 30 minutes. Whip cream with 2 tablespoons sugar until stiff; blend in lemon juice. Spread 1 cake layer with half the sliced strawberries and half the whipped cream. Top with second layer; spread with remaining sliced strawberries and remaining whipped cream. Garnish with reserved strawberries. Yield: 10-12 servings.

Photograph for this recipe on page 58.

RHUBARB-OATMEAL CRUNCH

4 c. finely diced rhubarb
3/4 c. sugar
2 tbsp. cornstarch
1 c. water
1/2 tsp. vanilla
1 c. sifted flour
3/4 c. oatmeal
1 c. (packed) brown sugar
1 tsp. cinnamon
1/2 c. melted butter

Place rhubarb in greased 11 x 7 x 2-inch pan. Combine sugar, cornstarch and water in saucepan; cook until thick and clear. Add vanilla; pour over rhubarb. Combine flour, oatmeal, brown sugar, cinnamon and melted butter; sprinkle over rhubarb. Bake at 350 degrees for 40 to 50 minutes. Yield: 8 servings.

Ruth Marceau, Sec.
Danville Grange No. 520
Groton, Vermont

SKILLET PIE

1/4 c. butter
1 c. flour
7/8 c. sugar
2 tsp. baking powder
1 c. milk
1 can fruit pie filling

Melt butter in 10-inch skillet. Combine flour, sugar, baking powder and milk; mix well. Pour batter into center of skillet. Spoon pie filling over batter. Bake in a preheated 375-degree oven for 45 minutes. Serve warm.

Mrs. Harold Nihiser, Sr.
Chm. of Women's Activities
Antioch Grange No. 2629
Rockbridge, Ohio

STRAWBERRY SHORTCAKE

2 c. packaged biscuit mix
2 tbsp. shortening, melted
1 egg, beaten
Strawberries

Combine biscuit mix, shortening and egg; mix to a soft dough with fork. Pat dough into an ungreased round cake pan. Bake in a preheated 450-degree oven for 15 to 20 minutes. Split warm cake lengthwise; fill with strawberries. Serve with whipped cream.

Beulah Sutton, CWA Chm., Ignacio
Mt. Allison Grange No. 308
Arbolis, Colorado

WATERMELON BOAT

1 watermelon
1 cantaloupe
1 honeydew melon
Fresh fruits
Shredded coconut
Lemon-lime carbonated beverage,
    chilled

Chill all fruits to be used. Slice watermelon lengthwise about 1/3 of the way down. Scoop out insides carefully. Cut into balls or cubes. Cut cantaloupe and honeydew meat into balls or cubes. Add to watermelon with other fresh fruits. Sprinkle with coconut. Chill until serving time. Add chilled beverage just before serving. Boat rim may be fluted, if desired.

Mary-Lee Steel, Sec., CWA Chm.
Potomac Grange No. 1
Washington, D. C.

Meringues, Tortes & Cheesecakes

Cheesecake — the word brings to mind a luscious, creamy dessert that seems to have just the right combination of tang and sweetness to please anyone's taste. The assortment of cheesecake recipes in this chapter will delight the dessert lovers in your family.

Also try the rich luscious tortes and fluffy, beautiful meringues, which are certain to lure appetites — or how about ice cream or ice cream pies? All this and more follow.

CHEESECAKE SUPREME

1 1/4 c. graham cracker crumbs
1/3 c. melted butter
5 egg yolks
1 c. sugar
1 c. milk
1 tsp. vanilla
Pinch of salt
Grated rind of 1 lemon
2 env. unflavored gelatin
1/2 c. cold water
1 lb. cream cheese, softened
1 pt. whipping cream

Combine crumbs and butter; spread evenly in 9-inch springform pan. Pat crumb mixture down firmly. Combine egg yolks, 1/2 cup sugar, milk, vanilla, salt and lemon rind in top of double boiler; cook until thickened, stirring constantly. Do not let custard boil. Soften gelatin in cold water; stir into hot custard until dissolved. Mix cream cheese and remaining sugar together until smooth; stir into custard. Mix well; let stand until cool. Whip cream until stiff; fold into cream cheese mixture. Pour into prepared shell; dust top with additional crumbs. Chill in re-frigerator for at least 2 hours; may chill over-night. Serve with sweetened strawberries, if desired.

Mary Moore, WAC Chm.
Pine Grove Grange No. 356
Hood River, Oregon

DIFFERENT CHERRY CHEESECAKE

1   3-oz. package fruit-flavored gelatin
1 c. boiling water
1/3 box graham crackers, crushed
1/4 c. melted margarine
1   8-oz. package cream cheese, softened
1 c. sugar
2 tsp. vanilla
1 can evaporated milk
1 can cherry pie filling

Stir gelatin in boiling water until dissolved; chill until partially congealed. Combine cracker crumbs and margarine; press over bottom of 9 x 12-inch pan. Mix cream cheese, sugar and vanilla together until smooth. Chill milk in refrigerator tray until icy crystals form around edges; whip with electric mixer until stiff peaks form. Fold in gelatin mixture. Add cheese mixture; stir to mix well. Pour into prepared pan; chill thor-oughly. Top with pie filling; chill for at least 1 hour before serving.

Mrs. Earl Mutchler, Women's Activities Chm.
Hanover Grange No. 2465
Loudonville, Ohio

CHERRY DELIGHT

2 c. graham cracker crumbs
1/2 c. melted butter
1/4 c. sugar
1   8-oz. package cream cheese, softened
1 c. confectioners' sugar
2 pkg. dessert topping mix
1 c. milk
1 No. 2 can cherry pie filling

Mix graham cracker crumbs, butter and sugar together; line 8 or 9-inch square pan to form a crust. Mix cream cheese with confec-tioners' sugar until smooth. Prepare dessert topping mix with milk according to package directions; fold into cream cheese mixture. Pour into crust; chill for 1 to 2 hours. Spread pie filling over top; chill thoroughly before serving.

Mrs. Charles N. Moore, Treas., WAC
Sharon Grange No. 691
Sharon, Wisconsin

CREAMY CHEESECAKE

1 c. graham cracker crumbs
2 tbsp. butter
Sugar
2 tbsp. flour
1/4 tsp. salt
2   8-oz. packages cream cheese, softened
1 tsp. vanilla
5 eggs, separated
1 c. whipping cream
1   1-lb. 6-oz. can cherry pie filling

Combine crumbs, butter and 2 tablespoons sugar; press down in 9-inch springform pan. Chill until firm. Blend 1/2 cup sugar, flour, salt and cream cheese together until smooth. Stir in vanilla. Add egg yolks, one at a time, beating well after each addition. Add cream; blend thoroughly. Fold in stiffly beaten egg whites; pour into crumb crust. Bake in 325-degree oven for 1 hour and 15 minutes or until cake tester inserted in center comes out clean. Remove from oven; let cool for 15 minutes. Spread pie filling over top; return to oven. Bake for 15 minutes longer. Let cool thoroughly; place in refrigerator. Let stand for several hours or until chilled. Do not remove from pan until well set.

Marjorie H. Campbell, Home and Comm. Com.
Guiding Star Grange No. 1
Greenfield, Massachusetts

DO-AHEAD CHERRY CHEESECAKE

1 2/3 c. fine graham cracker crumbs
1/4 c. butter, softened
1 8-oz. package cream cheese, softened
1 c. powdered sugar
1 env. dessert topping mix, prepared
1 can sweetened pie cherries

Combine cracker crumbs and butter; mix well. Press firmly in 7 x 11-inch pan. Bake at 375 degrees for 8 minutes. Cool. Whip cream cheese into powdered sugar; fold into the whipped topping. Pour into prepared pan; refrigerate until well set. Spread cherry filling evenly over the top; refrigerate until ready to serve. May be prepared the night before using.

Irene Granger, WAC Chm.
Rexville Grange No. 815
Anacortes, Washington

FAVORITE CHERRY CHEESECAKE

1 recipe graham cracker crust
1 8-oz. package cream cheese, softened
1 c. confectioners' sugar
1 c. sweetened whipped cream
1 can cherry pie filling

Press graham cracker mixture in 8-inch square pan to form crust. Bake in 325-degree oven for 10 minutes. Let cool thoroughly. Mix cream cheese and sugar together until smooth; fold in whipped cream gently. Pour into crust; refrigerate until chilled. Spread pie filling over top; chill until ready to serve.

Mrs. Leon Hoffman
Adams Grange No. 286
No. Adams, Michigan

QUICK CHERRY-TOPPED CHEESECAKE

1 8-oz. package cream cheese, softened
1/2 c. sugar
2 c. frozen dessert topping, thawed
1 9-in. graham cracker crust
1 c. cherry pie filling

Beat the cream cheese and sugar together until creamy; blend in dessert topping. Pour into graham cracker crust; top with pie filling. Chill for at least 3 hours before serving. Blueberry or other berry pie filling may be substituted for the cherry pie filling.

Mrs. Arthur Wurm
Delaware Co. Harlem Grange
Galena, Ohio

EASY CHEESECAKE

1 lb. cream cheese, softened
3 eggs, beaten
Sugar
1 tsp. almond extract
1 1/2 tsp. salt
1 c. sour cream
1 tsp. vanilla

Combine cream cheese, eggs, 1 cup sugar, almond extract and salt; mix until smooth. Spread into buttered pie plate. Bake at 350 degrees for 25 to 30 minutes or until firm. Remove from oven and let cool. Combine sour cream, 3 tablespoons sugar and vanilla; mix well. Spread over cheesecake. Top with · canned cherries or blueberries, if desired.

Mrs. Justin Price, Treas.
Price's Fork Grange No. 786
Blacksburg, Virginia

NO-BAKE CHEESECAKE

3 tbsp. melted butter or margarine
3/4 c. graham cracker crumbs
2 tbsp. sugar
1/4 tsp. each cinnamon and nutmeg

Combine all ingredients. Press 1/2 cup crumb mixture in 8 or 9-inch springform pan; reserve remaining crumb mixture for topping. One lightly greased 8-cup loaf pan may be used, if desired. Line with waxed paper cut to fit pan. Invert cheesecake on serving plate and remove waxed paper to serve.

Filling

2 envelopes unflavored gelatin
1 c. sugar
2 eggs, separated
1 c. milk
1 tsp. grated lemon rind
1 tbsp. lemon juice
1 tsp. vanilla
3 c. creamed cottage cheese
1 c. whipping cream, whipped

Combine gelatin and 3/4 cup sugar in medium saucepan. Beat egg yolks and milk together; stir into gelatin mixture. Place over low heat; cook for 3 to 5 minutes or until gelatin dissolves and mixture thickens slightly, stirring constantly. Remove from heat; stir in lemon rind, lemon juice and vanilla. Sieve cottage cheese or beat on high speed of electric mixer for 3 to 4 minutes or until smooth; stir into gelatin mixture. Chill until mixture mounds slightly when dropped from spoon, stirring occasionally. Beat egg whites until stiff but not dry; add remaining 1/4 cup sugar gradually and beat until very stiff. Fold into gelatin mixture; fold in whipped cream. Turn into prepared pan and sprinkle with reserved crumb mixture. Chill for 3 to 4 hours or until firm. Loosen side of pan with sharp knife; release springform. Half the filling mixture but full amount of crumb mixture in 8-inch round cake pan or 9-inch pie plate may be prepared for a smaller cheesecake. Yield: 12 servings.

PINEAPPLE CREAM CHEESECAKE

1 1/2 c. zwieback crumbs
2/3 c. sugar
3 tbsp. melted butter
1 c. well-drained, crushed pineapple

2 tbsp. flour
1/4 tsp. salt
2 3-oz. packages cream cheese,
    softened
1/2 tsp. vanilla
3 eggs, separated
2/3 c. light cream
1/2 c. whipping cream

Combine zwieback crumbs, 1/3 cup sugar and butter; pat into 10-inch pie dish. Spread crushed pineapple on top of the crumb mixture. Combine flour, remaining sugar, salt and cream cheese; beat until thoroughly blended. Add vanilla, egg yolks and cream; beat until smooth and creamy. Beat egg whites until fluffy; fold into cheese mixture. Pour over pineapple. Bake for about 1 hour at 325 degrees. Whip cream until stiff; spread over cheesecake to serve.

Margaret A. DeForest, Lecturer
Ogden Grange No. 111
Spencerport, New York

ANGEL FOOD PIE

1 c. sugar
1 1/2 c. water
1 tsp. vanilla
1/4 tsp. salt
3 tbsp. cornstarch
3 egg whites, stiffly beaten
1 10-in. baked pie shell

Combine sugar, water, vanilla, salt and cornstarch in a saucepan. Cook, stirring constantly, until thickened. Cool thoroughly. Pour over egg whites gradually, beating until fluffy. Pour into pie shell; chill thoroughly. Serve topped with whipped cream.

Mrs. Arthur Shaddick, Home Ec. Com.
Paw Paw Grange No. 1884
Paw Paw, Illinois

NUT ANGEL PIE

3 eggs, separated
1 c. sugar
11 graham crackers
1 tsp. baking powder
1/2 c. chopped nutmeats

Beat egg yolks until light and fluffy; add sugar, mixing well. Roll crackers into fine crumbs; add baking powder. Mix into egg yolk mixture. Fold in stiffly beaten egg whites and nutmeats. Pour into a greased 9-inch pie pan. Bake in preheated 350-degree oven for 30 minutes.

Mrs. Joe French, Home Ec. Chm.
Lincoln Grange No. 237
Wellsburg, New York

CRACKER MACAROON PIE

12 dates, chopped
14 saltine crackers, rolled fine
1/2 c. chopped pecans
1 c. sugar
1/4 tsp. salt
1 1/4 tsp. almond extract
3 egg whites

Combine dates, cracker crumbs, pecans, sugar, salt and almond extract; mix thoroughly. Beat egg whites until stiff peaks form. Fold cracker mixture into egg whites. Place in a buttered 9-inch pie pan. Bake in a preheated 300-degree oven for about 45 minutes. Cool; serve with whipped cream.

Mrs. Thelma P. Hylton, Master's Wife
Price's Fork Grange No. 786
Blacksburg, Virginia

COCONUT-CRUMB TORTE

1 c. graham cracker crumbs
1/2 c. flaked coconut
1/2 c. chopped walnuts
4 egg whites
1/4 tsp. salt
1 tsp. vanilla
1 c. sugar

Combine crumbs, coconut and walnuts. Combine egg whites, salt and vanilla in mixer bowl; beat with electric mixer until stiff peaks form, adding sugar gradually. Fold crumb mixture into egg mixture. Turn into well-greased 9-inch pie plate. Bake in preheated 350-degree oven for 30 minutes. Serve topped with ice cream.

Mrs. Elsie Dingus, Lecturer
Kincaid Grange No. 1482
Kincaid, Kansas

CHOCOLATE-FILLED MERINGUES

1/2 c. butter, softened
1/2 c. (firmly packed) brown sugar
3 tbsp. all-purpose flour
Salt
1 1-oz. square unsweetened chocolate, melted
1 1/2 c. rolled oats
4 egg whites
1/2 tsp. vinegar
1 tsp. vanilla
1 c. sugar

Preheat oven to 300 degrees. Place the butter in a mixing bowl; beat with an electric mixer until creamy. Blend in the brown sugar gradually. Stir in the flour, dash of salt, chocolate and oats, mixing well. Shape into 1/2-inch balls; set aside. Combine egg whites, vinegar, vanilla and 1/4 teaspoon salt in mixer bowl; beat with electric mixer until soft peaks form. Add sugar, 1 tablespoon at a time, beating until glossy and stiff peaks form. Drop by teaspoonfuls onto greased brown paper-lined cookie sheet. Place a chocolate ball in center of each meringue; press lightly into meringue. Bake for 30 to 35 minutes or until lightly browned. Let cool for several minutes before removing from cookie sheet.

Mrs. Rosamond Harding, Chaplain
Souhegan Grange No. 10
Amherst, New Hampshire

FORGOTTEN MERINGUE PIE

6 egg whites
1 c. sugar
1/4 tsp. salt
1/4 tsp. cream of tartar
1 1/2 tsp. vanilla
2 pkg. sweet cooking chocolate
6 tbsp. warm water
1 pt. heavy cream, whipped
1/2 c. finely chopped pecans

Preheat oven to 450 degrees. Beat egg whites until stiff peaks form, adding sugar gradually. Add salt, cream of tartar and 1/2 tea-

spoon vanilla; beat until glossy. Place in 2 well-greased 9-inch pie plates, shaping to the plate with back of spoon to form shell. Place meringue shell in oven; turn off heat. Do not open oven for at least 4 hours or overnight or until completely cool. Melt chocolate in top of double boiler over hot but not boiling water. Add warm water and remaining vanilla, blending well. Cool. Fold whipped cream and pecans in gently. Fill meringue shells; chill thoroughly.

Marion B. Comstock
New Haven Co. No. 5, Pomona CWA Chm.
Cheshire Grange No. 23
Yalesville, Connecticut

MERINGUE COOKIES

2 egg whites
Pinch of salt
2/3 c. sugar
1 c. chopped nuts
1 c. chocolate chips
1 tsp. vanilla
1/4 tsp. almond extract

Preheat oven to 350 degrees. Beat egg whites until stiff peaks form, adding salt and sugar gradually. Fold in nuts, chocolate chips and flavorings. Drop by teaspoonfuls onto greased cookie sheet. Turn off oven and place cookies in oven. Leave for 1 to 2 hours. May be left overnight, if desired.

James H. Kiles, Texas State Master
Leon Valley Grange No. 1581
San Antonio, Texas

NEVER-FAIL PIE MERINGUE

1 tbsp. cornstarch
1/2 c. boiling water
3 egg whites
6 tbsp. sugar

Dissolve cornstarch in 1 tablespoon cold water. Add to boiling water in small saucepan; cook, stirring constantly, until thick and clear. Remove from heat; set aside. Place egg whites in mixer bowl; beat with an electric mixer until soft peaks form. Add sugar gradually, beating until stiff peaks form.

Add cornstarch mixture slowly, beating constantly. Spoon onto pie, sealing edges well. Bake at 375 to 400 degrees until browned.

Erma Tschide, WAC Sec-Treas.
Ontario Heights Grange No. 917
Ontario, Oregon

FRESH PEACH MERINGUE

6 lg. egg whites
1/4 tsp. salt
1/2 tsp. cream of tartar
1 3/4 c. sugar
1 1/2 tsp. vanilla extract
1 1/2 lb. fresh peaches
2 tbsp. fresh lemon juice
1 envelope unflavored gelatin
2 tbsp. cold water
Vanilla Whipped Cream

Place egg whites, salt and cream of tartar in large bowl of electric mixer; beat until eggs have doubled in bulk. Beat in 1 1/2 cups sugar, 1 tablespoon at a time, being sure each addition of sugar is thoroughly dissolved before adding the next spoonful. It is impossible to beat this too much. Beat in vanilla extract; spoon into buttered 8-inch springform pan. Make a depression in center about 5 inches wide and 1 inch deep, using the back of a tablespoon. Place in preheated 400-degree oven. Close door; turn off heat. Let torte stand in oven for 12 hours or overnight; do not open oven door. Remove torte from oven; run spatula around side of pan to loosen. Release spring; lift off side gently. Slide torte carefully off pan onto serving plate. Peel and slice peaches; sprinkle with lemon juice and remaining sugar. Soften gelatin in water in small container; place in pan of hot water until dissolved. Combine with peaches; chill until juice has thickened. Pile into torte; top with Vanilla Whipped Cream. Serve at once. May garnish with sliced peaches and whipped cream piped around edge of torte, if desired. Yield: 6 servings.

Vanilla Whipped Cream

1/2 c. whipping cream
1 tbsp. sugar
1/4 tsp. vanilla extract

Whip cream until soft peaks form. Add sugar and vanilla slowly; beat until stiff.

CHOCOLATE TORTE

2 envelopes unflavored gelatin
2 4-oz. packages chocolate fudge
   pudding and pie filling mix
1/4 c. sugar
2 c. water
2 lg. cans undiluted velvetized
   evaporated milk
1/4 c. lemon juice
2 8 or 9-in. cake layers
Sliced blanched almonds
Stemmed red maraschino cherries
Chocolate curls

Combine gelatin, pudding and pie filling mix
and sugar in saucepan; stir in water and 2
cups evaporated milk. Cook until mixture
comes to a boil, stirring constantly. Cool
until chocolate mixture mounds when
dropped from a spoon. Chill remaining
evaporated milk in refrigerator tray for 10 to
15 minutes or until ice crystals form around
edges of tray. Whip for 1 minute or until
stiff. Add lemon juice; whip for 1 minute
longer or until very stiff. Fold into chocolate
mixture. Split cake layers crosswise into 4
layers. Spoon chocolate mixture over cake
layers and stack. Chill until firm. Decorate
torte with almonds, cherries and chocolate
curls.

Photograph for this recipe on page 70.

FROZEN SALAD DESSERT

1 8-oz. package cream cheese
1/4 c. maple syrup
2 pkg. dessert topping mix
1 c. drained crushed pineapple
1 c. miniature marshmallows
1/2 c. chopped nuts

Soften cream cheese at room temperature;
blend in maple syrup until smooth. Prepare
topping mix according to package directions;
fold into cream cheese mixture. Add pineapple, marshmallows and nuts, folding until
well blended. Turn into square pan or refrigerator tray; freeze. Garnish with chopped
cherries and nuts, if desired.

Grace Krach, Treas.
Salem Grange No. 964
DuBois, Pennsylvania

BUTTER PECAN ICE CREAM

1/2 c. sugar
1/2 tsp. salt
1 1/3 c. milk
1 c. broken pecans
2 tbsp. butter
2 eggs, separated
1 c. heavy cream
1 tsp. vanilla

Combine sugar, salt and milk; stir until dissolved. Brown pecans in butter; cool. Beat
egg whites until stiff, but not dry. Beat egg
yolks until thick and lemon colored. Whip
cream until thick enough to hold a soft
peak; add vanilla. Fold in egg yolks, egg
whites, milk and pecans. Pour into freezing
tray of refrigerator; freeze, stirring every 30
minutes, until mixture will hold shape.
Freeze until firm.

Mrs. Francis Abeln, Women's Act. Chm.
Gresham Grange No. 270
Gresham, Oregon

CUSTARD ICE CREAM

1 qt. milk
3 eggs
1 c. sugar
1/8 tsp. salt
1 c. cream
1 tbsp. vanilla

Scald milk in double boiler; cool. Beat eggs
until thick and lemon colored, adding sugar
and salt. Add egg mixture to milk. Cook,
stirring, for about 3 minutes. Cool; strain.
Stir in cream and vanilla. Freeze according
to freezer directions.

Mrs. Harry Neese, WA Chm.
Plum Creek Valley Grange No. 1702
Indiana, Pennsylvania

MA'S ICE CREAM

1 qt. milk
1 1/2 c. sugar
1 tbsp. cornstarch
1/2 tsp. salt
3 eggs, beaten
1 tbsp. vanilla

Scald milk in double boiler. Combine sugar, cornstarch, salt and eggs, mixing well. Add small amount of hot milk to egg mixture, stirring well. Return egg mixture to milk. Cook, stirring constantly, until of custard consistency. Remove from heat; stir in vanilla. Cool. Freeze according to freezer directions.

Ruth L. Lord, Pomona, Ceres Chebacco
Essex Grange
Ipswich, Massachusetts

COOKED HOMEMADE ICE CREAM

6 eggs
3 c. sugar
1/2 c. instant flour
3 qt. milk
1 pt. cream
1 lg. can evaporated milk
Flavoring to taste

Beat eggs until light; add sugar, beating until lemon colored. Add flour; beat until well mixed. Scald 2 quarts milk; add flour mixture. Cook and stir until thickened. Remove from heat; add cream, evaporated milk and flavoring. Stir in remaining milk. Pour into freezer container; freeze according to freezer directions. May be packed in plastic containers to store in home freezer.

Margaret A. Overla, Treas.
Broomfield Grange No. 1715
Mt. Pleasant, Michigan

HOMEMADE VANILLA ICE CREAM

9 eggs
2 c. sugar
1/2 c. instant flour
3 qt. milk
1 pt. cream
1 tall can evaporated milk
1 tbsp. vanilla
1 tsp. salt

Beat eggs until foamy; add sugar gradually, beating until thick. Add flour; mix well. Heat milk to lukewarm; add egg mixture.

Cook, stirring constantly, until of custard consistency. Remove from heat. Add cream, evaporated milk, vanilla and salt. Pour into container of 6-quart freezer. Freeze according to freezer directions.

Eunice Blackmer, Flora
Broomfield Grange No. 1757
Remus, Michigan

PINEAPPLE ICE CREAM

1 c. skim milk
1 can frozen pineapple juice
1/2 c. crushed pineapple, drained
2 tsp. sugar
1/2 tsp. vanilla

Chill milk in refrigerator tray until crystals form; beat until soft peaks form. Add pineapple juice, crushed pineapple, sugar and vanilla, folding until well mixed. Pour into refrigerator tray; freeze.

Mrs. Paul McCullough, Women's Activity
Big Beaver Grange
New Galilee, Pennsylvania

LEMON ICEBOX DESSERT

3 eggs, separated
1/2 c. sugar
4 tbsp. lemon juice
1/4 tsp. salt
2 c. heavy cream, whipped
1 1/2 c. crushed vanilla wafers

Beat egg yolks and 1 egg white in top of double boiler. Beat in sugar and lemon juice. Cook over hot water, stirring constantly, until smooth and thickened. Remove from heat; cool to room temperature. Beat remaining egg whites and salt until stiff peaks form. Fold whipped cream and egg whites into sugar mixture gently. Grease 8-inch square pan; cover bottom of pan with half the crushed wafers. Pour lemon mixture over wafers; top with remaining wafers. Freeze for several hours or until ready to serve.

Mrs. John B. Burgess
First Lady, Virginia State Grange
Woodpecker Community Grange
Chester, Virginia

LIME SHERBET DESSERT

2 c. coconut cookie crumbs
2 lg. cartons frozen dessert topping
Nuts (opt.)
1/2 gal. lime sherbet

Mix 1 cup cookie crumbs, 1 carton frozen dessert topping and nuts; spread in 9 x 13-inch pan. Cover with softened lime sherbet. Mix remaining crumbs and dessert topping. Spoon on top. Sprinkle top with nuts. Freeze. Yield: 12 servings.

Mrs. Luther Mylander, WA Chm.
Oak Harbor Grange No. 2218
Oak Harbor, Ohio

FROZEN LEMON CREAM PIE

1 egg
2 eggs, separated
3/4 c. sugar
1/3 c. lemon juice
1/4 tsp. salt
1 c. heavy cream, whipped
16 graham crackers, crushed
1/4 c. softened butter

Beat egg and 2 egg yolks until blended; add 1/2 cup sugar, lemon juice and salt. Cook, stirring, in double boiler until thickened. Cool. Beat egg whites until stiff; fold in whipped cream. Add egg white mixture to lemon mixture. Combine crumbs, butter and remaining sugar. Press half the crumb mixture into 9-inch pie plate. Chill. Pour filling into prepared crust; sprinkle with remaining crumbs. Freeze. Remove from freezer 1 hour before serving time.

Frances Leary, Master
Rye Grange No. 233
Rye, New Hampshire

FROZEN STRAWBERRY PIE

1 8-oz. package cream cheese,
    softened
1 c. sour cream
2 10-oz. packages frozen sliced
    strawberries, thawed
1 9-inch graham cracker crust

Blend cream cheese and sour cream. Reserve 1/2 cup berries and syrup; add remaining berries and syrup to cheese mixture. Pour into crust. Freeze until firm. Remove from freezer 5 minutes before serving. Cut into wedges; serve topped with reserved berries and syrup.

Margaret Sullivan, DWA
Price's Fork Grange No. 786
Blacksburg, Virginia

ICE CREAM PIE

1 1/2 c. graham cracker crumbs
1/4 c. softened butter or margarine
1 qt. vanilla ice cream, softened
1 pt. strawberries, sliced
1/4 c. light corn syrup

Blend crumbs and butter together well; press into 9-inch pie plate. Fill with ice cream. Combine strawberries and corn syrup; spoon over ice cream. Wrap pie in aluminum foil; freeze for at least 2 hours. Let soften for 15 to 20 minutes before serving.

Dorothy H. Barger, Chaplain, S&H Chm.
Putnam Valley Grange No. 841
Putnam Valley, New York

RASPBERRY SWIRL

3/4 c. graham cracker crumbs
3 tbsp. butter, melted
Sugar
3 eggs, separated
1 8-oz. package cream cheese,
    softened
1/8 tsp. salt
1 c. heavy cream
1 10-oz. package frozen raspberries,
    partially thawed

Combine crumbs, butter and 2 tablespoons sugar in small bowl; mix thoroughly. Press mixture into 7 x 11-inch pan. Bake at 375 degrees for 8 minutes or until set. Cool thoroughly. Beat egg yolks until thick and lemony; beat in cream cheese, 1 cup sugar and salt. Beat until smooth and fluffy. Beat egg whites until stiff peaks form. Whip cream until soft peaks form and cream is satiny. Fold egg whites and whipped cream into egg mixture; blend thoroughly. Pour over prepared crust. Place raspberries in blender container; puree. Swirl half the raspberry puree through filling. Spoon remaining puree over top; swirl gently with knife. Freeze, covered, until ready to use. Yield: 6-8 servings.

Mrs. John U. Cannon, Sec.
Marshall Grange No. 1840
Jeffersonville, Ohio

TANG-MILK SHERBET

8 c. milk
2 1/4 c. sugar
5 tbsp. lemon juice
3 tbsp. orange-flavored breakfast drink

Combine milk and sugar. Add remaining ingredients; stir until dissolved. Pour into 1-gallon freezer. Freeze according to freezer directions. Yield: 2 quarts.

Mrs. John Engelhardt, Past CWA Chm.
Richland Grange, Holmes County
Brinkhaven, Ohio

ICE CREAM KISSING BALL

1 qt. pistachio ice cream
1 qt. chocolate ice cream
1 pt. vanilla ice cream
1/4 c. chopped raisins
1/4 c. candied fruit
1/2 tsp. rum
3 c. heavy cream
1/4 c. confectioners' sugar

Line two 1-quart bowls with foil or plastic wrap. Line bowls with softened pistachio ice cream; freeze until firm. Repeat procedure with chocolate ice cream. Soften vanilla ice cream to room temperature; fold in raisins, candied fruit and rum. Spoon into center of chocolate layer. Freeze, covered, until ready to serve. Whip cream with confectioners' sugar until soft peaks form. Turn ice cream onto chilled serving dish; decorate with whipped cream. Serve immediately.

Mrs. Homer Sipe, Lecturer
Milford Grange
Somerset, Pennsylvania

CREME DE MENTHE PARFAITS

1 qt. vanilla ice cream
1/2 c. creme de menthe
Whipped cream (opt.)
Chopped nuts (opt.)

Soften ice cream slightly; swirl in creme de menthe. Spoon into parfait or dessert glasses. Freeze until serving time. Add a dollop of whipped cream and sprinkle with chopped nuts just before serving, if desired. May also be poured into 1-quart mold, sliced and served with cake.

Mrs. William A. Steel, Sec., CWA Chm.
Potomac Grange No. 1
Washington, D. C.

PEPPERMINT ICE CREAM ROLL

4 eggs, separated
3/4 c. sugar
1/2 tsp. vanilla
2/3 c. sifted flour
1/4 c. cocoa
1 tsp. baking powder
1/4 tsp. salt
1 qt. peppermint ice cream
1 c. frozen dessert topping, thawed
1/4 c. crushed peppermint candy

Beat egg yolks until thick and lemony; add 1/4 cup sugar gradually. Add vanilla; beat until smooth. Beat egg whites until soft peaks form; add remaining sugar gradually, beating until stiff peaks form. Fold egg whites into egg yolk mixture. Sift flour, cocoa, baking powder and salt together; fold into egg mixture gradually until smooth. Spread batter in greased and floured jelly roll pan. Bake at 375 degrees for 10 to 12 minutes or until cake tests done. Turn out on towel sprinkled with confectioners' sugar; roll up jelly roll fashion. Cool completely. Unroll cake; spread with softened ice cream. Roll jelly roll fashion; cover with plastic wrap. Freeze until ready to serve. Frost with dessert topping; sprinkle with candy. Serve immediately.

Mrs. Arthur Shaddick, Home Ec. Com.
Paw Paw Grange No. 1884
Paw Paw, Illinois

Pies & Pastries

Mom's Apple Pie . . . or any other type of pie she may bake . . .
enjoys a wide popularity with Americans. There is hardly a more
welcoming sight than a hot pie set on the windowsill to cool
. . . the juicy bubbling fruit encased in a light, flaky crust.

This chapter has a large assortment of pie and pastry recipes.
There are cream puffs, tarts, icebox pies, and fruit pies
from pumpkin to rhubarb. You'll find challenging recipes
for the experienced cook, and "easy-as-pie" pies
for the beginner in the kitchen.

APPLESCOTCH PIE

5 c. thinly sliced apples
1 c. (packed) brown sugar
1/4 c. water
1 tbsp. lemon juice
1/4 c. flour
2 tbsp. sugar
3/4 tsp. salt
1 tsp. vanilla
3 tbsp. butter
1 recipe 2-crust pie pastry

Combine apples, brown sugar, water and lemon juice in saucepan. Cover; cook over medium heat for 7 to 8 minutes or until apples are just tender. Mix flour, sugar and salt together. Stir into apple mixture in saucepan; cook, stirring constantly, until mixture comes to a boil. Boil for 1 minute, stirring constantly. Remove from heat; stir in vanilla and butter. Cool to room temperature. Place bottom pastry crust in pie pan; pour apple mixture into pastry. Place top crust over apples; cut for vents and seal edge. Bake in preheated 425-degree oven for 40 to 45 minutes.

Ina Brey
Hayes Grange No. 1490
Meriden, Kansas

APPLESAUCE-MARSHMALLOW PIE

2 c. applesauce
20 lg. marshmallows
1/2 c. sugar
1/4 tsp. cinnamon
1/4 c. butter or margarine
1 baked 9-inch pie shell
Whipped cream or whipped dessert
    topping mix

Combine first 5 ingredients in saucepan; simmer for 5 minutes or until marshmallows are melted, stirring occasionally. Cool slightly; pour into pie shell. Let stand until cold. Top with whipped cream to serve.

Mrs. W. J. Waterson, Ceres
Pine River Grange No. 197
Bayfield, Colorado

DANISH APPLE PIE

1/2 c. flour
1 tsp. baking powder
3/4 c. sugar
1 egg, slightly beaten
1 c. diced apples
1/2 c. chopped nuts

Sift flour, baking powder and sugar together. Stir in egg, apples and nuts; mix well. Pour into greased 8-inch pie pan. Bake for 25 to 30 minutes at 400 degrees. May serve warm or cold with whipped cream.

Mrs. Martha Sigler, Sec.
Hanover Grange No. 2465
Loudonville, Ohio

PERFECT APPLE PIE

2/3 c. sugar
1/3 c. (packed) dark brown sugar
2 tbsp. flour
1 tsp. cinnamon
Dash of nutmeg
6 c. tart apples, pared and
    thinly sliced
Pastry for 9-inch 2-crust pie
2 tbsp. butter

Combine sugars, flour and spices; mix with apples. Line 9-inch pie plate with half the pastry. Fill with apple mixture; dot with butter. Adjust top crust over apples; cut slits for escape of steam. Seal edge; sprinkle top with sugar. Bake at 400 degrees for 50 minutes or until done. Two 1-pound 4-ounce cans pie-sliced apples, drained, may be substituted for fresh apples.

Margaret Sullivan, DWA
Price's Fork Grange No. 786
Blacksburg, Virginia

APPLE PIE CAKE

1 c. flour
1 tsp. soda
1/4 tsp. salt
1 tsp. cinnamon
1 tsp. nutmeg

STRAWBERRY MOCHA CREAM TARTLETS

4 c. sifted all-purpose flour
2 tsp. salt
1 1/2 c. vegetable shortening
2 pt. fresh strawberries
Light corn syrup
1/2 c. strong coffee
1/2 c. sugar
6 egg yolks
1 tbsp. instant coffee powder
2 tbsp. cocoa
1 c. softened sweet butter

Combine the flour and salt in bowl. Cut in the shortening until uniform but coarse. Sprinkle with 1/2 cup water; toss with fork, then press into ball. Roll out 1/2 of the dough at a time on a lightly floured surface to a 1/8-inch thickness. Cut into 3-inch circles, then fit inside 2 1/4-inch tart pans. Prick with fork. Place on a baking sheet. Bake in a 425-degree oven for 10 minutes or until lightly browned. Cool; remove from tart pans. Brush the strawberries with corn syrup and let dry on racks. Combine the coffee and sugar; boil to the thread stage or until candy thermometer registers 234 degrees. Beat the egg yolks with the instant coffee powder and cocoa until fluffy and thick. Add the hot syrup gradually to yolks, pouring in a thin steady stream and beating constantly. Continue beating until light in color and cold, then beat in butter. Chill slightly, if necessary. Pipe a ring of the butter mixture around the inside edge of each cooled tartlet shell. Place a strawberry in each shell and chill until served. Yield: 50 servings.

Photograph for this recipe on page 85.

BLACK BEANS AND RICE

1 6-oz. package herb rice
1/4 c. chopped onion
1 c. cooked black beans or kidney beans
1 tomato, cut in wedges
Finely chopped parsley

Cook rice according to package directions, adding onion at beginning of cooking. Stir in part of the beans. Turn out onto a large square of heavy-duty aluminum foil. Top with tomato; add remaining beans. Fold foil over top, sealing to make a tight package. Place on grill for 10 to 15 minutes or until heated through. Sprinkle with parsley when ready to serve. Rice mixture may be cooked the day before and chilled, if desired. Yield: 6 servings.

Photograph for this recipe on page 85.

SEAFOOD CREAM WITH AVOCADO HALVES

1 lb. fresh mushrooms, sliced
1 c. sliced onion
1 c. butter or margarine
2/3 c. flour
2 1/2 tsp. salt
1 tsp. monosodium glutamate
1/2 tsp. dry mustard
1/2 tsp. pepper
1/4 tsp. thyme leaves
5 c. milk
2 c. light cream
2 eggs, slightly beaten
2 c. grated Swiss cheese
8 7-oz. cans solid white tuna
1 c. sauterne
2 tsp. grated lemon peel
Lemon juice
6 5-oz. cans lobster, drained
2/3 c. chopped toasted blanched almonds
12 ripe avocados
Watercress

Saute the mushrooms and onion in butter until lightly browned; remove with slotted spoon. Quickly stir in the flour and seasonings. Stir in the milk and cream gradually. Cook and stir until the sauce boils for 1 minute. Stir a small amount of hot sauce into eggs, then return to the saucepan. Stir the cheese into hot sauce over low heat until melted. Drain the tuna; separate into large pieces. Add sauterne, lemon peel, 2 tablespoons lemon juice, tuna, lobster, almonds, sauteed mushrooms and onion to the sauce. Heat to serving temperature. Cut the avocados in half lengthwise, twisting gently to separate halves. Whack a sharp knife directly into seeds and twist to lift out. Peel avocado halves and brush with lemon juice. Arrange on a serving platter with watercress. Garnish with lime slices. Serve hot seafood mixture over avocado halves. Garnish with buttered, toasted fine bread crumbs and sliced truffles. Yield: 24 servings.

Photograph for this recipe on page 85.

BAHAMIAN-BARBECUED CHICKEN

1/4 c. lime juice
1/4 c. honey
1/4 c. light rum
4 1/2 tsp. monosodium glutamate
1/4 c. salad oil
2 tbsp. soy sauce
1/2 tsp. dried leaf tarragon
4 broiler-fryer chickens, halved
4 tsp. salt
1 tsp. pepper
Lime slices (opt.)

Line bottom of grill with heavy-duty aluminum foil and prepare fire. Blend the lime juice and honey in a bowl. Warm the rum slightly, then ignite. Add to honey mixture when flame has burned out. Add 1/2 teaspoon monosodium glutamate, oil, soy sauce and tarragon and beat until blended. Sprinkle both sides of chickens with the salt, pepper and remaining monosodium glutamate. Place chickens, skin side up, on grate 6 inches from heat and cook, turning occasionally, for 45 minutes to 1 hour and 15 minutes depending on weight of chicken. Brush with barbecue sauce during last 30 minutes of cooking time. Chicken leg should twist easily out of thigh joint and pieces should feel tender when probed with a fork when done. Garnish chicken with lime slices.

Photograph for this recipe on page 86.

TROPICAL FRUIT BAKE

1/2 c. (packed) brown sugar
1/4 c. butter, melted
1 tsp. grated lemon rind
2 tbsp. lemon juice
1/8 tsp. nutmeg
3 bananas
1 papaya
1 c. honeydew melon balls
1 c. cantaloupe balls
Flaked coconut

Combine brown sugar, butter, lemon rind and juice and nutmeg. Peel bananas; cut in half crosswise and lengthwise. Peel papaya; discard seeds and cube fruit. Combine all fruits; divide among 6 squares of heavy-duty aluminum foil. Sprinkle brown sugar mixture over each and sprinkle with coconut. Seal foil to make tight packages. Place on grill for 10 to 15 minutes or until heated through. Yield: 6 servings.

Photograph for this recipe on page 86.

HERBED PINWHEELS

1 c. butter, softened
1/4 c. chopped parsley
1/2 tsp. oregano leaves
1/4 tsp. tarragon leaves
1/4 tsp. ground thyme
1/8 tsp. pepper
4 c. sifted all-purpose flour
2 tbsp. baking powder
2 tsp. salt
2/3 c. vegetable shortening
1 1/2 c. milk
1 egg

Whip the butter with parsley, oregano, tarragon, thyme and pepper; let stand for 1 hour to blend flavors. Mix the flour, baking powder and salt in a bowl; cut in shortening until mixture looks like coarse meal. Stir in the milk. Knead about 10 times on a floured board and divide the dough in half. Roll out each half into a 12 x 10-inch rectangle. Spread half the herb mixture on each rectangle; roll up each rectangle from 12-inch side and seal edge. Cut each roll into 24 1/2-inch pinwheels and place pinwheels in ungreased muffin pans. Beat the egg with 2 tablespoons water and brush over pinwheels. Bake in a 425-degree oven for 10 to 15 minutes or until golden brown.

Photograph for this recipe on page 86.

1/4 c. butter or margarine
1 c. sugar
1 egg
1 tsp. vanilla
2 tbsp. hot water
2 1/2 c. chopped, peeled and cored
   apples
1/2 c. chopped nuts
Slightly sweetened whipped cream or
   frozen dessert topping

Sift flour once. Measure; add soda, salt and spices. Sift again. Cream butter and sugar until light and fluffy. Add egg; beat again. Add vanilla; blend well. Add water, apples and nuts; mix well. Pour into a 9-inch pie pan or 8 x 8 x 2-inch baking pan. Bake in 350-degree oven for about 45 minutes or until done. Top with whipped cream to serve.

Mrs. Marion Judd, Master
Lake Habor Grange No. 1185
Muskegon, Michigan

BLUEBERRY PIE

Sugar
2 1/2 tbsp. cornstarch
1/4 tsp. salt
3 c. blueberries
2 tbsp. butter
1/2 tsp. lemon juice
1 c. heavy cream
1   9-in. baked pie shell

Combine 3/4 cup sugar with cornstarch, salt, 1 cup blueberries and 2/3 cup water in saucepan. Bring to a boil; cook, stirring constantly, until thickened and clear. Remove from heat; stir in butter and lemon juice. Cool to room temperature; fold in remaining blueberries. Beat cream, adding 2 tablespoons sugar, until soft peaks form. Spread half the whipped cream over bottom of pie shell. Spoon filling carefully over cream; top with remaining cream. Chill until ready to serve.

Mrs. Albert J. Halsey
Sub. Sec., Pomona Lecturer
Southampton Grange No. 1281
Southampton, New York

CREAM CHEESE PIE

2 c. sifted flour
1/2 tsp. baking powder
1 tsp. salt
2/3 c. shortening
1   8-oz. package cream cheese
1   15-oz. can sweetened condensed
   milk
1/3 c. lemon juice
1 tsp. vanilla
1 can cherry pie filling

Sift flour, baking powder and salt together. Pour 1/3 cup boiling water over shortening; mix with fork until creamy. Add flour mixture; mix into dough. Roll half the pastry out on floured surface 1 inch larger than 9-inch pie plate. Fit pastry into pan; trim and flute edge. Remaining pastry may be frozen. Bake pie shell in a preheated 375-degree oven until golden brown. Cool. Soften cream cheese; whip until fluffy. Add condensed milk gradually, beating well. Add lemon juice and vanilla; spoon into pie pastry. Chill for 2 hours. Pour cherry pie filling over cream cheese layer.

Mary S. Harris, Sec.
Taft Settlement Grange No. 473
Mattydale, New York

NO-ROLL CHERRY PIE

1/2 c. butter
Sugar
1 1/4 c. flour
1 c. cherry pie filling
1 egg
1/4 c. milk

Combine butter and 1 tablespoon sugar in saucepan; cook over low heat until butter is melted. Add 1 cup flour; stir vigorously until mixture forms a ball. Press pastry into 9-inch pie pan, lining side and bottom. Spoon pie filling over pastry in pan. Beat egg and 1/2 cup sugar; blend in remaining flour and milk until smooth. Pour egg mixture over pie filling. Bake in a preheated 350-degree oven for 50 minutes to 1 hour.

Mrs. Hazel Murray, Sec.
Pennfield Grange No. 85
Battle Creek, Michigan

CHERRY PAN DOWDY

1 1/4 c. sugar
1/4 c. cornstarch
Dash of salt
1 1/4 tsp. cinnamon
1/8 tsp. nutmeg
2 No. 303 cans red sour pitted
   cherries
1/2 tbsp. lemon juice
1/4 tsp. almond flavoring
2 tbsp. butter or margarine
Few drops of red food coloring
2 c. biscuit mix
2/3 c. milk

Combine 1 cup sugar, cornstarch, salt, 1/4 teaspoon cinnamon and nutmeg; add to cherries and juice in saucepan. Cook over low heat, stirring constantly, until thick. Remove from heat; add lemon juice, almond flavoring, butter and food coloring. Pour into greased 8 x 8 x 2-inch baking dish. Mix biscuit mix and milk just until blended. Mix remaining sugar and cinnamon; drop biscuit mixture by tablespoonfuls into cinnamon mixture. Place biscuits on top of cherry filling. Bake in 400-degree oven for about 30 minutes. Yield: 6-8 servings.

CHERRY-RHUBARB PIE

7 graham crackers, crushed
1/4 c. melted butter
1 tbsp. sugar
1   3-oz. package strawberry gelatin
1/2 c. rhubarb jam
1 1/2 c. cherry pie filling
1 pkg. whipped topping mix

Combine graham crackers, butter and sugar in bowl; blend thoroughly. Press crumb mixture on bottom and side of 9-inch pie pan; chill until ready to use. Dissolve gelatin in 1/4 cup water, stirring constantly, over low heat. Combine gelatin, jam and pie filling; blend thoroughly. Pour into prepared pie shell. Prepare whipped topping according to package directions. Spread over pie filling. Chill for at least 2 hours.

Mrs. Clare E. Case, Past Chm., S and H Com.
Canandaigua Grange No. 1062
Canandaigua, New York

CHERRY AND CHEESE PIE

20 graham crackers, crushed
1/4 c. sugar
1/2 c. margarine, melted
1 pkg. dessert topping mix
1 8-oz. package cream cheese
1 c. confectioners' sugar
1 can cherry pie filling

Combine crackers, sugar and margarine; mix well. Press crumb mixture on bottom and side of pie pan. Prepare topping mix according to package directions. Blend cream cheese and confectioners' sugar until fluffy. Combine topping and cream cheese mixture, blending well; spoon into prepared shell. Pour pie filling over cream cheese layer. Chill well before serving.

Mrs. Deward Franklin, Sec.
Plymouth Grange No. 1535
Plymouth, New York

CHOCOLATE SUNDAE PIE

1 c. evaporated milk
1/4 tsp. nutmeg
3 eggs, separated
1/4 c. sugar
1/8 tsp. salt
1 tbsp. gelatin
1 tsp. vanilla
1 baked 9-in. pie shell
Whipped cream
Grated semisweet chocolate

Combine evaporated milk, 1/2 cup water and nutmeg in double boiler; heat through. Beat egg yolks until thick and lemon-colored, adding sugar and salt gradually. Add small amount hot milk mixture to egg yolk mixture, beating well. Return egg yolk mixture to hot milk mixture. Cook, stirring constantly, until thickened. Soften gelatin in 3 tablespoons cold water for 5 minutes. Add gelatin mixture to hot egg yolk mixture, stirring to dissolve. Cool well. Fold in vanilla and stiffly beaten egg whites. Spoon into pie shell; chill until set. Cover with whipped cream; sprinkle with grated chocolate just before serving.

Dorothy Bajema, Treas.
Northwood Grange No. 264
Lynden, Washington

NO-BAKE CHOCOLATE PIE

1/2 c. butter
3/4 c. sugar
1 tsp. vanilla
1 1/2 sq. chocolate, melted
2 eggs
1 graham cracker crust

Cream butter and sugar until light and fluffy. Add vanilla and chocolate; beat well. Add eggs, one at a time, beating for 5 minutes after each addition. Spoon filling into pie shell. Chill until ready to serve.

Clara Gindlesberger, Lady Asst. Steward
Fulton Grange No. 2421 of Stark Co., Ohio
Canal Fulton, Ohio

CHOCOLATE BAR PIE

1/2 c. milk
15 marshmallows
6 milk chocolate bars
1/2 c. chopped nuts
1 c. whipping cream, whipped
1/2 c. butter, melted
1 tbsp. powdered sugar
18 graham crackers, crushed

Combine milk and marshmallows in double boiler; heat until marshmallows are melted. Add chocolate bars and nuts; cool. Fold in whipping cream. Combine butter, powdered sugar and crackers; mix well. Press crumb mixture into 9-inch pie plate, reserving small amount for topping. Spoon filling into prepared shell; sprinkle with reserved crumbs. Chill for 2 hours.

Mrs. Jerry Blackstone
Women's Activities Chm.
Bruno Center Grange No. 2696
Thornville, Ohio

FRENCH SILK CHOCOLATE PIE

1/2 c. butter
3/4 c. sugar
1 sq. unsweetened chocolate, melted
1 tsp. vanilla
2 eggs
1 baked 9-in. pie shell
Whipped cream

Cream butter and sugar; blend well. Add melted chocolate and vanilla. Add eggs, one at a time, beating for 5 minutes after each addition. Pour filling into pie shell; chill for 2 hours. Top with whipped cream just before serving.

Mrs. William E. Sheets, Sec.
Kingston Grange
Sunbury, Ohio

IT'S-SO-GOOD COCONUT PIE

2 c. milk
1/2 c. sugar
1/4 tsp. salt
2 tbsp. cornstarch
2 eggs, separated
1 tsp. vanilla
1/2 c. coconut
1 baked pie shell

Heat milk until hot in double boiler. Combine sugar, salt and cornstarch; add beaten egg yolks, mixing well. Add hot milk to egg yolk mixture, a small amount at a time, stirring constantly. Return egg yolk mixture to double boiler; cook until thick. Remove from heat; add vanilla and coconut. Fold in stiffly beaten egg whites carefully; pour into pie shell. Bake in 300-degree oven until brown.

Mrs. Clarence Solomon, WA Com.
Jackson Grange No. 228
Findlay, Ohio

THREE-MINUTE PIE

1/4 c. butter, softened
1 1/4 c. sugar
3 eggs
1 c. frozen coconut
1/4 c. buttermilk

1 tsp. vanilla
1 frozen pie shell

Combine butter, sugar, eggs, coconut, buttermilk and vanilla in a mixer bowl; beat well. Pour into pie shell. Bake for 35 to 40 minutes in 375-degree oven.

Mate L. Bradley, Sec.
Floris Grange No. 749
Herndon, Virginia

SHERRY-COCONUT CREAM PIE

1 c. sugar
1/2 c. cornstarch
1/4 tsp. salt
2 1/2 c. hot milk
3 egg yolks, well beaten
1 tsp. vanilla
1/2 tsp. almond extract
1/2 c. California sherry
2 c. flaked coconut
1 baked 9-in. pie shell
1 c. whipping cream

Combine sugar, cornstarch and salt in top of a double boiler; stir in hot milk gradually. Bring to boil, stirring constantly; boil for 1 minute. Remove from heat. Stir part of the hot mixture into egg yolks; stir egg yolks into remaining hot mixture. Add vanilla, almond extract and sherry. Replace pan over hot water; cook for about 5 to 10 minutes or until custard is thick enough to mound from a spoon. Stir in half the coconut; turn into baked pie shell. Cover top with waxed paper or foil; refrigerate for 3 to 4 hours or until filling is set. Beat cream until stiff; spread over filling. Sprinkle remaining coconut over top. Garnish with spearmint candy leaves or candied fruit, if desired.

Lela Hughes, CWA Chm., Dir., Treas.
Porterville Grange No. 718
Porterville, California

BANANA DELIGHT COCONUT PIE

1/4 c. melted butter
2 c. coconut
1 pkg. vanilla pudding and pie mix
2 c. milk
1 c. sliced bananas

Cinnamon (opt.)
Whipped cream

Combine butter and coconut; press evenly in ungreased 8-inch pie pan to form crust. Bake at 300 degrees for 20 to 30 minutes or until golden brown. Cool thoroughly. Combine pudding and pie mix and milk in saucepan; cook over medium heat until mixture comes to a full boil, stirring constantly. Remove from heat; cool for 5 minutes, stirring twice. Pour half the pie filling into coconut crust; cover with layer of sliced bananas. Add remaining pie filling; sprinkle with cinnamon. Chill thoroughly. Spread whipped cream over top of pie just before serving.

Mrs. Jesse I. Hawkins, Cookbook Sales Chm.
Alpha Grange No. 154
Chehalis, Washington

REFRIGERATOR COCONUT-CREAM PIE

1 pkg. instant vanilla pudding
1 1/2 c. milk
1 c. whipping cream
1 baked pie shell
1/2 c. toasted coconut, chilled

Prepare instant pudding according to package directions, using 1 1/2 cups milk. Let stand in refrigerator until set. Whip cream until stiff; let stand in refrigerator until cold. Fold whipped cream into pudding; pour into pie crust. Top with coconut; refrigerate until ready to serve.

Ruth Ann Kensinger, Sec.
Lincoln Grange No. 914
Altoona, Pennsylvania

SNOW PIE

1/2 c. sugar
2 tbsp. (heaping) cornstarch
1/4 tsp. salt
1 tsp. vanilla
3 egg whites, stiffly beaten
3/4 c. coconut
1 baked pie shell
Whipped cream

Combine sugar, cornstarch, salt and 1 cup boiling water in heavy saucepan; cook until thick, stirring constantly. Add vanilla; let cool to lukewarm. Fold into egg whites; fold in 1/2 cup coconut. Pour into pie shell. Cover with whipped cream; sprinkle with remaining coconut.

Mrs. Ralph Fielding, Home Ec Chm.
Riverview Grange No. 243
Blackfoot, Idaho

TOASTED COCONUT PIE

3 eggs, beaten
1 1/2 c. sugar
1/4 c. melted butter or margarine
4 tsp. lemon juice
1 tsp. vanilla
1 1/3 c. flaked coconut
1 unbaked pastry shell

Combine eggs, sugar, butter, lemon juice and vanilla; stir in coconut. Pour into pastry shell. Bake in 350-degree oven for 40 to 45 minutes.

Mrs. Mildred Jones, CWA Sec.
Glen Avon Grange No. 591
Riverside, California

MAINE CUSTARD PIE

4 eggs
1/2 c. plus 1 tbsp. sugar
1/3 tsp. salt
3 1/2 c. hot milk
Vanilla to taste
1 unbaked 9-in. pie shell, chilled
Nutmeg

Beat eggs slightly; add sugar and salt. Stir in milk gradually, beating well. Add vanilla. Spoon filling into pie shell; sprinkle with nutmeg. Bake in a preheated 400-degree oven for 10 to 15 minutes. Reduce oven temperature to 325 degrees. Bake for about 45 minutes longer or until knife inserted in center comes out clean.

D. Brackett, Chm., CWA
Sabbathday Lake Grange No. 365
Poland Spring, Maine

MARION'S CUSTARD PIE

4 eggs
2/3 c. sugar
1 tbsp. flour
1/4 tsp. salt
2 1/2 c. milk
1 tsp. vanilla
Dash of nutmeg
1 lg. unbaked pie shell

Beat eggs and sugar together well; stir in flour and salt. Add milk, vanilla and nutmeg. Spoon filling into pie shell. Bake in a preheated 400-degree oven until a knife inserted in center comes out clean.

Mrs. Marion Schilliger, Home Ec. Chm.
Ashley Grange
Ashley, Ohio

OLD-FASHIONED CUSTARD PIE

5 eggs
1 qt. milk
Pinch of salt
3/4 c. sugar
Vanilla to taste
1 unbaked pie shell
Nutmeg

Beat eggs slightly; add milk, salt, sugar and vanilla. Mix well. Spoon filling into pie shell; sprinkle with nutmeg. Bake in a preheated 400-degree oven for 10 minutes. Reduce oven temperature to 325 degrees. Bake until knife inserted in center comes out clean.

Rebecca Stiff, Pres., Women's Aux.
East Spokane Grange No. 148
Spokane, Washington

FRESH BERRY PIE

1 1/4 c. graham cracker crumbs
1/2 c. margarine, melted
Sugar
3 tbsp. cornstarch
1   3-oz. package blackberry or
    strawberry gelatin
Blackberries or strawberries

Combine crumbs, margarine and 3 tablespoons sugar; mix well. Press into pie plate to form shell. Bake in preheated 350-degree oven for 10 minutes; cool. Combine 1 cup sugar, cornstarch and 1 cup water in saucepan; cook, stirring constantly, until thick. Add gelatin; mix thoroughly. Arrange berries in pie shell; pour gelatin mixture over berries. Chill thoroughly. Serve with whipped cream. May use any berry or fruit with same flavor gelatin, if desired.

Mrs. Justin Price, Treas.
Price's Fork Grange No. 786
Blacksburg, Virginia

GOOSEBERRY PIE

1 qt. gooseberries
1 egg, beaten
1 1/3 c. sugar
2 tbsp. flour
1 recipe 2-crust pie pastry

Wash gooseberries; drain thoroughly. Combine egg, sugar and flour in large bowl; stir in gooseberries. Line 9-inch pie pan with pastry. Pour gooseberry mixture into pie shell; moisten edge of pastry. Arrange top crust over filling; seal and flute edge. Brush with milk; sprinkle with additional sugar, if desired. Cut steam vents in top crust. Bake at 425 degrees for 35 to 40 minutes or until crust is golden brown.

Mrs. Floyd Milburn, Women's Act. Chm.
Clear Creek Grange No. 233
De Soto, Kansas

MAGIC LEMON PIE

1 can sweetened condensed milk
Juice of 1 lemon
Grated rind of 1 lemon
2 eggs, separated
16 graham crackers, crushed
6 tbsp. butter, melted
1/4 tsp. cream of tartar
2 tbsp. sugar

Combine condensed milk, lemon juice, grated rind and egg yolks. Beat together thoroughly. Combine cracker crumbs and melted butter; press into 9-inch pie plate. Spoon filling into prepared shell. Beat egg whites until foamy; add cream of tartar. Add sugar gradually, beating until stiff peaks form. Spread meringue over pie, sealing edge. Bake in a preheated 400-degree oven until meringue is lightly browned.

Evelyn H. Pressey, Ceres
Deering Grange No. 535
Portland, Maine

SOUR CREAM-LEMON PIE

1 c. sugar
1/4 c. cornstarch
1 1/4 c. milk
3 egg yolks, slightly beaten
1 tsp. grated lemon rind
1/3 c. lemon juice
1/4 c. margarine
1 c. sour cream
1 baked 9-in. pastry shell
Whipped cream (opt.)

Combine sugar and cornstarch in 2-quart saucepan; add milk gradually, stirring until smooth. Stir in egg yolks, lemon rind and lemon juice until blended. Add margarine. Cook over medium heat until mixture comes to boil, stirring constantly; boil for 1 minute. Pour into bowl; cover surface of pudding with waxed paper or plastic film. Chill thoroughly. Fold in sour cream; turn into pastry shell. Chill until ready to serve. Top with whipped cream; serve immediately.

LEMON CAKE PIE

1 c. sugar
3 tbsp. flour
2 eggs, separated
2 tbsp. butter or margarine, melted
Grated rind of 1 lemon
Juice of 1 lg. lemon
1 c. milk
1 unbaked 9-in. pie shell

Beat sugar, flour, egg yolks and melted butter together until of creamy consistency. Add grated lemon rind and lemon juice. Add milk; mix slightly. Fold in stiffly beaten egg whites. Turn into pastry shell. Bake in a preheated 300-degree oven for 30 minutes.

Mrs. W. J. Waterson, Ceres
Pine River Grange No. 197
Bayfield, Colorado

LEMON PIE DELUXE

1 3/4 c. sugar
1/4 c. flour
1/4 c. cornstarch
1/2 tsp. salt
4 eggs, separated
1/3 c. lemon juice
Grated rind of 2 lemons
1 baked 9-in. pie shell

Mix 1 1/2 cups sugar, flour, cornstarch and salt together in double boiler. Add 2 cups boiling water, stirring constantly. Cook over medium heat, stirring, until thickened. Add small amount of hot mixture to beaten egg yolks, beating well. Return egg yolk mixture to double boiler; cook, stirring, for 2 minutes longer. Stir in lemon juice and rind; cool. Pour filling into pie shell. Beat egg whites until foamy. Add remaining sugar gradually, beating until stiff peaks form. Spread meringue over pie, sealing edges. Bake in a preheated 400-degree oven until meringue is lightly browned.

Caroline Minegar
Trowbridge Grange No. 296
Allegan, Michigan

LEMON VELVET PIE

1 1/3 c. sugar
6 tbsp. cornstarch
1/2 tsp. salt
2 eggs, separated
2 tbsp. butter
1/3 c. lemon juice
1 tsp. grated lemon rind
1 tsp. vanilla
1 tbsp. gelatin
1 c. coffee cream
1 graham cracker pie shell

Combine sugar, cornstarch and salt in double boiler. Add 1 1/2 cups boiling water gradually, stirring constantly. Cook over medium heat, stirring, until smooth and thickened. Cook for 15 minutes longer. Add small amount of hot mixture to beaten egg yolks, mixing well. Return egg yolk mixture to double boiler; cook for 2 minutes, stirring.

Remove from heat; stir in butter, lemon juice, rind and vanilla. Reserve 1 cup lemon filling for topping. Soften gelatin in 1/4 cup cold water. Add to hot mixture in double boiler, stirring to dissolve. Cool. Stir in cream. Chill until slightly thickened; fold in stiffly beaten egg whites. Spoon filling into pie shell. Chill until firm. Spread reserved filling over pie.

Eloise Potts, CWA
Lamont Grange No. 889
Lamont, Washington

OLD-FASHIONED LEMON PIE

1/3 c. butter
1 3/4 c. sugar
4 eggs
1/4 tsp. salt
2 tbsp. flour
Juice of 2 lemons
Grated rind of 2 lemons
1 unbaked pie shell

Cream butter until fluffy, adding sugar gradually. Beat in eggs, one at a time, beating well after each addition. Add salt, 1/3 cup water, flour, lemon juice and grated rind. Pour filling into pie shell. Bake in a preheated 375-degree oven for 40 to 50 minutes.

Mrs. Byron Brumback, Sec.
Middletown Grange No. 761
Middletown, Virginia

LEMON-PINEAPPLE PIE

5 tbsp. sugar
1 pkg. lemon pie filling
2 eggs, separated
1 10 1/2-oz. can crushed pineapple
1 baked pie shell

Combine 3 tablespoons sugar with lemon pie filling in top of double boiler; stir in 1/2 cup water. Beat egg yolks until thick and lemony; stir into pie filling mixture. Drain pineapple, reserving liquid. Add water to reserved liquid to make 2 cups liquid. Bring to a boil in small saucepan; remove from heat.

Stir small amount of egg mixture into hot liquid; return to egg mixture. Stir to blend well; stir in pineapple. Cook, stirring constantly, over hot water for 10 minutes; pour into prepared shell. Beat egg whites with 2 tablespoons sugar until stiff peaks form. Spoon meringue over filling, sealing edge well. Bake at 400 degrees for 10 minutes or until meringue is lightly browned.

Mrs. Russell F. Borst, Master
Worthington Grange No. 90
Huntington, Massachusetts

OLD-FASHIONED COCONUT-LEMON PIE

1 1/4 c. sugar
2 tbsp. flour
1/8 tsp. salt
1/4 c. soft butter
3 eggs
1 c. shredded coconut
2 tsp. grated lemon rind
1/4 c. lemon juice
1 recipe 2-crust pie pastry

Cream sugar, flour and salt with butter in large bowl. Beat eggs until thick and lemony; add to sugar mixture, blending thoroughly. Stir in coconut, 1/2 cup water, lemon rind and juice; mix well. Line 9-inch pie pan with pastry; pour filling into pastry. Moisten edge of pastry; arrange top pastry over filling, sealing and fluting edges. Cut slits in top crust; brush with water and sprinkle with additional sugar, if desired. Bake at 400 degrees for 35 minutes or until crust is golden. Cool before serving.

Agnes K. Woike, CWA Chm.
Westfield Grange No. 50
Cromwell, Connecticut

FLORIDA ORANGE PIE

1 c. orange juice
1 c. diced orange sections
2 tbsp. grated orange rind
Sugar
5 tbsp. cornstarch
3 eggs, separated
Lemon juice
2 tbsp. butter
1 baked pie shell
1/4 tsp. cream of tartar

Combine orange juice, sections and rind with 1 cup sugar and cornstarch in saucepan. Cook, stirring constantly, over low heat until sugar is dissolved and syrup is clear. Beat egg yolks until thick and lemony. Add small amount of hot mixture to egg yolks; blend well. Return egg yolk mixture to hot mixture; cook, stirring constantly, for 5 minutes or until thickened. Remove from heat; stir in 2 tablespoons lemon juice and butter. Pour mixture into pie shell. Beat egg whites with 1 teaspoon lemon juice and cream of tartar until frothy; add sugar to taste gradually, beating until stiff peaks form. Spread meringue over filling, sealing edge well. Bake at 350 degrees until meringue is lightly browned.

Irene Granger, WAC Chm.
Rexville Grange No. 815
Anacortes, Washington

ORANGEMALLOW PIE

3 tbsp. butter
1/2 c. flaked coconut
1 6-oz. can frozen orange juice
   concentrate
36 lg. marshmallows
2 env. dessert topping mix

Melt butter in medium skillet over medium heat; stir in coconut. Cook, stirring constantly, until coconut is golden. Press on bottom and side of 9-inch pie pan. Cool to room temperature. Thaw orange juice concentrate; combine with marshmallows in saucepan. Cook, stirring constantly, over low heat just until marshmallows are dissolved. Chill until thickened. Prepare topping mix according to package directions. Blend topping mix into orange juice mixture gently; pour into prepared shell. Chill for 2 to 3 hours or until ready to serve. Garnish with additional coconut, if desired.

Irene Granger, WAC Chm.
Rexville Grange No. 815
Anacortes, Washington

LEMON-PEACH CHIFFON PIE

1 envelope unflavored gelatin
1/2 c. cold water
5 eggs, separated
1 c. sugar
1/2 c. lemon juice
1/4 tsp. salt
1 c. finely chopped or mashed
    fresh peaches
1 baked 9-inch pie shell
Fresh peach slices
Whipped cream

Soften gelatin in cold water; set aside. Place egg yolks in top of double boiler; beat slightly. Add half the sugar; beat until well mixed. Stir in lemon juice; cook over boiling water until thick, stirring constantly. Add softened gelatin; stir until dissolved. Remove from heat; let cool. Add salt to egg whites; beat until stiff but not dry. Add remaining 1/2 cup sugar gradually; beat until very stiff. Set aside. Stir chopped peaches into cooked lemon gelatin mixture; fold in egg whites gently. Pile carefully into baked pie shell; chill until firm. Top with whipped cream and garnish with sliced fresh peaches just before serving.

Photograph for this recipe on page 82.

PEACH CRUMB PIE

4 c. sliced fresh peaches
3/4 c. sugar
2 1/2 tbsp. tapioca
1 tbsp. lemon juice
1/4 tsp. salt
1 9-in. pastry shell
1/3 c. (packed) brown sugar
1/4 c. flour
2 1/2 tbsp. soft butter
1/2 tsp. cinnamon

Combine peaches, sugar, tapioca, lemon juice and salt; spoon into pastry shell. Combine brown sugar, flour, butter and cinnamon; mix until crumbly. Sprinkle over peaches. Bake at 425 degrees for 45 to 50 minutes.

Mrs. Glenn Lowe, Sec.
Chester Grange No. 1930
West Salem, Ohio

PEACH-CHEESE PIE

16 graham crackers
Sugar
1/3 c. melted butter
1 8-oz. package cream cheese
1/3 c. milk
2 eggs, beaten
1/4 tsp. vanilla
2 c. canned peach slices, drained

Roll graham crackers into crumbs; add 3 tablespoons sugar and melted butter. Blend well. Pack into 9-inch pie pan. Bake at 350 degrees for 10 minutes. Blend cream cheese and milk. Add 1/3 cup sugar, eggs and vanilla; beat with rotary beater until smooth. Place peach slices in pie shell. Pour cheese mixture over peaches. Bake at 350 degrees for 30 minutes. Garnish top with additional peach slices, if desired.

Mrs. Martha Sigler, Sec.
Hanover Grange No. 2465
Loudonville, Ohio

PEAR PIE

1 unbaked pie shell
Sliced pears
1 c. sugar
1/8 tsp. salt
1 tsp. cornstarch
1 tsp. grated lemon rind
1 tbsp. lemon juice
1/2 tsp. cinnamon
1/2 tsp. ginger
1/4 tsp. mace
1/2 c. flour
1/4 c. butter, softened

Fill pie shell with pears. Combine half the sugar, salt, cornstarch, lemon rind and lemon juice; mix well. Spread over pears. Mix remaining sugar, spices and flour together; add to butter. Stir with fork until of crumb consistency; sprinkle over pears. Bake in preheated 450-degree oven for 15 minutes; reduce oven temperature to 350 degrees. Bake for about 30 minutes longer.

Patricia Jo Bonham, Publ. Chm.
Whitethorn Grange No. 792
Whitethorn, California

PENNSYLVANIA DUTCH SHOO-FLY PIE

3/4 c. molasses
1/2 tsp. soda
3/4 c. boiling water
1 unbaked 9-in. pie shell
1 1/2 c. flour
3/4 c. (packed) brown sugar
1/4 c. shortening
Pinch of salt
1/2 tsp. baking powder

Combine molasses, soda and 3/4 cup boiling water; pour into pie shell. Combine flour, brown sugar, shortening, salt and baking powder in bowl; blend to consistency of coarse meal. Spread crumb mixture over molasses mixture. Bake at 375 degrees for 35 to 40 minutes or until pie tests done.

Mrs. Helen Readinger
National Ceres
Fleetwood, Pennsylvania

PINEAPPLE SPONGE PIE

2 c. crushed pineapple
1 c. sugar
1 tbsp. (rounded) cornstarch
2 tbsp. melted butter
2 eggs, separated
Pinch of salt
1/3 tsp. lemon extract
1 unbaked pie shell

Combine pineapple, sugar, cornstarch and melted butter in bowl. Beat egg yolks until thick and lemony; stir into pineapple mixture. Add salt and lemon extract; blend well. Beat egg whites until stiff peaks form; fold into pineapple mixture. Pour into pie shell. Bake at 350 degrees for 50 minutes or until filling is set.

Mrs. Elva L. Benner, Chaplain
Acorn Grange No. 418
Friendship, Maine

PEANUT BUTTER PIE

1 c. confectioners' sugar
1/2 c. peanut butter
1 baked pastry shell
1/4 c. cornstarch
Sugar
1/4 tsp. salt
2 c. milk, scalded
3 eggs, separated
1 tbsp. butter
1/4 tsp. vanilla

Combine confectioners' sugar and peanut butter in small bowl; blend to consistency of cornmeal. Spread half the mixture over pastry shell. Combine cornstarch, 2/3 cup sugar, salt and milk in top of double boiler over hot water; blend thoroughly. Beat egg yolks until thick and lemony. Stir small amount of hot mixture into egg yolks; return to hot mixture. Cook, stirring constantly, until smooth and thickened; stir in butter and vanilla. Pour into pastry shell. Beat egg whites with 6 tablespoons sugar until stiff peaks form. Spoon meringue over filling, sealing edge well. Sprinkle remaining peanut butter mixture over meringue. Bake at 325 degrees for 15 minutes or until meringue is browned.

Rita P. Armstrong, Lecturer
Nute Ridge Grange No. 316
Farmington, New Hampshire

CAROLINA-STYLE PECAN PIE

1/2 c. sugar
1/4 c. butter or margarine
3 eggs
3/4 c. white corn syrup
1 tsp. vanilla
1 c. pecan halves
1 unbaked 9-in. pie shell

Cream sugar and butter until fluffy. Add eggs, one at a time, beating well after each addition. Add corn syrup and vanilla. Fold in pecans. Spoon filling into pie shell. Bake in a preheated 400-degree oven for 15 minutes. Reduce oven temperature to 350 degrees. Bake for 30 to 35 minutes longer or until knife inserted in center comes out clean.

Gladys A. Ridley, WAC Chm.
Mousam Lake Grange
Springvale, Maine

DELICIOUS PECAN PIES

6 eggs
1   1-lb. box brown sugar
2 c. dark corn syrup
2 tsp. vanilla
2 c. shelled pecans
2 unbaked 9-in. pie shells

Beat eggs and brown sugar together well. Add syrup and vanilla, mixing well. Place 1 cup pecans in each pie shell. Spoon half the filling into each shell. Bake in a preheated 350-degree oven for about 50 minutes or until knife inserted in center comes out clean.

Mrs. Carrie Baumbarger
Providence Grange No. 2572
Grand Rapids, Ohio

KEY LIME PIE

Sugar
3 tbsp. cornstarch
2 tbsp. flour
Pinch of salt
2 c. boiling water
3 eggs, separated
1/4 c. lime juice
Grated rind of 1 lime
1 baked 9-in. pastry shell

Combine 1 cup sugar, cornstarch, flour and salt in the top of a double boiler. Add boiling water gradually, beating constantly. Cook over direct heat, stirring constantly, until thickened. Place over boiling water; cook for about 10 minutes longer. Beat egg yolks until light and lemon colored; beat a small amount of the hot mixture gradually into yolks. Add yolk mixture slowly to hot mixture, stirring constantly. Cook for several minutes until thick. Remove from heat; beat in lime juice and rind. Turn into pastry shell. Beat egg whites until stiff, adding 6 tablespoons sugar gradually. Spread over the filling, sealing to edge. Bake in preheated 425-degree oven for 5 to 6 minutes or until browned. Cool before serving.

Eugenie R. de Graff, Women's Activities Chm.
Nobleboro Grange No. 369
Waldoboro, Maine

GRAHAM CRACKER-CREAM PIE

16 graham crackers, finely crushed
1/2 c. melted margarine
1 tbsp. flour
1/2 c. sugar
1 tsp. cinnamon
3 eggs, separated
2 c. milk
1/4 c. sugar
2 tbsp. cornstarch
1 tsp. vanilla

Combine graham crackers, margarine, flour, sugar and cinnamon; blend thoroughly. Press on bottom and side of 9-inch pie pan. Bake at 375 degrees for 7 minutes; cool. Beat egg yolks until thick and lemony; beat in milk, sugar, cornstarch and vanilla. Pour into top of double boiler; cook, stirring constantly, over hot water until mixture coats spoon. Pour into prepared pie shell; beat egg whites with 3 tablespoons additional sugar until stiff peaks form. Spread meringue over filling, sealing edge well. Bake at 400 degrees for 10 to 15 minutes or until meringue is browned.

Mrs. Malio Liotti, Master's Wife
Pike Grange No. 1669
Canton, Ohio

SPICY PUMPKIN PIE

2 eggs, separated
1 c. canned pumpkin
3/4 c. sugar
1 tsp. salt
1 1/2 c. milk
1/2 tsp. ginger
1 tsp. cinnamon
1/4 tsp. allspice
1/4 tsp. cloves
1/4 tsp. nutmeg
1/8 tsp. mace (opt.)
1 unbaked 10-in. pie shell

Beat egg yolks thoroughly; add pumpkin, sugar, salt, milk and spices. Beat egg whites until stiff peaks form; add to pumpkin mixture, folding until well mixed. Pour into pie shell. Bake at 400 degrees for 10 minutes. Reduce temperature to 350 degrees. Bake for 45 to 50 minutes longer or until knife inserted in center comes out clean.

Mrs. Mary Engelhardt, Master
Petaluma Grange No. 23
Petaluma, California

PUMPKIN CHIFFON PIE

1/2 c. (packed) brown sugar
1 env. unflavored gelatin
1 tsp. salt
1 tsp. cinnamon
1/4 tsp. nutmeg
1/8 tsp. cloves
2 eggs, slightly beaten
1/2 c. evaporated milk
1 c. pumpkin
1 pkg. dessert topping mix
1 baked pie shell

Combine sugar, gelatin, salt and spices in saucepan; mix well. Add eggs, milk and pumpkin. Cook, stirring constantly, over medium heat until gelatin is dissolved. Cool thoroughly. Prepare topping mix according to package directions; fold into pumpkin mixture. Pour into pie shell; chill for 2 to 3 hours or until firm.

Mrs. Mark W. Cheesbrough
Montour Valley Grange No. 2005
Oakdale, Pennsylvania

RAISIN PIE SUPREME

1   15-oz. package raisins
3 tbsp. lemon juice
2 c. sugar
4 tbsp. cornstarch
Butter
1/2 c. chopped walnuts
1 unbaked 9-in. pie shell
1 c. flour

Cover raisins with boiling water; let stand overnight. Bring to a boil; boil for 15 minutes or until plump. Stir in lemon juice and 1 1/2 cup sugar. Combine cornstarch with small amount of water; add to raisin mixture. Cook, stirring constantly, over medium heat until clear and thickened; stir in 1 tablespoon butter and walnuts. Pour into prepared pie shell. Combine flour, remaining sugar and 1/2 cup butter in small bowl; work with fork until crumbly. Sprinkle over filling. Bake at 450 degrees for 20 minutes; reduce oven temperature to 400 degrees. Bake for 15 minutes longer.

Margaret Bennett, Home Ec.
Pike Grange No. 1669
East Sparta, Ohio

RAISIN PIE DELUXE

1 c. raisins
4 eggs, well beaten
1 c. sugar
1 c. dark corn syrup
1 tsp. vanilla
1 c. flaked coconut
1 unbaked 10-in. pie shell
Butter

Soak raisins in boiling water to cover for 15 minutes; drain thoroughly. Combine eggs, sugar, corn syrup, vanilla and coconut in large bowl; blend thoroughly. Pour into pie shell; dot with butter. Bake at 325 degrees for 45 minutes or until golden brown and filling is set.

Mrs. John Cannon, Sec.
Marshall Grange No. 1840
Washington Court House, Ohio

FRESH RHUBARB PIE

2 c. chopped rhubarb
1 unbaked 9-in. pie crust
3 eggs, slightly beaten
1 c. sugar
1/3 c. melted butter
1 c. light corn syrup
1 tbsp. cornstarch
Nutmeg

Place rhubarb in pie crust. Mix eggs, sugar, butter, syrup and cornstarch together; pour over rhubarb. Sprinkle with nutmeg. Bake in a preheated 375-degree oven for 40 to 50 minutes. Frozen rhubarb may be used instead of fresh rhubarb.

Mrs. John O. Smith, Women's Activities Chm.
Fairview Grange No. 2177
Goshen, Indiana

CENTENNIAL RHUBARB PIE

1 c. sugar
2 tbsp. flour
2 eggs, separated
3 c. diced rhubarb
1 unbaked 8-in. pie shell

Combine sugar, flour and beaten egg yolks. Coat rhubarb with flour mixture. Fold in stiffly beaten egg whites. Spoon rhubarb mixture into pie shell. Bake in a preheated 425-degree oven for 10 minutes. Reduce oven temperature to 375 degrees; bake until rhubarb is tender and pie is set.

Mrs. Helen Readinger
National Ceres
Fleetwood, Pennsylvania

FAMOUS RHUBARB PIE

1 1/2 c. sugar
1 egg, beaten
2 tbsp. all-purpose flour
Juice of 1/4 orange
Grated rind of 1/4 orange
4 c. diced rhubarb
1 recipe 2-crust pie pastry

Combine sugar, egg, flour, orange juice and grated orange rind; mix well. Coat rhubarb with flour mixture. Place bottom pastry in 9-inch pie pan. Spoon rhubarb mixture into prepared pan. Place top pastry over filling, trimming edges. Flute edge; cut vents in top. Bake in a preheated 350-degree oven for about 1 hour or until crust is golden brown.

Mrs. Larry Hicks
West Oshtemo Grange
Kalamazoo, Michigan

ST. PATRICK'S DAY PIE

1 pkg. pineapple cream pudding
   and pie mix
1 3-oz. package lime gelatin
1 env. whipped topping mix
1 baked 9-in. crumb crust

Combine pudding and pie filling and gelatin with 2 1/4 cups water. Cook, stirring con-stantly, over medium heat until mixture comes to a boil and is clear and thickened. Remove from heat; chill until partially set. Prepare topping mix according to package directions; reserve 1/3 cup topping mix. Blend remaining topping mix with gelatin mixture; pour into prepared crust. Form shamrock in center of pie with reserved top-ping, using decorator tube. Chill for at least 3 hours before serving.

Mrs. Ester Leighton, Sec.
Mt. Forist Grange No. 351
Berlin, New Hampshire

SOUR CREAM PIE

1 c. sour cream
1/2 c. sugar
1 c. chopped raisins
2 eggs, separated
1 tbsp. flour
1 tsp. nutmeg
1 tsp. cinnamon
1 tsp. butter
1 baked pie shell

Combine sour cream, sugar, raisins, egg yolks, flour, nutmeg, cinnamon and butter in top of double boiler. Cook, stirring con-stantly, over hot water until smooth and thickened. Remove from heat; cool. Pour into prepared pie shell. Beat egg whites until stiff peaks form. Spoon over filling, sealing edge well. Bake at 400 degrees for 10 min-utes or until meringue is lightly browned.

Mary Avery, Master
South Barre Grange No. 467
Barre, Vermont

FRENCH STRAWBERRY GLACE PIE

1 qt. strawberries
1 c. sugar
3 tbsp. cornstarch
1 3-oz. package cream cheese,
   softened
1 9-in. baked pie shell

Wash, hull and drain strawberries. Combine 1 cup strawberries and 2/3 cup water in sauce-

PATE MAISON

1/2 env. unflavored gelatin
1/2 c. bouillon or consomme
Pimento
Capers
Truffles and ripe olives
1 lb. chicken livers
1/2 tsp. monosodium glutamate
2 tbsp. minced onion
6 tbsp. butter or margarine
1/2 tsp. salt
1 tsp. dry mustard
1/4 tsp. cloves
1/8 tsp. nutmeg
2 tbsp. brandy

Sprinkle gelatin over bouillon in saucepan. Place over low heat, stirring constantly, until gelatin is dissolved. Pour thin layer of bouillon mixture in bottom of 8 x 4 x 2 1/2-inch pan. Chill until thickened. Press a design of pimento, capers, truffles and ripe olives into thickened bouillon. Pour remaining bouillon mixture over design and chill while preparing pate. Sprinkle chicken livers with monosodium glutamate. Saute with onion in 2 tablespoons butter for 6 to 7 minutes. Remove from heat. Turn into blender. Sprinkle with salt, dry mustard, cloves and nutmeg. Blend until smooth. Add remaining butter and brandy. Blend until smooth. Turn into prepared pan. Chill. Dip quickly into pan of hot water up to top to unmold. Loosen with sharp knife. Turn onto platter. Yield: 24 servings.

Photograph for this recipe on page 103.

RIPE OLIVE RIGOLETTOS

2 c. canned pitted ripe olives
2 8-oz. packages cream cheese
1 tsp. salt
6 drops of hot sauce
2 tbsp. lemon juice
2 tbsp. tomato paste
1/2 c. mashed avocado
8 candied cherries, chopped
1 tbsp. chopped sugared ginger
1/4 c. chopped nuts
1 bunch hearts of celery
1 cucumber
1 green pepper
1 tomato
1 red onion
1 pkg. Cheddar cheese

Chop 1 1/2 cups ripe olives very fine. Cut remaining olives into halves, quarters and rings for garnish. Soften the cream cheese in a bowl. Add the chopped olives, salt, hot sauce and lemon juice and mix well. Spoon equal amounts into 3 bowls. Add tomato paste to 1 bowl, mashed avocado to 1 bowl and cherries, ginger and nuts to remaining bowl. Stuff celery with cherry mixture and press together to form bunch. Roll in waxed paper and chill. Cut the cucumber into slices. Cut green pepper and tomato into wedges, scooping out seeds and membrane. Cut the onion into wedges and separate. Cut cheese into triangles. Pipe cream cheese mixtures onto canape bases with a pastry tube and garnish with reserved ripe olives. Cut celery into slices. Chill all canapes well before serving.

Photograph for this recipe on page 103.

LOBSTER BARQUETTES

1 10-oz. package pie crust mix
1 tbsp. butter
1 5-oz. can lobster, finely chopped
1 tbsp. chopped onion
1 tbsp. chopped parsley
2 tbsp. brandy
1/2 tsp. monosodium glutamate
2 tsp. lemon juice
1/3 c. warm light cream
1 egg yolk
Grated Parmesan cheese
Buttered bread crumbs

Prepare pie crust mix according to package directions. Roll dough on lightly floured board to 1/8-inch thickness. Invert 3-inch barquette molds on dough. Cut 1/3 inch around each mold with knife. Fit piece of pastry into each mold; press to bottom and sides. Trim excess around rim of mold. Prick bottom with a fork. Fill pastry shells with rice to prevent pastry from bubbling. Bake at 375 degrees for 10 to 12 minutes or until shells are golden brown. Remove rice. Cool. Melt butter in a skillet. Add lobster, onion and parsley. Cook until onion is tender but not brown. Stir in brandy. Sprinkle with monosodium glutamate and lemon juice. Combine cream and egg yolk; stir into skillet. Spoon mixture into baked barquettes. Sprinkle with Parmesan cheese and bread crumbs. Brown under broiler to serve immediately. Refrigerate until ready to serve if prepared in advance. Reheat in a 350-degree oven for 15 minutes. Brown lightly under broiler.

Photograph for this recipe on page 104.

CRAB MEAT QUICHE

1 8-in. unbaked pie shell
2 eggs
1 c. light cream
1 tsp. monosodium glutamate
3/4 tsp. salt
Dash of cayenne pepper
3 oz. Swiss cheese, grated
3 oz. Gruyere cheese, grated
1 tbsp. flour
1 6 1/2-oz. can crab meat, flaked

Prick bottom and sides of pie shell with fork. Bake in a 450-degree oven for about 10 minutes or until delicate brown. Combine eggs, cream, monosodium glutamate, salt and cayenne pepper; beat well. Combine cheeses, flour and crab meat; sprinkle evenly in pie shell. Pour in cream mixture. Bake at 325 degrees for 45 minutes to 1 hour or until tip of knife inserted in center comes out clean. Cut into small wedges.

Photograph for this recipe on page 104.

ALMOND MUSHROOMS

18 lg. mushrooms
Monosodium glutamate
1/3 c. fine dry bread crumbs
2 tsp. lemon juice
1/8 tsp. rosemary
1 tsp. marjoram
1/4 tsp. salt
1/4 c. finely chopped almonds
1 tbsp. capers
3 tbsp. butter
3 tbsp. chopped parsley

Wash mushrooms and remove stems. Sprinkle inside of mushroom caps with monosodium glutamate. Chop stems finely; combine with bread crumbs, lemon juice, herbs, salt, almonds and capers. Spoon mixture into caps. Place in greased shallow baking pan. Dot each mushroom with butter. Bake at 350 degrees for 20 to 25 minutes. Sprinkle with parsley.

Photograph for this recipe on page 104.

RIPE OLIVE QUICHE

1 10-oz. package frozen patty shells
1 8-oz. package cream cheese
2 eggs
2 c. canned pitted ripe olives, drained
1 2-oz. can rolled anchovies with capers

1/2 c. grated Fontina or imported
    Swiss cheese
1/2 c. grated Parmesan cheese

Thaw patty shells in refrigerator. Knead patty shells together and roll out. Press into 10-inch fluted tart pan. Mix cream cheese with eggs; pour into pastry. Cut olives into halves and chunks. Sprinkle evenly over cheese filling. Arrange anchovies on top; sprinkle with cheeses. Bake in 400-degree oven for 40 minutes or until brown. Serve warm or cold.

Photograph for this recipe on page 104.

VEGETABLES VINAIGRETTE

White Beans

3 c. cooked white beans
1/2 tsp. monosodium glutamate
1 onion, chopped
2 tbsp. chopped parsley
1/2 c. French dressing
1 clove of garlic, slashed

Place beans in a large bowl; add remaining ingredients. Mix well. Chill for several hours. Remove garlic before serving.

Cucumbers

3 cucumbers
1/2 tsp. monosodium glutamate
1/2 c. vinegar
2 tbsp. sugar
1 clove of garlic, slashed
Chopped dill

Peel cucumbers and slice thinly. Sprinkle with monosodium glutamate. Combine vinegar, sugar and 2 tablespoons water; pour over cucumbers. Add garlic. Sprinkle with dill. Chill. Remove garlic before serving.

Artichoke Hearts

2 1-lb. cans artichoke hearts
1 tsp. monosodium glutamate
1/2 c. French dressing
2 tbsp. lemon juice

Drain artichoke hearts and place in bowl. Sprinkle with monosodium glutamate. Add dressing and lemon juice. Marinate for several hours. Garnish with diced pimento and capers.

Photograph for this recipe on page 104.

pan; simmer for 3 minutes. Blend sugar and cornstarch with 1/3 cup water; add to strawberry mixture. Bring to a boil; boil, stirring constantly, for 1 minute. Remove from heat; cool. Spread cream cheese over bottom of pie shell. Arrange remaining strawberries over cream cheese. Pour cooled mixture over strawberries. Chill for at least 2 hours. May be served with whipped cream, if desired.

Mrs. Loretta Girouard
Bethlehem Grange No. 121
Bethlehem, Connecticut

FROZEN STRAWBERRY PIE

1 qt. frozen strawberries
2 tbsp. cornstarch
1 c. sugar
1 tsp. red food coloring
1 9-in. baked pie shell
Whipped cream or topping

Thaw strawberries; drain well, reserving juice. Place reserved juice in saucepan; add cornstarch, combined with small amount of water. Cook, stirring constantly, until clear and thickened; stir in sugar and food coloring. Cook, stirring, until sugar is dissolved. Remove from heat; cool to room temperature. Stir in strawberries; pour into crust. Chill thoroughly. Top with whipped cream before serving.

Mrs. John O. Smith, Women's Act. Chm.
Fairview Grange No. 2177
Goshen, Indiana

STRAWBERRY CHIFFON PIE

1 3-oz. package strawberry gelatin
1 c. fresh strawberries
1/2 c. sugar
1 c. whipped cream
1 9-in. baked pie shell

Dissolve gelatin in 1 cup boiling water. Slice strawberries; cover with sugar. Let stand for 1 hour; drain well, reserving juice. Add reserved juice to gelatin mixture; blend well. Chill until partially set; whip until mixture is light and fluffy. Fold in berries and whipped cream. Pour into prepared pie shell. Chill for

several hours or until set. Frozen strawberries and whipped topping may be substituted. Additional whipped cream may be spread over pie before serving, if desired.

Mrs. Merrill L. Going, CWA Chm.
Coventry Grange No. 75
Andover, Connecticut

STRAWBERRY ICEBOX PIE

1 1-lb. package marshmallows
2 c. sweetened fresh strawberries
1 c. heavy cream, whipped
1 baked 9-in. pastry shell

Place marshmallows in top of double boiler over hot water. Drain strawberries, reserving 2 tablespoons juice. Add reserved juice to marshmallows; cook, stirring frequently, until marshmallows are dissolved. Stir in strawberries. Chill for 2 hours. Fold in whipped cream; pour into cooled prepared shell. Chill until ready to serve. One package frozen strawberries may be substituted, if desired.

Grace R. Lord, Master
Crooked River Grange No. 32
Harrison, Maine

STRAWBERRY PIE DELUXE

1 qt. fresh strawberries
1 9-in. baked pie shell
1 12-oz. package frozen strawberries
1 c. sugar
3 tbsp. cornstarch
1/4 tsp. salt
1 tbsp. butter

Wash and hull strawberries; drain well. Arrange in pie crust. Combine frozen strawberries with 1/2 cup water, sugar, cornstarch and salt in saucepan. Cook, stirring constantly, until clear and thickened. Add butter. Cool slightly; pour over strawberries in pie shell. Chill for at least 3 hours before serving. Serve topped with whipped cream, if desired. Yield: 6 servings.

Beatrice Sturtevant, Maine State Sec.
Stevens Mills Grange No. 294
Auburn, Maine

EASY PIE CRUST

5 1/2 c. all-purpose flour
1/2 tsp. salt
1 lb. lard
1 egg
1 tbsp. vinegar

Sift flour with salt into large bowl; cut in lard with pastry blender until mixture resembles coarse meal. Place egg and vinegar in measuring cup; stir lightly. Add water to egg mixture to make 1 cup liquid; add to flour mixture. Blend well to form dough. May be refrigerated until ready to use. Yield: 5 pastry shells.

Mrs. Dorothy Hale
Mile Branch Grange No. 933
Alliance, Ohio

NEVER-FAIL PIE CRUST

3 c. all purpose flour
1 1/4 c. vegetable shortening
1 tbsp. sugar
2 tsp. salt
1 egg
1 tbsp. vinegar

Combine flour, shortening, sugar and salt. Mix with pastry blender until crumbly. Beat egg; add 1/2 cup water and vinegar, mixing well. Combine flour mixture and egg mixture gradually until dry ingredients are moistened. Chill dough for 1 hour before rolling out. May be kept in refrigerator for 1 week or may be frozen. Yield: 2 double crust 9-inch pie shells.

Coramae C. Bailey, S and H Com., Treas.
East Bloomfield Grange No. 94
Holcomb, New York

PERFECTION PIE CRUST

4 c. flour
2 tsp. salt
1 tbsp. sugar
2 c. vegetable shortening
1 egg, beaten
1 tbsp. vinegar

Sift flour with salt and sugar. Blend in shortening until mixture resembles small peas. Blend in egg, vinegar and 1/2 cup cold water; work into flour mixture to form soft easy to handle dough. Dough will keep, refrigerated, for 1 week.

Lillian Wagner, Grange Sec.
Fulton Grange No. 2421
Canal Fulton, Ohio

REFRIGERATOR PIE CRUST

5 c. flour
2 tbsp. sugar
1 tsp. salt
2 c. lard
1 egg

Sift flour with sugar and salt into large bowl; add lard. Blend with pastry blender until of consistency of coarse meal. Place egg in measuring cup; stir lightly. Add water to egg to measure 1 cup liquid. Add to flour mixture, blending well to form dough. Refrigerate until ready to use.

Mrs. Woodrow Valentine, Wife of State Master
Indiana State Grange
Portland, Indiana

RICH PIE CRUST

4 c. flour
1 tbsp. sugar
2 tsp. salt
1 3/4 c. vegetable shortening
1 lg. egg
1 tbsp. vinegar

Spoon flour lightly into cup when measuring. Combine flour, sugar and salt in large bowl; blend well. Add shortening; blend with pastry blender until mixture resembles coarse meal. Place egg in measuring cup; add vinegar, stirring lightly to blend. Add 1/2 cup water to egg mixture, blending well. Add to dry ingredients; blend well to form dough. Wrap dough in plastic wrap; chill for at least 1/2 hour or until needed.

Grace R. Lord, Master
Crooked River Grange No. 32
Harrison, Maine

SESAME PIE CRUST

1 c. flour
1/2 c. oatmeal
1/2 c. sesame seed
1/2 c. salad oil
1/4 c. milk or water
1 tbsp. sugar
1/2 tsp. salt

Combine all ingredients; mix thoroughly. Press onto bottom and side of 9-inch pie pan; prick well. Bake at 350 degrees until golden. Wheat or soy flour may be substituted. Part of dough may be crumbled over top of filling, if double crust is desired.

Sandra Pearce, Sec.
Golden Gate Grange No. 451
Golden, Colorado

SIMPLE PIE CRUST

3 c. flour
1 tsp. salt
1 1/4 c. shortening
1 egg
1 tbsp. vinegar

Sift flour and salt together; cut in shortening until crumbly. Blend egg, 5 tablespoons water and vinegar together; beat well. Add vinegar mixture to flour mixture, mixing well. Roll into ball. May be kept in refrigerator for 2 to 3 weeks if well wrapped. Yield: 3 pie shells.

Ann Schaad, Lecturer, WAC
Waterford Grange No. 231
Waterford, Ohio

APPLE PAN PIE

5 c. flour
Sugar
1/2 tsp. salt
1/2 tsp. baking powder
1 1/2 c. shortening
2 egg yolks
3 to 5 tart apples
3/4 c. (firmly packed) brown sugar
1/4 tsp. salt
1 tsp. cinnamon
1/2 tsp. nutmeg
3 to 4 tsp. lemon juice (opt.)
Milk
1/2 c. confectioners' sugar

Combine flour, 4 teaspoons sugar, salt and baking powder in large bowl; cut in shortening. Beat egg yolks in measuring cup; add enough cold water to make 1 cup liquid, stirring to blend. Add to flour mixture; mix well. Divide pastry in 2 equal parts. Roll out 1 part to fit 15 1/2 x 1 1/2-inch jelly roll pan; fit into pan. Peel and slice apples. Place half the apples in crust. Combine 3/4 cup sugar, brown sugar, salt and spices. Sprinkle half the sugar mixture over apples. Add remaining apples and sugar mixture. Drizzle lemon juice over all. Roll out remaining pastry; fit over apples. Brush with milk; sprinkle lightly with additional sugar. Prick in several places with fork. Bake at 400 degrees for 50 minutes. Combine 1 tablespoon milk and confectioners' sugar; drizzle over top of pie.

Mrs. Alfred Barger, Chaplain, S and H Chm.
Putnam Valley Grange No. 841
Putnam Valley, New York

AUNT LUCY'S FRIED PIES

2 c. flour
2 tsp. baking powder
1/2 tsp. salt
1/4 c. butter
1 egg
Milk
Thick applesauce

Sift flour, baking powder and salt together into large bowl. Cut in butter until mixture resembles cornmeal. Add egg and enough milk to hold dough together. Roll out on floured board; cut in rounds. Spoon applesauce in center of round. Fold in half; seal edge well. Fry in 360-degree deep fat until brown. Drain on paper towels; dust with confectioners' sugar. Mincemeat may be substituted for applesauce.

Ruth L. Lord, Chebacco Pomona, Ceres
Essex Grange
Ipswich, Massachusetts

EASY CREAM PUFFS

1/4 lb. butter
1 c. boiling water
1 c. flour
4 eggs
1 tsp. salt

Add butter to water; bring to a boil. Add flour all at once; stir vigorously until ball forms in center of pan. Cool slightly. Add eggs, one at a time, beating after each addition. Add salt; blend well. Mixture should be very stiff. Drop by spoonfuls; shape on oiled cookie sheet. Bake at 450 degrees for 15 minutes. Reduce temperature to 350 degrees; bake for 30 minutes longer. Turn off heat; leave oven door open for about 30 minutes.

Mrs. LaVerne Eagan, Master
Clinton Grange No. 77
Clinton, Connecticut

MICHIGAN CREAM PUFFS

1 c. water
1/2 c. butter or margarine
1 c. flour
4 eggs

Preheat oven to 400 degrees. Bring water and butter to a rolling boil. Remove from heat; stir in flour. Beat in eggs, all at one time. Continue beating until smooth. Drop in 12 portions onto ungreased cookie sheet. Bake for 35 to 40 minutes or until puffed and golden. Cool and fill.

Mrs. Thomas Latterner, Lady Asst. Steward
W. Oshtemo Grange
Kalamazoo, Michigan

FRUIT FRITTERS

1 c. flour
1 1/2 tsp. baking powder
1/4 tsp. salt
3 tbsp. confectioners' sugar
1/3 c. milk
1 egg, beaten
2 c. fruit

Sift flour, baking powder, salt and sugar together. Add milk gradually; beat until smooth. Add egg; mix well. Dip fruit in batter. Fry in 375-degree shallow fat or salad oil until delicate brown. Drain on absorbent paper. Serve hot. Sprinkle with confectioners' sugar, if desired. Serve with sauce or whipped cream. Apples, bananas, drained peaches or pineapple may be used.

Pearl Estabrook, Pomona
Bolton No. 142 P of H
Bolton, Massachusetts

ITALIAN TURNOVERS

1 lg. orange, peeled
1 sm. jar peach preserves
1 1/2 c. sugar
1/2 tsp. cinnamon
1/2 tsp. nutmeg
1 tsp. cocoa
1 c. finely chopped walnuts
5 to 6 c. all-purpose flour
4 tsp. baking powder
1 tsp. grated orange peel
4 eggs
3/4 c. salad oil
3/4 c. milk
2 tsp. vanilla

Chop orange coarsely. Combine orange pulp, juice, peach preserves, 1 cup sugar, cinnamon, nutmeg, cocoa and walnuts in saucepan. Cook, stirring constantly, over medium heat for 15 to 20 minutes or until well blended and thickened. Remove from heat; cool slightly. Combine flour, baking powder, remaining sugar and grated orange peel in large bowl; blend well. Make well in center of flour mixture; add eggs, salad oil, milk and vanilla to well. Blend thoroughly to smooth dough. Roll out on lightly floured surface 1/4 inch thick. Cut into 2 1/2-inch squares. Place 1 teaspoon filling in center of each square. Bring four corners together; pinch and twist to seal. Place on greased baking sheet. Bake at 350 degrees for 45 minutes or until golden.

Theresa Caliendo, CWA
Southington Grange No. 25
Southington, Connecticut

DANISH PUFF

2 c. flour
1 c. butter
1 tsp. almond extract
3 eggs

Preheat oven to 350 degrees. Place 1 cup flour in bowl; cut in 1/2 cup butter with pastry blender until mixture resembles coarse meal. Sprinkle 2 tablespoons water over mixture; mix with fork until mixture forms ball. Divide in half. Pat into two 12 x 3-inch strips; place 3 inches apart on ungreased baking sheet. Combine remaining butter with 1 cup water in saucepan; bring to a boil. Stir in almond extract; remove from heat. Stir in remaining flour until smooth and thickened. Beat in eggs, one at a time, beating well after each addition. Divide mixture in half; spread over pastry strips. Bake for 60 minutes; cool slightly. Frost with confectioners' icing and sprinkle generously with nuts, if desired.

Mrs. James Willoughby, Wife of Master
Newark Grange No. 1004
Granville, Ohio
Betty Behn, Flora
Cromwell Grange No. 67
Middletown, Connecticut

PINEAPPLE SQUARES

4 c. flour
1 tsp. salt
1 1/2 c. shortening
1 c. milk
3 c. crushed pineapple
1 1/2 c. sugar
6 tbsp. tapioca
2 c. confectioners' sugar
1/4 c. soft butter
1/2 tsp. vanilla

Sift flour and salt together. Cut in shortening; stir in milk. Divide dough in half; roll first half to fit into a 10 1/2 x 15 1/2 x 1-inch jelly roll pan, allowing pastry to extend up the sides to top of pan. Mix pineapple, sugar and tapioca; spread over bottom crust. Roll remaining dough to fit. Cover filling; pinch edges of dough together. Bake at 450 degrees for 45 minutes or until golden

brown; cool. Combine confectioners' sugar, butter and vanilla; spread on top pastry. Cut into squares.

Mrs. Mary Carey, Master's Wife
Curriers Grange No. 1273
Sardinia, New York

PECAN TARTS

1 8-oz. package cream cheese
1/2 c. melted butter
1 c. sifted flour
2 lg. eggs, beaten
1 1/2 c. (packed) brown sugar
2 tbsp. soft butter
1 tsp. vanilla
1 c. chopped pecans

Mix cream cheese, melted butter and flour together; chill for 30 minutes. Roll chilled dough into 1/2-inch balls. Place balls in miniature muffin tins, pressing against side and bottom to form cups. Mix remaining ingredients together; fill cups 3/4 full. Bake in a preheated 325-degree oven for 45 minutes.

Mrs. Howard Huck, Sec.
Hall of Fame Grange No. 2003
Kansas City, Kansas

QUICK TARTS

3/4 c. graham cracker crumbs
1/4 c. butter
1 8-oz. package cream cheese
1/4 c. sugar
1 egg, beaten
1 tsp. vanilla
1 can cherry pie filling

Combine crumbs and butter, mixing well. Press crumb mixture into bottoms of paper muffin cups. Blend cream cheese, sugar, egg and vanilla together. Spoon filling into muffin cups about 1/2 full. Bake in a preheated 350-degree oven for about 10 minutes. Cool. Top cream cheese layers with cherry pie filling.

Janice N. Going, Lecturer
Coventry Grange No. 75
Coventry, Connecticut

Chilled Desserts

In addition to their refreshing qualities on a hot day, chilled desserts are a convenient "make-ahead" item for your dinner menu. Hurried, on-the-go homemakers are grateful for dishes you will find in this chapter. They are quickly made, slipped into the refrigerator, and "forgotten" until serving time.

The molded gelatins included in this section possess lively color and shape. You'll find they add an appetizing touch of beauty to your table. Gelatins are a light dessert choice, well-suited to finish a filling meal.

BERRY DELIGHT

1 1/2 c. graham cracker crumbs
1/4 c. melted butter or margarine
1/2 c. milk
1/2 lb. miniature marshmallows
1 c. heavy cream
1   1-lb. 3-oz. can sweetened berries
1/4 c. sugar
3 tbsp. cornstarch
1 tbsp. lemon juice

Combine cracker crumbs and butter. Reserve 3 tablespoons for topping. Pat remaining crumbs into 8 x 12-inch pan. Combine milk and marshmallows in double boiler. Heat until marshmallows are melted. Cool. Whip cream; fold into marshmallow mixture. Place berries and juice in saucepan. Combine sugar and cornstarch; add to berries. Mix well. Cook over medium heat, stirring, until thickened. Stir in lemon juice; cool. Spread half the marshmallow mixture over graham cracker crust. Cover with berry mixture. Add remaining marshmallow mixture. Sprinkle reserved crumbs over top; chill for several hours. Yield: 8-10 servings.

Mrs. Dale Wimp, Master's Wife, Treas.
Elbow Creek Grange No. 733
Visalia, California

BLUEBERRY DESSERT

1   1-lb. box vanilla wafers
2 eggs, separated
1/2 c. butter or margarine
1 c. powdered sugar
1 can blueberry pie filling
2 env. dessert topping mix

Crush vanilla wafers; spread in 9 x 11-inch pan. Combine egg yolks, butter and powdered sugar; beat until fluffy. Fold in stiffly beaten egg whites and pie filling. Spoon blueberry mixture into prepared pan. Prepare topping mix according to package directions; spread over filling. Sprinkle with additional crumbs.

Mrs. Donald Pickinpaugh
LA Steward, Women's Activities Chm.
Sharon Grange No. 1561
Caldwell, Ohio

BUSY DAY DESSERT

1 c. mandarin oranges, drained
1 c. pineapple tidbits, drained
1 c. sour cream
1 c. miniature marshmallows
1 c. flaked coconut

Combine all ingredients; let stand overnight in refrigerator.

Hazel Haier, WAC
Kirtland Grange No. 1245
Kirtland, Ohio

CALIFORNIA FRUIT DESSERT

1 can fruit cocktail
1 can mandarin oranges
1 can pineapple chunks
1 qt. cream, whipped
4 tbsp. powdered sugar
2 tsp. vanilla
1   8-oz. package cream cheese, softened
2 c. miniature marshmallows

Drain all fruit well. Whip cream; add sugar, vanilla, and cream cheese. Add fruit and marshmallows. Chill before serving. Will keep for several days in refrigerator.

Mrs. Homer Sipe, Lecturer
Milford Grange
Somerset, Pennsylvania

CHERRY PUDDING

22 graham crackers
1/2 c. sugar
1/4 lb. melted margarine
1 env. dessert topping mix
1/2 c. milk
1/2 tsp. vanilla
2 c. miniature marshmallows
1 can cherry pie filling

Roll graham crackers into crumbs. Add sugar and margarine; mix well. Pat into bottom of long baking pan. Combine dessert topping mix, milk and vanilla in medium bowl. Whip on high speed until soft peaks form. Add marshmallows; spread over crust. Pour cherry pie filling over marshmallow mixture; sprinkle with additional sugar. Let stand overnight or for several hours before serving.

Ethel Diediker, Steward
Reseda Grange No. 703
Sepulveda, California

CHERRY-SOUR CREAM DESSERT

1 angel food cake
2 cans cherry pie filling
1 pkg. instant vanilla pudding mix
1 1/2 c. milk
1 c. sour cream

Break cake into pieces; spread half the pieces in 9 x 13-inch pan. Spread 1 1/2 cans pie filling over cake. Arrange remaining cake on top. Combine pudding mix, milk and sour cream. Beat until smooth. Spread over cake. Garnish with remaining cherry filling. Refrigerate overnight. Yield: 12-15 servings.

Mrs. Shirley Van Buren, Ceres
Kahlotus Grange No. 939
Pasco, Washington
Helen M. Hill, Overseer
Mt. Belknap Grange No. 4
Laconia, New Hampshire

CHOCO-BANANA PUDDING CAKE

1 pkg. no-bake Dutch chocolate pie
3/4 c. finely chopped pecans
3 tbsp. sugar
1/4 c. margarine, melted
1 med. banana, sliced
Cold milk
1 pkg. instant banana cream pudding

Combine graham cracker crumbs from pie package, pecans, sugar and margarine; press firmly against side and bottom of 8-inch springform pan. Refrigerate crust for 15 minutes. Line bottom crust with banana slices. Pour 1 1/4 cups cold milk into small deep mixing bowl. Add pie filling; beat at medium speed with electric mixer or rotary beater for 3 minutes, scraping side of bowl occasionally. Pour over banana slices. Pour 1 1/2 cups cold milk into mixing bowl. Add banana cream pudding; beat for about 1 minute or until well blended. Pour slowly over chocolate filling. Pour 1/3 cup cold milk into small deep bowl. Add topping from pie package; beat at high speed for 3 to 4 minutes or until soft peaks form. Spread over banana pudding; chill until firm.

DATE DELIGHTS

12 packaged cream-filled chocolate
  cookies, crushed
1 8-oz. package pitted dates, cut up
3/4 c. water
1/4 tsp. salt
2 c. miniature marshmallows
1/2 c. chopped walnuts
1 c. whipping cream
1/2 tsp. vanilla
Walnut halves

Reserve 1/4 cup cookie crumbs; spread remaining crumbs in 10 x 6 x 1 1/2-inch baking dish. Combine dates, water, and salt in saucepan; bring to a boil. Reduce heat; simmer for 3 minutes. Remove from heat; add marshmallows, stirring until melted. Cool to room temperature. Stir in chopped walnuts. Spread date mixture over crumbs in dish. Combine cream and vanilla; beat until soft peaks form. Swirl over dates. Sprinkle with reserved crumbs; top with walnut halves. Chill overnight. Cut in squares. Yield: 8 servings.

Mary Moore, WAC Chm.
Pine Grove Grange No. 356
Hood River, Oregon

CHOCOLATE COOKIE ICEBOX CAKE

1/2 c. butter or margarine
1 c. powdered sugar
3 eggs, separated
1 tsp. vanilla
Pinch of salt
1 pkg. large chocolate wafers
1/2 c. finely chopped nuts

Cream butter and powdered sugar until smooth; add egg yolks, one at a time, blending well. Mix in vanilla and salt. Fold in stiffly beaten egg whites. Grind cookies; spread half the cookie crumbs in waxed paper-lined 9-inch square pan. Sprinkle half the nuts over crumbs. Pour in butter mixture. Top with remaining nuts; cover with remaining cookie crumbs. Press down; let stand for 24 hours in refrigerator. Cut in squares; top with sweetened whipped cream

and chopped nuts, if desired. Yield: 9 servings.

Mrs. Laura Taylor, Subordinate Pomona
Blue Mt. Grange No. 345
LaGrande, Oregon

BUTTERSCOTCH TOFFEE DESSERT

2 c. graham cracker crumbs
1 c. soda cracker crumbs
1/2 c. melted margarine
1 pkg. instant vanilla pudding
1 pkg. instant butterscotch pudding
2 c. milk
1 qt. vanilla ice cream
1 pkg. dessert topping mix
2 lg. Butterfinger candy bars

Combine crumbs and margarine; mix well. Reserve 3/4 cup crumb mixture; press remaining mixture in 9 x 13-inch pan. Combine puddings and milk; beat with mixer until smooth and thick. Add ice cream; mix well. Pour over crust in pan. Prepare topping mix according to package directions; spread over filling. Chop candy bars fine; add to reserved crumbs. Spread over top; chill for several hours before serving.

Betty Page, Sec.
Ridges Grange No. 1616
Bronson, Kansas

ENGLISH TOFFEE PUDDING

2 c. confectioners' sugar
2 tbsp. cocoa
1/2 tsp. salt
1/2 c. butter
2 eggs, separated
1 tsp. vanilla
1 c. chopped nuts
1 3/4 c. vanilla wafer crumbs

Combine sugar, cocoa and salt; stir until well blended. Add butter; cream until fluffy. Add egg yolks; beat well. Stir in vanilla and nuts. Fold beaten egg whites into crumbs. Spread half the crumb mixture into waxed paper-lined 9-inch square pan. Spoon in toffee mixture; cover with remaining crumb mixture. Refrigerate until serving time. Yield: 6-9 servings.

Mrs. William E. Sheets, Sec.
Kingston Grange
Sunbury, Ohio

EGGNOG DESSERT

4 c. miniature marshmallows
1/4 c. milk
2 eggs, beaten
1 1/2 tsp. rum flavoring
1 c. heavy cream, whipped
1/2 c. chopped candied fruits

Melt marshmallows in milk in double boiler; stir until smooth. Stir small amount of hot mixture into eggs, mixing well. Return egg mixture to double boiler. Cook, stirring constantly, for 2 to 3 minutes. Remove from heat; add rum flavoring. Chill until slightly thickened. Fold in whipped cream and candied fruits. Spoon into individual serving dishes. Top with additional candied fruit, if desired. Chill for several hours or overnight. Yield: 6-8 servings.

Della Grove, WAC Chm.
Blackhawk Grange
Leaf River, Illinois

IGLOOS

1/4 c. butter
1/2 c. sugar
1 egg, separated
1/2 tsp. vanilla
1/2 c. crushed pineapple, slightly
    drained
1/2 c. pecans
Vanilla wafers
1 c. whipping cream

Cream butter and sugar until fluffy; add beaten egg yolk. Mix in vanilla and pineapple; add pecans, mixing well. Fold stiffly beaten egg white into creamed mixture. Spread mixture between vanilla wafers, stacking 4 high. Let stand overnight in refrigerator. Whip cream; spread around sides and

on top of each serving about 4 hours before serving. Sprinkle with coconut; top with maraschino cherries, if desired. Yield: 12 servings.

Eloise Potts, CWA
Lamont Grange No. 889
Lamont, Washington

FIVE-CUP SALAD DESSERT

1 c. crushed pineapple, drained
1 c. diced apples
1 c. chopped pecans
1 c. flaked coconut
1 c. sour cream

Combine all ingredients in serving bowl. Chill well. Garnish with maraschino cherries and nuts, if desired.

Mrs. Leon Hoffman
Adams Grange No. 286
North Adams, Michigan

PATTY'S BANANA SPLIT DESSERT

[handwritten: DELICIOUS]

2 c. crushed graham crackers
Butter
2 c. powdered sugar
1 tsp. vanilla
2 eggs, slightly beaten
Firm bananas
1 lg. can crushed pineapple
2 c. whipped cream
1/4 c. crushed nuts
Maraschino cherries

[handwritten: Use this alternate: Crust 3 Cups Crax, 3/4 cup margarine. FILLING #1: 1 LB Conf. Sugar, (or) 8 oz Cream cheese, 1 Tsp vanilla, 1/2 Cup margarine. Same. use Lite Cool Whip unsweetened Pineapple. I used soft Cream Cheese]

Combine cracker crumbs and 6 tablespoons melted butter, mixing well. Press crumb mixture into bottom of 13 x 9-inch pan. Combine 1/2 cup butter, sugar, vanilla and eggs; beat well until fluffy. Spread sugar mixture over crumb layer. Slice bananas lengthwise over sugar mixture. Spoon pineapple over bananas; cover pineapple layer with whipped cream. Garnish with nuts and cherries. Chill for 6 hours before serving.

Mrs. John Larson
Lady Asst. Steward, Home Ec. Chm.
Big Lake Grange
Big Lake, Minnesota

GLORIFIED RICE

2/3 c. rice
Butter
1 No. 303 can crushed pineapple
1 6-oz. package miniature marshmallows
3 c. whipped cream
Vanilla to taste
Sugar to taste

Cook rice in salted water to cover and small amount of butter. Drain; run cold water over rice to cool. Drain pineapple; add to rice. Add marshmallows; fold in whipped cream, vanilla and sugar. Chill until ready to serve.

Ruth Holst, CWA Chm.
Thurston Grange
Springfield, Oregon

PEACH-FILLED ANGEL FOOD CAKE

1 pkg. angel food cake mix
1 pkg. vanilla pudding mix
2 c. milk
1 No. 2 can peach pie filling
1 c. heavy cream, whipped

Prepare cake according to package directions, using 10-inch tube pan. Cool. Cut 1-inch layer off top of cake; reserve sliced layer. Hollow out cake, leaving 1-inch shell. Prepare pudding mix according to package directions, using 2 cups milk. Cool. Combine half the pie filling and pudding; spoon into cake cavity. Replace reserved layer of cake. Fold remaining pie filling into whipped cream; frost cake. Chill until serving time.

Robin Lindsey Quist, Ceres, Youth Com.
Boylston Grange No. 111
Boylston, Massachusetts

PINEAPPLE ICEBOX CAKE

1 7-oz. package vanilla wafers
3/4 c. butter
3 c. sifted powdered sugar
3 eggs, separated
1/4 tsp. almond extract
1 pt. whipping cream, whipped
1 lg. can crushed pineapple, drained

Crush wafers into crumbs; spread half the crumbs into 9 x 13-inch dish. Cream butter and sugar until light; add lightly beaten egg yolks. Fold in stiffly beaten egg whites and almond extract. Spread egg mixture over crumbs in dish. Combine whipped cream and pineapple; pour over egg mixture. Sprinkle remaining crumbs over pineapple mixture. Chill for several hours or overnight.

Lucile Hamann, CWA Chm.
Blue Mt. Grange No. 345
LaGrande, Oregon

PINEAPPLE-MARSHMALLOW DESSERT

1 No. 2 can crushed pineapple
1 lb. marshmallows
1 lg. can evaporated milk, chilled
Graham cracker crumbs

Drain pineapple; reserve juice. Combine marshmallows and 1/2 cup reserved juice in top of double boiler; cook, stirring, until marshmallows are melted. Let cool. Whip milk until soft peaks form. Add pineapple to marshmallow mixture; fold in whipped milk. Line large pan with graham cracker crumbs; pour marshmallow mixture over crumbs. Chill until firm.

Mrs. Willard J. Beckley
Washington Hall Grange No. 2216
Carrollton, Ohio

RUTH'S DESSERT

1 sm. box yellow cake mix
1 8-oz. package cream cheese
2 c. milk
1 3-oz. package instant vanilla
    pudding mix
1 No. 2 can crushed pineapple
1 lg. carton frozen dessert topping

Prepare cake mix according to package directions, using 9 x 13-inch pan. Cool. Beat cream cheese until fluffy; add milk gradually, creaming well. Add pudding mix; blend well. Beat until thick. Spread cream cheese mixture over cake. Drain pineapple; spread over pudding layer. Spread dessert topping over pineapple layer. Garnish with nuts and red cherries, if desired. One-half large box yellow cake mix may be used. Yield: 12 servings.

Mrs. Luther Mylander
Women's Activities Chm.
Oak Harbor Grange No. 2218
Oak Harbor, Ohio

STRAWBERRY ANGEL DESSERT

1 lg. package strawberry gelatin
1 env. dessert topping mix
1 angel food cake
1 med. can fruit cocktail, drained
1 qt. frozen strawberries, thawed

Prepare gelatin according to package directions; chill until partially thickened. Prepare topping mix according to package directions; fold into gelatin. Break cake into bite-sized pieces; add cake, fruit cocktail and strawberries to gelatin mixture. Spoon cake mixture into oblong cake pan; chill until firm.

Mrs. Willard J. Beckley, Lecturer
Washington Hall Grange No. 2216
Carrollton, Ohio

ANGEL DELIGHT

1 angel food cake
1 env. unflavored gelatin
1 sm. can frozen orange juice
   concentrate
1 tbsp. lemon juice
1 c. sugar
2 c. heavy cream, whipped

Tear angel food cake into bite-sized pieces; place in 9 x 13-inch baking pan. Soften gelatin in 1/4 cup cold water; dissolve in 1/4 cup hot water. Stir in orange juice concentrate, lemon juice and sugar; blend thoroughly. Fold whipped cream into gelatin mixture; spoon over cake. Sprinkle with chopped nuts and maraschino cherry halves, if desired. Chill overnight.

Dorothy Rippee, Sec.
Williams Grange No. 399
Murphy, Oregon

APPLE FLUFF

1 pkg. fruit-flavored gelatin
1 1/2 c. applesauce
1 tsp. grated lemon rind
1/4 tsp. cinnamon
1/8 tsp. ground cloves

Dissolve gelatin in 1 cup boiling water; stir in 2/3 cup water. Chill until partially set; beat until fluffy. Fold in applesauce, lemon rind, cinnamon and cloves; blend well. Pour into mold. Chill until firm. May be served with whipped cream, if desired.

Lila M. Byerley, Rec. Sec.
Berryton Grange No. 1430
Berryton, Kansas

APRICOT SALAD DESSERT

2 pkg. apricot gelatin
1 No. 2 can crushed pineapple
2 bananas, sliced
2 c. miniature marshmallows
3/4 c. sugar
2 tbsp. flour
1 egg, beaten
1   8-oz. package cream cheese
1 env. dessert topping mix
Flaked coconut

Dissolve gelatin in 2 cups boiling water; stir in 2 cups cold water. Drain pineapple, reserving 1/2 cup juice. Add pineapple, bananas and marshmallows to gelatin; chill until firm. Combine sugar and flour in saucepan; blend well. Stir in reserved juice; bring to a boil. Cook, stirring constantly, until slightly thickened. Pour small amount of hot mixture over egg, stirring constantly. Return egg mixture to hot mixture; cook, stirring, for about 5 minutes longer. Add cream cheese; stir until smooth. Cool. Prepare dessert topping mix according to package directions; fold into cooled sauce. Spread topping over apricot salad; chill until firm. Sprinkle with coconut, if desired.

Mrs. Zollie Cornett, DWA
Goodwill Grange No. 959
Grayson, Virginia

APRICOT DELIGHT

2 3-oz. boxes apricot gelatin
1 No. 2 can crushed pineapple
2 bananas, sliced
1 c. miniature marshmallows
1 egg, beaten
1/2 c. sugar
2 tbsp. butter
2 tbsp. flour
1 3-oz. package cream cheese, softened

Prepare gelatin according to package directions. Pour in 9 x 13-inch pan; chill until partially set. Drain pineapple, reserving 1/2 cup juice. Add pineapple, bananas and marshmallows; blend well. Chill until firm. Beat egg and sugar together until lemon colored. Melt butter in saucepan; blend in flour. Stir in reserved juice; cook, stirring constantly, until mixture coats spoon. Stir small amount of hot mixture into egg mixture; return to saucepan. Cook, stirring constantly, for about 5 minutes longer. Stir in cream cheese until smooth; cool. Spread over gelatin mixture. Chill until firm.

Mrs. John E. Jones, WA Chm.
Amity Grange No. 1540, Washington Co.
Washington, Pennsylvania

HONEY-BANANA MOLD

1 3-oz. package orange gelatin
1 c. boiling water
2 med. ripe bananas
1/2 c. honey
3 tbsp. lemon juice
2/3 c. evaporated milk, chilled

Dissolve gelatin in boiling water; let cool. Mash bananas in large bowl of electric mixer, using medium speed; blend in honey, lemon juice and cooled gelatin. Chill until partially congealed. Whip gelatin mixture at low speed, gradually adding chilled evaporated milk. Turn speed to high; whip until mixture doubles in volume and becomes thick. Turn into lightly oiled 5-cup mold; chill for about 3 hours or until firm. Garnish with quartered orange slices and maraschino cherries, if desired. Yield: 6 servings.

Photograph for this recipe on page 112.

DARK CHOCOLATE SPONGE

1 envelope unflavored gelatin
1/3 c. cold water
2 sq. unsweetened chocolate
1/2 c. sugar
1/8 tsp. salt
1 tall can evaporated milk
Cointreau Sauce

Sprinkle gelatin over cold water; set aside. Melt chocolate in small saucepan over low heat; stir in sugar and salt. Add evaporated milk gradually, stirring to keep smooth. Add softened gelatin; cook over low heat for 5 minutes, stirring constantly. Chill until mixture begins to set. Beat chocolate mixture in small bowl of electric mixer at high speed until double in bulk and thick; pour into lightly oiled 4-cup mold. Chill for about 3 to 4 hours or until set. Serve with Cointreau Sauce.

Cointreau Sauce

1 c. sugar
2 tbsp. cornstarch
Juice of 1 orange
1/2 c. Cointreau
1 tbsp. orange rind

Combine sugar and cornstarch in small saucepan; stir in orange juice and Cointreau.

Boil for 1 minute, stirring constantly. Remove from heat; add orange rind. Let cool completely.

LIME AND COTTAGE SALAD DESSERT

2 pkg. lime gelatin
3 1/2 c. hot water
12 oz. cottage cheese
1/2 c. mayonnaise
1 14-oz. can fruit cocktail, drained
1 can mandarin oranges, drained
8 maraschino cherries, chopped
1/2 c. colored marshmallows
1/2 c. drained chunk pineapple

Dissolve gelatin in hot water; stir in cottage cheese and mayonnaise. Chill until partially congealed. Beat for 5 minutes at high speed of electric mixer. Add remaining ingredients; stir carefully until well mixed. Pour into pan or mold; chill until firm.

Grace Gratzer, Pomona
Taft Settlement Grange No. 473
Syracuse, New York

LUSCIOUS LIME DESSERT

1 can evaporated milk
1 pkg. lime gelatin
1 3/4 c. hot water
3/4 c. sugar
1/4 c. lime juice
22 cream-filled chocolate cookies
1/2 c. butter or margarine, softened
Shaved semisweet chocolate squares

Chill evaporated milk overnight. Dissolve gelatin in hot water. Add sugar and lime juice; stir until sugar is dissolved. Chill until partially congealed. Crush cookies; mix with butter until well combined. Spread in bottom of large pan. Whip chilled milk until soft peaks form. Add gelatin mixture; beat until well mixed. Pour over cookie crust; refrigerate until firm. Sprinkle top with shaved chocolate before serving.

Bonnie Heath, CWA Chm.
Huntsburg Grange No. 2541
Huntsburg, Ohio

FRUIT SURPRISE

3 3-oz. packages strawberry
   gelatin
2 pkg. frozen strawberries
1 No. 2 can crushed pineapple
4 lg. bananas, mashed
1 pt. sour cream

Dissolve gelatin in 2 1/2 cups boiling water; cool. Thaw strawberries partially. Combine strawberries, pineapple and bananas with gelatin mixture. Pour half the gelatin mixture into 13 x 9-inch dish; chill until firm. Spread sour cream over firm gelatin mixture. Pour remaining gelatin mixture over sour cream carefully. Chill until firm. Serve with whipped cream and maraschino cherries, if desired. Yield: 12-15 servings.

Hazel Swanson, Ex CWA Chm.
Pleasant Valley Grange No. 537
Tillamook, Oregon

MAI TAI BANANA MOLD

Sugar
1 env. unflavored gelatin
Dash of salt
2 eggs, separated
1/2 c. pineapple juice
3/4 c. Mai Tai mix
1/2 c. heavy cream, whipped
2 c. sliced bananas

Combine 1/2 cup sugar, gelatin and salt in saucepan. Beat egg yolks until thick and lemony; add to sugar mixture. Blend in pineapple juice. Cook, stirring constantly, until gelatin is dissolved and mixture is thickened. Stir in Mai Tai mix; remove from heat. Chill until partially set. Beat egg whites until soft peaks form. Add 2 tablespoons sugar gradually, beating until stiff peaks form. Fold egg whites into gelatin mixture; fold in whipped cream. Chill until mixture mounds from spoon; fold in bananas. Turn into large mold. Chill for at least 4 hours or until firm. Yield: 6-8 servings.

Sophie E. Potempo, Master
Reseda Grange No. 703
Sepulveda, California

COTTAGE CHEESE-FRUIT DESSERT

2 1-lb. cartons cottage cheese
1 3-oz. package orange gelatin
1 lg. carton frozen dessert topping
1 No. 2 can crushed pineapple, drained
1/2 c. chopped nuts

Combine all ingredients in large bowl; mix until well blended. Pour into mold or shallow 13 x 9-inch dish; chill until ready to serve.

Mrs. Geraldine Keeler, Pomona
Laurel Hill Grange
Milan, Pennsylvania

DESSERT SALAD DELIGHT

1 pkg. lemon gelatin
1 pkg. orange gelatin
1 can crushed pineapple
1 c. finely diced celery
1 c. finely diced carrots
2 c. fine curd cottage cheese
1 c. whipped cream
1/2 c. finely chopped nuts
1/2 c. mayonnaise

Dissolve lemon and orange gelatins in 1 cup boiling water; chill until slightly thickened. Stir in pineapple, celery, carrots, cottage cheese, whipped cream, nuts and mayonnaise. Pour into mold; chill for several hours or until firm.

Kathryn C. Byrne
Huntsburg Grange No. 2541
Middlefield, Ohio

ENGLISH TRIFLE

1 3-oz. package ladyfingers
1 3-oz. package orange gelatin
1 can mandarin oranges, drained
1 pkg. vanilla pudding

Split ladyfingers; place around side and bottom of 2-quart glass bowl. Prepare gelatin according to package directions; chill until partially set. Fold in mandarin oranges; spoon mixture over ladyfingers. Chill until firm. Prepare pudding according to package directions; cool slightly. Pour pudding over gelatin; chill until set. Garnish with whipped cream, maraschino cherries and additional mandarin orange sections, if desired.

Hazel Haier, WAC
Kirtland Grange No. 1245
Kirtland, Ohio

FLUFFY DESSERT

1 pkg. lemon gelatin
1 c. sugar
Juice of 1 lemon
1 tall can evaporated milk
Crushed vanilla wafers

Dissolve gelatin in 1 cup boiling water; stir in sugar and lemon juice. Beat well. Chill until partially thickened. Place milk in freezer until icy crystals form; beat until stiff. Beat gelatin mixture until fluffy; fold in milk. Arrange wafer crumbs in 11 x 6-inch pan. Pour gelatin mixture into prepared pan. Top with crushed wafers.

Mrs. Laura B. Gillett, Ceres
Central Square Grange No. 583
Central Square, New York

GELATIN FRUIT CAKE

1 box white cake mix
2 3-oz. packages strawberry gelatin
3 c. fruit cocktail

Prepare cake mix according to package directions; bake in 9 x 13 x 2-inch glass baking dish. Cool completely. Dissolve gelatin in 2 cups boiling water; stir in 2 cups cold water. Chill until partially set; stir in fruit cocktail. Spoon gelatin mixture over cake; chill for at least 1 hour. May be served with whipped cream or vanilla ice cream. Yellow cake mix may be substituted; any flavor gelatin may be used.

Edith M. Nail, CWA Vice Chm.
Central Union Grange No. 559
Lemoore, California

FRUIT-MARSHMALLOW DESSERT

2 env. unflavored gelatin
2 c. hot fruit juice
2/3 c. sugar
1/2 tsp. salt
4 tbsp. lemon juice
1 c. diced peaches
1 c. sliced bananas
1 c. cream, whipped
2 egg whites, stiffly beaten
2 c. miniature marshmallows

Soften gelatin in 1/2 cup water. Stir in fruit juice, sugar and salt, stirring until sugar and gelatin are dissolved. Stir in lemon juice; chill until partially set. Fold in peaches, bananas, whipped cream, egg whites and marshmallows. Spoon into 9 x 13-inch baking dish; chill until firm. Cut into squares; place maraschino cherry or nut on each square before serving.

Mrs. Milburn G. Travis, Sec.
Sharon Grange No. 691
Sharon, Wisconsin

GRAHAM CRACKER-STRAWBERRY DESSERT

1 pkg. strawberry gelatin
1 sm. can crushed pineapple
1 c. whipping cream
2 tbsp. sugar
1 tsp. vanilla
1/2 c. chopped nuts
Graham crackers

Dissolve gelatin in 1 cup hot water. Drain pineapple well; reserve juice. Add 1 cup reserved juice to gelatin; chill until partially set. Whip cream, adding sugar and vanilla; fold in nuts and 2/3 cup pineapple. Line bottom of 9 x 13-inch dish with graham crackers. Spoon cream mixture over crackers; top with additional graham crackers. Spoon gelatin mixture over all. Chill until firm. May be served with whipped cream, if desired.

Dorothy Rippee, Sec.
Williams Grange No. 399
Murphy, Oregon

MAPLE FLUFF

2 env. unflavored gelatin
2 c. (packed) maple or brown sugar
2 eggs, separated
1/2 c. chopped walnuts
1/2 c. sugar
2 tbsp. flour
1 c. milk
1 tsp. vanilla

Soften gelatin in 1/2 cup water. Combine maple sugar with 1 1/2 cups water in saucepan; bring to a boil. Boil for 10 minutes. Combine sugar syrup and gelatin, stirring until gelatin is dissolved. Chill until partially set. Beat egg whites until stiff peaks form; fold into chilled mixture. Fold in walnuts; stir in 1/2 teaspoon maple flavoring if brown sugar is used. Pour into mold; chill until set. Beat egg yolks until thick and lemony; add sugar, flour and milk, blending well. Pour into saucepan; cook, stirring constantly, over medium heat until smooth and thickened. Stir in vanilla; cool. Serve sauce with Maple Fluff.

Mrs. Hannah E. Williams, Sec.
Wapping Grange No. 30
Manchester, Connecticut

ORANGE SHERBET DESSERT

1 can mandarin oranges
1 pkg. orange gelatin
1 pt. orange sherbet
1 c. whipping cream, whipped
1 med. angel food cake, cubed

Drain oranges, reserving juice; add enough water to reserved juice to measure 1 cup liquid. Bring to a boil; stir in gelatin until dissolved. Cool until warm. Stir in sherbet until melted; fold in whipped cream. Pour half the gelatin mixture into pan; arrange cake cubes over gelatin mixture. Cover with oranges; top with remaining gelatin mixture. Chill until firm. Yield: 8-9 servings.

Judy Fernald, Ceres
Wonder Grange
Medway, Maine

FRESH ORANGE REFRIGERATOR CAKE

4 c. fresh orange juice
1 1/4 c. sugar
3 envelopes unflavored gelatin
1/3 c. fresh lemon juice
1/8 tsp. salt
1 c. whipping cream
1 c. orange sections
15 (about) ladyfingers

Heat 1 cup orange juice and sugar in sauce-pan until sugar is dissolved; remove from heat. Soften gelatin in another 1 cup orange juice. Add hot juice; stir until gelatin is dissolved. Add remaining 2 cups orange juice, lemon juice and salt; chill until partially congealed. Whip cream until stiff; fold into gelatin mixture. Fold in orange sections. Line bottom and side of 8-inch springform pan with split ladyfingers; fill with orange mixture. Chill for at least 4 hours or until firm. Remove side of pan; place cake on serving plate. Garnish with fresh strawberries, if desired. Serve immediately.

QUICK ORANGE DESSERT

1 can mandarin oranges
1 3-oz. package orange gelatin
2 c. vanilla ice cream

Drain oranges, reserving juice; add enough water to reserved juice to make 1 cup liquid. Heat liquid to boiling point; stir in gelatin until dissolved. Soften ice cream in blender; add to gelatin. Cut up mandarin oranges; add to gelatin mixture. Chill until firm. May be served with topping, if desired.

Helen L. Chandler, Master
Quinnatissett Grange No. 65
North Grosvenordale, Connecticut

PEARL'S DELIGHT

1 lg. package lemon gelatin
1 c. sugar
Juice and grated rind of 2 lemons
1 can evaporated milk, chilled
Graham cracker crumbs to taste

Dissolve gelatin in 1 1/2 cups boiling water; chill until partially set. Whip gelatin until light and fluffy; beat in sugar, lemon juice and rind. Whip evaporated milk until soft peaks form; fold into gelatin mixture. Sprinkle crumbs over bottom of shallow 1-quart dish; pour gelatin mixture carefully over crumbs. Top with additional crumbs; chill until firm.

Mrs. Laura Taylor, Subordinate Pomona
Blue Mountain Grange No. 345
LaGrande, Oregon

RIBBON DESSERT

1 3-oz. package lime gelatin
1 can crushed pineapple
1 3-oz. package lemon gelatin
1 8-oz. package cream cheese
2 c. heavy cream
1 3-oz. package cherry gelatin

Dissolve lime gelatin in 1 cup boiling water. Drain pineapple well; reserve juice. Add 1/2 cup reserved juice and 1 cup pineapple to gelatin mixture; mix well. Pour into large shallow baking dish; chill until firm. Soften cream cheese to room temperature. Beat cream until soft peaks form; beat in cream cheese gradually, blending thoroughly. Beat lemon gelatin into whipped cream mixture. Spread mixture over firm pineapple mixture. Chill. Dissolve cherry gelatin in 2 cups boiling water; cool to room temperature. Pour cherry mixture carefully over whipped cream layer; chill until firm.

Marie Weller, Ladies Activity
Economy Grange
Sewickley, Pennsylvania

ANGEL DELIGHT

2 sm. packages strawberry gelatin
4 c. boiling water
1 c. whipping cream
1/2 c. sugar
1 c. strawberries
1 lg. angel food cake, broken or sliced

Dissolve gelatin in boiling water; chill until partially congealed. Whip until fluffy. Whip cream until soft peaks form; add sugar gradually, whipping until stiff. Fold into gelatin mixture; fold in strawberries. Line bottom of 9 x 13-inch pan with half the cake; pour in half the gelatin mixture. Repeat layers; refrigerate for several hours or until firm.

Martha Beck, Women's Activities Com.
Salem Grange No. 964
Sykesville, Pennsylvania

KANSAS-STYLE STRAWBERRY WHIP

1 pkg. strawberry gelatin
1 c. boiling water
1 pkg. frozen strawberries
1 c. whipped cream or topping

Dissolve gelatin in boiling water. Drain strawberries, reserving juice; add enough cold water to juice to make 1 cup liquid. Add juice to gelatin. Let chill until partially congealed. Whip gelatin mixture slightly. Add remaining ingredients; whip slightly. Chill until firm.

Mrs. Charles Lewis, HEC
New York Valley Grange
Yates Center, Kansas

STRAWBERRY WHIP CAKE

1 box strawberry gelatin
1 tbsp. lemon juice
1 pt. fresh strawberries, crushed
1/2 c. confectioners' sugar
1 c. whipping cream, whipped
2 cake layers

Dissolve gelatin in 1 cup boiling water; add 1/2 cup cold water and lemon juice. Chill until partially congealed. Beat until fluffy. Sweeten strawberries with sugar; stir into gelatin mixture. Fold in whipped cream. Spread strawberry mixture between cake layers; chill thoroughly in refrigerator. Decorate with additional whipped cream, if desired.

Mrs. Eva Ingram, Treas.
Putnam Valley Grange No. 841
Peekskill, New York

STRAWBERRY SALAD DESSERT

1 No. 2 can crushed pineapple
2 3-oz. packages strawberry gelatin
1 1-lb. package frozen strawberries, thawed
1 banana, mashed
1 c. sour cream

Drain pineapple, reserving juice; add enough water to reserved juice to measure 1 3/4 cups liquid. Heat to boiling point; stir in gelatin until dissolved. Cool slightly. Add pineapple, strawberries and banana; chill until syrupy. Beat sour cream for 5 minutes; fold into strawberry mixture. Pour into mold; chill until firm.

Mrs. Geraldine Keeler, Pomona
Laurel Hill Grange
Milan, Pennsylvania

STRAWBERRY MALLOW RUSSE

1 c. chocolate wafer crumbs
1/4 c. margarine, melted
Chocolate wafer halves
1 3-oz. package strawberry gelatin
1 c. boiling water
1 10-oz. package frozen strawberries
1 c. heavy cream, whipped
2 c. miniature marshmallows

Combine crumbs and margarine; press over bottom of 9-inch springform pan. Line sides of springform pan with wafer halves. Dissolve strawberry gelatin in boiling water. Add frozen strawberries; stir until strawberries separate and gelatin mixture thickens. Fold in whipped cream and marshmallows; pour into chocolate crust. Chill until firm. Yield: 8-10 servings.

Della Grove, WAC Chm.
Blackhawk Grange
Leaf River, Illinois

STRAWBERRY SPECIAL

2 tbsp. unflavored gelatin
1/2 c. cold water
1/2 c. hot water

Dash of salt
3 c. heavy cream
1 c. confectioners' sugar
Red food coloring
2 boxes frozen strawberries, partially thawed
1 med. angel food cake

Soften gelatin in cold water. Add hot water and salt; stir until dissolved. Let stand in refrigerator until syrupy. Whip cream until soft peaks form. Add confectioners' sugar and food coloring to tint a deep pink; beat until stiff. Stir strawberries into syrupy gelatin; fold into whipped cream mixture. Break cake into crumbs; spread on bottom of pan. Spread layer of strawberry mixture over cake. Repeat layers until all ingredients are used. Chill until ready to serve. May be refrigerated overnight.

Mrs. H. E. Wilds, CWA Chm.
Dorris Grange No. 393
Dorris, California

STRAWBERRY ANGEL FOOD DESSERT

1 3-oz. package strawberry gelatin
1 tbsp. sugar
Pinch of salt
1 1/4 c. boiling water
1 10-oz. package frozen strawberry slices
1 c. whipping cream, whipped and sweetened
1/2 10-in. angel food cake

Dissolve gelatin, sugar and salt in boiling water; stir in strawberries. Chill until partially congealed. Combine gelatin mixture and whipped cream, stirring carefully to give a marbled effect. Tear cake into pieces; place half the pieces in 8 or 9-inch square pan. Spoon half the strawberry mixture over cake pieces. Repeat layers; refrigerate for several hours or until firm. Cut into squares to serve.

Jeanette Shepard, S and H Chm.
Delhi Grange No. 1192
Delhi, New York

EMERALD ISLE PINEAPPLE DESSERT

1/2 c. non-dairy coffee creamer
1 sm. package lime gelatin
1 c. boiling water
1 c. pineapple juice
1 c. drained crushed pineapple
1 c. softened cream cheese

Combine creamer and gelatin; add boiling water. Stir until dissolved. Add pineapple juice. Chill until slightly set; beat with rotary beater. Fold in pineapple and cream cheese. Pour into individual molds; chill until firm.

Mrs. G. T. Wallbillich, Lecturer
Rocksburgh Grange No. 116
Phillipsburg, New Jersey

ORANGE-PINEAPPLE DESSERT

1 3-oz. package orange gelatin
1 No. 2 can crushed pineapple
1 env. dessert topping mix
1/2 c. cold milk
1 tsp. vanilla

Dissolve gelatin in 1 1/2 cups boiling water. Drain pineapple, reserving 1/2 cup juice. Pour juice into gelatin mixture; mix well. Chill until slightly set. Combine topping mix, milk and vanilla; beat until soft peaks form. Fold topping, pineapple and gelatin mixture together until blended. Chill until firm.

Marie L. Wagner, Ec. Chm.
Eno Grange No. 2080
Bidwell, Ohio

PINEAPPLE BUTTERFLY MOUSSE

1 envelope unflavored gelatin
1 13 1/4-oz. can crushed pineapple
1/2 c. sugar
2 eggs, separated
1 c. sour cream
1 tsp. vanilla
1/2 tsp. grated lemon peel
1 tbsp. lemon juice
1/2 tsp. salt

32 vanilla wafers
Currant jelly

Sprinkle gelatin over undrained pineapple in saucepan; let stand for 5 minutes. Add 1/4 cup sugar and lightly beaten egg yolks; cook slowly until gelatin dissolves and mixture thickens slightly, stirring constantly. Cool to room temperature. Stir in sour cream, vanilla, lemon peel and juice; chill until partially congealed. Beat egg whites with salt until soft peaks form. Beat in remaining 1/4 cup sugar gradually; beat until stiff. Fold into thickened gelatin. Spread half the vanilla wafers with currant jelly; top with remaining wafers. Spoon pineapple mousse into 8 serving dishes; place 1 wafer sandwich in each serving. Spoon remaining mousse over sandwiches. Cut remaining wafer sandwiches into halves; arrange 2 halves, butterfly fashion, on top of each serving. Garnish with crushed pineapple, if desired. Chill for several hours or overnight until set. Yield: 8 servings.

Candies

Candy is the joy of anyone who possesses a "sweet tooth" . . .
and almost everyone falls into that category. Children love it
and adults never outgrow it.

Homemade candy is a perfect gift, particularly at Christmas time.
It expresses the desire to give a little of yourself by investing
some time and effort in a gift. Candy is also an excellent selection
for a gift because it keeps well and is easily packaged. You may
even mail it to out-of-towners. Our candy entries include
recipes for fudge, toffee, and numerous confections.

BEEF CANDY

2 c. sugar
1/2 c. white corn syrup
1/2 c. ground beef, cooked
1 c. milk
3 tbsp. butter
1 tsp. vanilla
1/2 c. chopped nuts

Combine sugar, corn syrup, ground beef, milk and butter in saucepan. Cook to soft-ball stage or 238 degrees on candy thermometer. Cool to 120 degrees. Beat until thick; stir in vanilla and nuts. Spoon into greased pan or dish; cool. Cut into squares to serve.

Shirley Engler, Ceres
Mt. Allison Grange No. 308
Ignacio, Colorado

BROWN SUGAR FUDGE

2 c. (firmly packed) brown sugar
Dash of salt
3/4 c. cream
2 tbsp. butter
3/4 c. chopped walnuts
1 tsp. vanilla

Combine sugar, salt and cream in saucepan; stir until dissolved. Cook to 234 degrees on candy thermometer or to soft-ball stage. Remove from heat; add butter, walnuts and flavoring. Let cool; beat until creamy. Press in buttered pan; cut in squares.

Mrs. Loren Garverick, Past Deputy
Jugs Corners Grange No. 3680
Mansfield, Ohio

CREAM CANDY

5 c. sugar
1/2 tsp. salt
1/4 tsp. soda
1 c. milk
1/2 c. butter
1 tsp. vanilla

Combine sugar, salt and 1 cup water in heavy kettle; bring to a boil, stirring just until sugar dissolves. Reduce heat; cook over medium heat to 240 degrees on candy thermometer. Stir in soda; add milk, one teaspoon at a time, stirring to blend. Add butter in small pieces, stirring until melted. Cook until mixture browns or to 270 degrees on candy thermometer. Stir in vanilla; pour out on cool well-greased surface. Pull candy when cooled; cut into pieces with scissors. Candy will cream when completely cooled. May be wrapped in small pieces of waxed paper and stored in airtight container. May be made only on cold, clear day.

Hazel Bryant, CWA
Marion Grange
Logan, Ohio

COCOA FUDGE

2/3 c. cocoa
3 c. sugar
1/8 tsp. salt
1 1/2 c. milk
1/4 c. butter
1 tsp. vanilla

Combine cocoa, sugar and salt in a large saucepan; add milk gradually, mixing thoroughly. Bring to a boil over high heat, stirring constantly. Reduce heat to medium; boil, without stirring, to 232 degrees on candy thermometer or until a small amount of cocoa mixture dropped in cold water forms a soft ball. Remove from heat; add butter and vanilla. Do not stir until cool. Beat by hand until well mixed; pour into 8 x 8 x 2-inch pan. Cool until hardened; cut in squares.

Mrs. Doris Merriam, Chaplain, S and H Chm.
Genesee Valley Grange No. 1109
Wellsville, New York

DEPRESSION DAY FUDGE

5 c. sugar
1/4 c. cocoa
1 c. corn syrup
1 1/2 c. evaporated milk
1 tsp. vanilla
1/2 tsp. orange extract
2 tbsp. margarine or butter

3/4 c. crunchy peanut butter
1/2 c. chopped nuts

Combine sugar, cocoa, corn syrup and milk in heavy kettle. Cook over medium heat to soft-ball stage or 234 degrees on candy thermometer, scraping side of kettle several times during early part of cooking. Remove from heat; add flavorings, margarine, peanut butter and nuts. Place kettle in cold water; beat candy until thick and creamy. Pour into greased 8-inch square pan; cool. Cut into 1-inch squares to serve. Yield: 16 squares.

Lillian M. Overmyer, Fund Raising
Cleon Grange No. 633
Copemish, Michigan

CREAMY FUDGE

1/2 c. margarine, melted
4 1/2 c. sugar
1 can evaporated milk
3 sm. packages chocolate chips
1 7 1/2-oz. jar marshmallow fluff
Chopped nuts

Combine margarine, sugar and milk in a heavy saucepan; bring to a boil. Reduce heat; boil slowly for 10 minutes, stirring occasionally. Remove from heat. Add chocolate bits and marshmallow fluff; beat until smooth. Stir in nuts; pour into greased pan. Cool thoroughly; cut into squares. Yield: 5 pounds candy.

Mrs. Clara Avery
Stafford Grange No. 1, Inc.
Stafford Springs, Connecticut

MARSHMALLOW-CHOCOLATE FUDGE

2 pkg. semisweet chocolate chips
1 c. sweetened condensed milk
1/2 tsp. salt
1 tsp. vanilla
1 c. chopped nuts
2 1/2 c. miniature marshmallows
1/2 c. candied cherries (opt.)

Melt chocolate chips in top of double boiler over hot water; stir in milk and salt. Blend in

remaining ingredients, cooking until marshmallows are dissolved. Remove from heat; pour into well-greased 8-inch square pan. Cool; cut into squares.

Mrs. Russell Albrecht, S and H Com.
Wide Awake Grange No. 747
Phelps, New York

MARSHMALLOW CREME FUDGE

1 10-oz. jar marshmallow creme
1 1/2 c. sugar
2/3 c. evaporated milk
1/4 c. butter or margarine
1/4 tsp. salt
2 6-oz. packages semisweet chocolate bits
1/2 c. chopped nuts
1 tsp. vanilla

Combine creme, sugar, milk, butter and salt in saucepan; bring to a boil, stirring constantly. Remove from heat; stir in chocolate until melted. Add nuts and vanilla; mix well. Pour into greased 8-inch square pan. Chill until firm. Yield: 2 1/2 pounds candy.

Mrs. Lorenzo Nitcher, Sec.-Treas.
Greenwood Grange No. 1615
Pomona, Kansas

PUDDING FUDGE

1/2 c. margarine
1 sm. package vanilla pudding mix
1 sm. package chocolate pudding mix
1/2 c. milk
4 c. confectioners' sugar
Vanilla
Chopped nuts

Melt margarine in heavy saucepan; add puddings. Stir in milk; cook for 1 minute. Stir in sugar; add vanilla and nuts to taste. Pour into pan; let cool.

Mrs. Diane Doyle
Holland Grange No. 1023
Holland, New York

QUICK CHOCOLATE FUDGE

1/4 c. margarine
3 oz. unsweetened chocolate
1 lb. confectioners' sugar
1/3 c. instant nonfat dry milk
1/2 c. corn syrup
1 tbsp. water
1 tsp. vanilla
1/2 c. chopped nuts or 1 c. miniature
   marshmallows (opt.)

Melt margarine and chocolate in top of 2-quart double boiler. Sift confectioners' sugar and dry milk together; set aside. Stir corn syrup, water and vanilla into chocolate mixture over boiling water; add sugar mixture in 2 additions, stirring well after each addition. Remove from boiling water; mix in nuts. Turn into greased 8-inch square pan; let cool. Cut into squares. Yield: 1 3/4 pounds.

Quick Blonde Fudge

Follow recipe for Quick Chocolate Fudge omitting chocolate and water, using light corn syrup and increasing vanilla to 2 teaspoons.

Quick Brown Sugar Fudge

Follow recipe for Quick Chocolate Fudge omitting chocolate and water, melting 1/2 cup firmly packed brown sugar with margarine and using dark corn syrup.

Quick Peanut Butter Fudge

Follow recipe for Quick Chocolate Fudge omitting chocolate, melting 1/3 cup peanut butter with margarine and using light corn syrup.

Stuffed Fruit

Prepare Quick Chocolate or Blonde Fudge; stuff into dried fruit.

Fudge Roll

Grease two 9-inch square pans. Cover bottom of 1 pan with 2 cups chopped nuts. Prepare 1 recipe Quick Chocolate Fudge. Pour over nuts; spread and smooth. Prepare 1 recipe Quick Blonde Fudge; pour into second pan. Let stand until set but not firm. Turn out chocolate fudge onto waxed paper, then invert so that nuts are on bottom. Roll blonde fudge into tight roll; place on one end of chocolate fudge. Do not stretch blonde fudge. Roll up jelly roll fashion, using waxed paper as aid. Chill until firm; slice with sharp knife.

MILLION DOLLAR FUDGE

4 1/2 c. sugar
1 lg. can evaporated milk
Pinch of salt
1 c. butter or margarine
3 pkg. chocolate chips
1 can marshmallow fluff
2 c. chopped nuts
2 tsp. vanilla

Combine sugar, milk, salt and butter in a heavy saucepan; cook until a small amount of the sugar mixture dropped in cold water forms a soft ball. Remove from heat; stir in remaining ingredients until well combined and thick. Pour into oiled 10 x 14-inch pan. Let stand until hardened.

Mrs. Russell Albrecht, S & H Comm.
Wide Awake Grange No. 747
Phelps, New York

RAISIN-COCONUT FUDGE

2 c. sugar
3 tbsp. cocoa
2 tbsp. light corn syrup
2/3 c. evaporated milk
2 tbsp. butter
1 tsp. vanilla
1 c. raisins
1 c. coconut flakes

Combine sugar, cocoa, syrup and milk in saucepan. Stir until sugar is dissolved. Cook over low heat until temperature reaches 234 degrees on candy thermometer or until mixture forms a soft ball when small amount is dropped in cold water. Remove from heat. Add butter; beat until cooled to lukewarm. Add vanilla. Chop raisins and coconut in blender; add to candy. Beat until thick; pour into greased shallow pan. One cup nuts may be added, if desired.

Mrs. Grover Grigsby, State Master's Wife
Lansing, Michigan

ORANGE CARAMEL FUDGE

1 lg. orange
4 c. sugar
1 tall can evaporated milk
1/4 c. butter
1 c. chopped walnuts

Remove peel with very small layer of white from orange; cut peel into thin strips. Cut strips into very small pieces to measure 1/3 to 1/2 cup; set aside. Place 1 cup sugar in large, deep aluminum skillet or chicken fryer. Place remaining sugar, evaporated milk and butter in heavy 3-quart aluminum saucepan. Place skillet with 1 cup sugar over very low heat. This will warm sugar and skillet for ease in caramelizing. Cook 3 cups sugar mixture over medium heat, stirring frequently, until sugar is dissolved. Cook, stirring occasionally, for about 25 minutes or to 234 degrees on candy thermometer. Remove from heat. Turn heat up to medium under the 1 cup sugar in skillet; stir until sugar is melted and golden brown. Remove skillet from heat; stir in milk mixture, gradually, blending thoroughly. Add orange peel and walnuts to mixture in skillet; beat until mixture begins to stiffen. Turn into lightly-buttered 8-inch square pan; spread evenly with spatula. Cool thoroughly before cutting into squares. Yield: 2 pounds.

Photograph for this recipe on page 128.

HONEY FUDGE

2 c. sugar
1/4 tsp. salt
1 c. evaporated milk
1/3 c. honey
2 tbsp. butter
1 c. chopped nuts

Combine sugar, salt and milk in heavy kettle; bring to a boil. Boil for 5 minutes; stir in honey. Cook to soft-ball stage or to 234 degrees on candy thermometer. Remove from heat; stir in butter. Cool to lukewarm. Beat until creamy; add nuts. Pour into shallow well-greased pan; cool. Cut into squares.

Mary Grafton, Matron
Pleasant Hill Grange No. 1757
Steubenville, Ohio

PEANUT BUTTER FUDGE

3 c. sugar
1/2 c. light corn syrup
1 1/4 c. evaporated milk
1/4 c. margarine
1 tsp. vanilla
1 c. peanut butter
Nuts to taste (opt.)

Combine sugar, corn syrup, milk and margarine in large heavy kettle; bring to a boil. Cook, stirring just until sugar is dissolved, to firm-ball stage or 244 degrees on candy thermometer. Remove from heat; stir in vanilla, peanut butter and nuts. Cool slightly; beat until mixture loses its glossiness. Pour into greased 11 x 8 x 2-inch pan. Cool completely; cut into squares. Yield: 2 pounds candy.

Zada Ehl, Ceres
Broomfield Grange No. 1757
Mt. Pleasant, Michigan

PINEAPPLE-CREAM FUDGE

3 c. sugar
1 1/4 c. light cream
1/4 tsp. salt
1/2 c. crushed pineapple
1 tbsp. butter

Bring sugar, cream and salt to a boil in heavy kettle; boil for 10 minutes. Add pineapple gradually, cooking until mixture forms soft ball or to 234 degrees on candy thermometer. Remove from heat; add butter. Cool slightly; set pan in pan of cold water. Beat until creamy and mixture loses its glossiness. Pour into well-greased 13 x 9 x 2-inch pan. Cool completely; cut into squares. Store in airtight container.

Mrs. Harry Brazlan
Bolton Grange No. 142
Bolton, Massachusetts

PINEAPPLE-NUT FUDGE

1 c. (packed) brown sugar
2 c. sugar
1/2 c. light cream
1 No. 2 can crushed pineapple,
    drained
2 tbsp. butter or margarine
1 tsp. ginger
2 tsp. vanilla
1 c. chopped nuts
1/2 c. maraschino cherries (opt.)

Combine brown sugar, sugar, cream and pineapple in large heavy saucepan; cook to soft-ball stage or 234 degrees on candy thermometer. Remove from heat; stir in butter, ginger and vanilla. Beat until mixture loses glossiness. Add nuts and cherries; blend well. Pour into greased 8 x 8 x 2-inch pan. Cool; cut in squares. Store in airtight container.

Mrs. Glenn Silvernail
North Urbana Grange
Hammondsport, New York

VANILLA FUDGE

3 c. sugar
1/2 c. light corn syrup
1 1/4 c. evaporated milk
1/2 c. margarine or butter
1 tsp. vanilla
1/2 c. chopped nuts

Combine sugar, syrup, milk and margarine in large heavy kettle. Cook over medium heat to firm-ball stage or 244 degrees on candy thermometer. Remove from heat; stir in vanilla and nuts. Beat until mixture loses its glossy appearance. Place in well-greased 11 x 8 x 2-inch pan; cool. Cut into squares. Yield: 2 pounds candy.

Zada Ehl, Ceres
Broomfield Grange No. 1757
Mt. Pleasant, Michigan

PEANUT BUTTER-MARSHMALLOW CANDY

2 c. sugar
2/3 c. milk
1 c. miniature marshmallows
1 c. peanut butter
1 tsp. vanilla

Combine sugar and milk in heavy saucepan; cook to soft-ball stage. Fold marshmallows, peanut butter and vanilla into hot mixture. Beat well until marshmallows are melted and mixture is blended. Spoon into greased pan; cool. Cut into squares to serve.

Sharon Buehrer, Master's Wife
Asst. to Home Ec. Chm.
Aetna Grange No. 310
Delta, Ohio

OLD-FASHIONED BUTTER CRUNCH

1 c. butter
1 1/4 c. sugar
2 tbsp. light corn syrup
2 tbsp. water
1 c. almond chips, toasted
1 6-oz. package semisweet
   chocolate
1 c. ground almonds

Melt butter in heavy pan; add sugar, corn syrup and water. Cook, stirring, to 300 degrees on candy thermometer or to hard-crack stage. Remove from heat; stir in almond chips. Pour quickly into well-greased 9 x 13-inch pan. Let cool until firm; turn out in thin sheet onto waxed paper. Melt chocolate; spread 1/2 of the chocolate over top of candy. Sprinkle with half the ground almonds. Let candy stand until hard. Turn candy; spread with remaining chocolate and sprinkle with remaining ground almonds. Let stand until firm; break into pieces.

Mrs. Russell Metzger, Master
Central Grange No. 1650
Germansville, Pennsylvania

QUICK BUTTER CANDY

1 c. butter
1 c. sugar
Melted chocolate
Chopped nuts

Melt butter in heavy saucepan; stir in sugar until dissolved. Cook, stirring constantly, until mixture begins to turn light brown. Pour quickly onto buttered cookie sheet, making a very thin layer. Let stand until candy is set. Spread with half the melted chocolate; sprinkle with half the nuts. Let stand until hard. Turn candy over. Spread with remaining chocolate; sprinkle with remaining nuts.

Mrs. Nellore Rice, Master
Terre Haute Grange No. 2480
Urbana, Ohio

CHOCOLATE MINT MERINGUES

2 egg whites
1/8 tsp. salt
1/2 tsp. cream of tartar
3/4 c. sugar
5 or 6 drops of green food coloring
1 6-oz. package chocolate mint chips

Combine egg whites, salt and cream of tartar in mixer bowl; beat with electric mixer until soft peaks form. Add sugar gradually, beating until stiff peaks form. Fold in food coloring and chocolate mint chips. Drop by teaspoonfuls onto waxed paper-lined cookie sheet. Preheat oven to 375 degrees for 15 minutes. Turn oven off; place meringues in oven. Let stand overnight. Store in airtight container.

Mrs. Harold E. Roderuck, WAC
Glade Valley Grange No. 417
Walkersville, Maryland

COCONUT AND PEANUT BUTTER EGGS

2 1-lb. boxes powdered sugar
1 c. soft butter
1 8-oz. package cream cheese
1 tsp. vanilla
1 c. peanut butter
1 c. flaked coconut
2 sq. unsweetened chocolate
1 6-oz. package semisweet chocolate bits
1/2 box paraffin

Blend sugar, butter, cream cheese and vanilla together well. Divide mixture into 2 parts. Add peanut butter to one part, mixing well. Add coconut to other part. Shape into small balls; chill for several hours. Combine unsweetened chocolate, chocolate bits and paraffin in double boiler. Heat until ingredients are melted. Dip balls into chocolate mixture; place on waxed paper to cool.

Mrs. Russell Metzger, Master
Central Grange No. 1650
Germansville, Pennsylvania

BUTTERSCOTCH SPOONOODLES

1 3-oz. can chow mein noodles
1 c. coarsely chopped nuts
1/3 c. honey
1/4 c. sugar
2 tbsp. butter

1/2 tsp. vanilla
1/8 tsp. salt
1 6-oz. package butterscotch morsels

Combine chow mein noodles and nuts in mixing bowl; set aside. Combine honey, sugar, butter, vanilla and salt in saucepan; bring to a full boil over moderate heat, stirring constantly. Remove from heat. Add butterscotch morsels; stir until melted and smooth. Pour over noodles and nuts; mix gently until coated. Drop by heaping teaspoonfuls onto waxed paper on baking sheet. Let stand until set or chill until firm. Yield: 32 spoonoodles.

CARAMEL CORN CONFECTION

2 c. brown sugar
1/2 c. dark corn syrup
1 c. margarine
1/2 tsp. cream of tartar
1 tsp. soda
6 qt. popcorn

Combine brown sugar, syrup, margarine and cream of tartar in saucepan. Bring to a hard boil; boil for 5 minutes. Remove from heat; add soda. Stir; pour over popcorn. Bake in 250-degree oven for about 1 hour, stirring 1 or 2 times. Store in tightly covered containers.

Mrs. Berlin Hinton, WAC Chm.
Elmdale Grange No. 2162
Chillicothe, Ohio

OLD-FASHIONED NEEDHAMS

1 sm. boiled potato
1 pkg. flaked coconut
1 1-lb. box powdered sugar
1 tsp. vanilla
Melted chocolate

Peel potato; mash while hot. Add coconut, powdered sugar and vanilla. Spread in greased pan. Chill; cut into squares. Dip each square in melted chocolate; cool on waxed paper.

Evelyn H. Pressey, Ceres
Deering Grange No. 535
Portland, Maine

CHOW MEIN CANDY

1 pkg. chocolate bits
1 c. butterscotch bits
1 can chow mein noodles
1 c. chopped cashew nuts

Melt chocolate and butterscotch bits in double boiler. Remove from heat; stir in chow mein noodles and cashew nuts. Drop by spoonfuls onto waxed paper. Cool.

Mrs. Robert Latterner, WA Chm.
W. Oshtemo Grange
Kalamazoo, Michigan

CREAMED CANDY

4 c. powdered sugar
4 c. flaked coconut
3/4 c. cold mashed potatoes
1 tbsp. vanilla

Combine powdered sugar, coconut, potatoes and vanilla, mixing well. Shape into small balls. May be tinted with food coloring and rolled in chopped nuts or dipped in melted chocolate, if desired. May be shaped into flat rectangle and spread with peanut butter. Roll as for jelly roll; cut into slices.

Marie L. Wagner, Ec Chm.
Eno Grange No. 2080
Bidwell, Ohio

DING BATS

1 c. sugar
1 c. chopped dates
1/2 c. margarine
1 egg, slightly beaten
2 c. oven-toasted rice cereal
1/2 c. chopped nuts
1 pkg. flaked coconut

Combine sugar, dates, margarine and egg in double boiler. Cook, stirring, until dates are softened. Cool. Add rice cereal and nuts. Shape into small balls; roll in coconut.

Nellie M. Hill, Master
Kegar Lake No. 440
North Lovell, Maine

GRAHAM CRACKER ROLL

2 lb. graham crackers, crushed
1 lb. dates, cut up
1 lb. marshmallows, cut up
1 1/2 c. chopped nuts
1/2 c. sugar
Cream

Combine cracker crumbs, dates, marshmallows, nuts, sugar and enough cream to moisten. Shape into a roll; wrap in waxed paper. Store in refrigerator. Slice to serve.

Mrs. Paul F. Vogel, Ceres
McCutchen Grange No. 2360
Fostoria, Ohio

HONEY-MILK BALLS

1/2 c. honey
1/2 c. peanut butter
1 c. instant nonfat dry milk
1 c. quick-cooking oats, uncooked

Combine honey and peanut butter; add dry milk and oats gradually. Shape into small balls; place on waxed paper.

Mrs. Doris Koenig, Past Lady Asst. Steward
Pennsylvania State Grange
Central Grange No. 1650
Slatington, Pennsylvania

PEANUT BUTTER BALLS

2 1/2 c. graham cracker crumbs
1 1-lb. box confectioners' sugar
1 c. margarine
1 1/2 c. peanut butter
1 c. finely chopped nuts
1 12-oz. package butterscotch bits
1/2 bar paraffin

Combine crumbs and sugar; mix well. Add margarine, peanut butter and nuts; blend thoroughly. Shape into balls. Melt butterscotch bits and paraffin in top of double boiler over hot water. Dip balls, using wooden picks, into butterscotch mixture. Place on waxed paper to cool.

Mrs. Mae Long, DWA
Lafayette Grange No. 773
Elliston, Virginia

Cookies

In this chapter we suggest some excellent contributions for your cookie jar. Cookies are family pleasers, custom-made for after school or anytime snacks. And like candy, they are a gift that expresses your personality and creativity.

The many possible sizes, shapes, textures and flavorings are the reason there are more varieties of cookies than of any other baked product. Look for easy-to-make drop cookies, shaped cookies that are pretty and party-going, refrigerated cookies and chocolate brownies in this section.

SCOTCHBREAD DOMINOES

1 c. butter
3/4 c. confectioners' sugar
2 3/4 c. sifted all-purpose flour
1/2 c. blanched almonds,
    finely chopped
1/2 tsp. salt
1 tsp. almond extract
Semisweet chocolate morsels

Cream butter; work in sugar, flour, almonds, salt and almond extract until mixture is fine-crumbed. Press into greased 11 x 7 x 1 1/2-inch pan. Cut into 1 x 1 1/2-inch bars; decorate with semisweet chocolate morsels to resemble dominoes. Bake in 350-degree oven for 30 to 35 minutes. Remove from pan carefully. Yield: 4 dozen bars.

Photograph for this recipe on page 138.

CHEWY BUTTERSCOTCH SQUARES

1/2 c. chopped dates
1/2 c. raisins
1/2 c. evaporated milk
1/2 c. soft butter
1/4 c. confectioners' sugar
1 c. flour
1/4 c. sugar
1 egg, beaten
1 4-oz. package butterscotch pudding mix
1/2 tsp. baking powder
1 2/3 c. flaked coconut

Combine dates and raisins in mixing bowl; pour milk over fruits. Let stand for about 10 minutes. Cream butter and confectioners' sugar until fluffy. Blend in flour, mixing until crumbly. Press crumb mixture into greased 8-inch square pan evenly. Bake in a preheated 350-degree oven for 20 minutes or until lightly browned. Beat sugar into egg gradually; stir in butterscotch pudding mix, baking powder, coconut and date mixture. Spread over baked crust. Bake for 40 minutes or until well browned. Cool; cut into squares. Yield: 16 squares.

Mrs. Mary Rockhill, Ceres
Westville Grange No. 1047
Constable, New York

BROWN SUGAR CHEWS

1 egg
1 c. (packed) brown sugar
1 tsp. vanilla
1/2 c. sifted flour
1/4 tsp. salt
1/4 tsp. soda
1 c. coarsely chopped walnuts

Mix egg, brown sugar and vanilla; add flour, salt and soda. Stir in walnuts. Pour into greased 8-inch square pan. Bake at 350 degrees for 18 to 20 minutes or until cookies are golden. Cool in pan; cut into squares.

Nannette Larson
Humboldt Grange No. 501
Eureka, California

EASY BROWNIES

2/3 c. sifted flour
1/2 tsp. baking powder
1/4 tsp. salt
1/2 c. cocoa
1 c. sugar
1/3 c. shortening
3 eggs, well beaten
1/2 c. chopped nuts
1 tsp. vanilla

Sift flour with baking powder, salt, cocoa and sugar. Cream shortening in large mixer bowl; beat in eggs. Beat in flour mixture until smooth. Stir in nuts and vanilla; blend well. Pour into well-greased 8 x 8 x 2-inch pan. Bake at 350 degrees for 30 to 35 minutes. Cool; cut into squares.

Caroline Minegar
Trowbridge Grange No. 296
Allegan, Michigan

BEST-EVER BROWNIES

1 c. sugar
1/4 c. butter
4 eggs
1 tsp. vanilla
1 16-oz. can chocolate syrup
1 c. plus 1 tbsp. flour
1/2 tsp. baking powder
Salt to taste
1/2 c. nuts

Cream sugar and butter until fluffy. Add eggs, one at a time, beating well after each addition. Add vanilla and chocolate syrup. Sift flour, baking powder and salt together; add to batter, beating well. Stir in nuts. Spoon into brownie pan. Bake in a preheated 350-degree oven for 30 minutes.

Frosting

1 c. sugar
1/4 c. butter
1/4 c. milk
1   6-oz. package chocolate bits

Combine all ingredients except chocolate bits in saucepan; bring to a boil. Remove from heat; add chocolate chips, stirring until melted. Spread over brownies; cut into squares.

Erma Tschida, WAC Sec.-Treas.
Ontario Heights Grange No. 917
Ontario, Oregon

DISAPPEARING MARSHMALLOW BROWNIES

1/2 c. butterscotch bits
1/4 c. butter
3/4 c. flour, sifted
1/3 c. (packed) brown sugar
1 tsp. baking powder
1/4 tsp. salt
1/2 tsp. vanilla
1 egg, beaten
1 c. miniature marshmallows
1 c. semisweet chocolate bits
1/4 c. chopped nuts

Combine butterscotch bits and butter in heavy pan; heat until melted. Add flour, brown sugar, baking powder, salt, vanilla and egg. Fold marshmallows, chocolate bits and nuts into butterscotch mixture just until combined. Spread batter in 9-inch square pan. Bake in a preheated 350-degree oven for 20 to 25 minutes.

Mrs. James Willoughby, Master's Wife
Newark Grange No. 1004
Granville, Ohio

DELUXE BROWNIES

1/2 c. sifted flour
1/2 tsp. baking powder
1/4 tsp. salt
1   6-oz. package semisweet chocolate bits
1/3 c. butter
2 eggs
1/2 c. sugar
1 tsp. vanilla
1 c. chopped nuts

Sift flour, baking powder and salt together. Combine chocolate bits and butter in double boiler; heat until melted. Beat eggs until fluffy, adding sugar gradually; beat until thick. Add sifted dry ingredients, chocolate mixture and vanilla, mixing well. Fold in nuts. Spread batter in greased 8-inch square pan. Bake in a preheated 375-degree oven for about 30 minutes. Cool; cut into squares.

Helen Sturdevant, Home Ec. Com.
Lincoln Grange
Wellsburg, New York

APPLE-WALNUT BROWNIES

1/2 c. butter
2 sq. unsweetened chocolate
2 eggs
1 c. sugar
1 c. sifted cake flour
1/4 tsp. baking powder
1/4 tsp. salt
1 c. chopped walnuts
1 c. finely chopped apples
1 tsp. vanilla

Combine butter and chocolate in top of double boiler over hot water; cook, stirring constantly, until smooth. Cool. Beat eggs until light and lemony, adding sugar gradually. Stir in chocolate mixture; beat for 1 minute. Sift flour, baking powder and salt; add to egg mixture. Stir in nuts, apples and vanilla. Spoon into well-greased 8-inch square pan. Bake at 350 degrees for 35 to 40 minutes. Cool; cut into squares.

Mrs. Joann Berg, Flora
White Pigeon Grange No. 1732
Blaine, Kansas

CHOCOLATE CAKE BROWNIES

2 c. flour
2 c. sugar
1/2 tsp. salt
3/4 tsp. cinnamon
1 1/2 c. margarine
6 tbsp. cocoa
2 eggs
1/2 c. buttermilk
1 tsp. soda
2 tsp. vanilla
Confectioners' sugar
3 tbsp. milk
1/2 c. chopped nuts

Sift flour, sugar, salt and cinnamon into large bowl. Bring 1 cup margarine, 1 cup water and 3 tablespoons cocoa to boil; blend well. Mix with dry ingredients. Add eggs; beat well. Add buttermilk, soda and 1 teaspoon vanilla. Pour into greased jelly roll pan. Bake at 350 degrees for 20 to 25 minutes. Melt remaining margarine in medium saucepan over low heat. Add confectioners' sugar, remaining cocoa and milk to margarine; blend to desired consistency. Stir in remaining vanilla. Frost brownies while warm; sprinkle with nuts. Cool; cut into squares.

Mrs. Donald E. Morton, Wife of Pomona Master
Lamont Grange No. 889
Lamont, Washington

FARMER'S BROWNIES

Cocoa
Butter
2 1/2 c. flour
1 tsp. soda
1/2 tsp. salt
2 c. sugar
2 eggs, slightly beaten
1/2 c. buttermilk or sour milk
1 tsp. vanilla
1 c. chopped nuts
Confectioners' sugar

Mix 1/4 cup cocoa with 1 cup hot water in large mixer bowl; beat in 3/4 cup butter. Cool. Sift flour with soda, salt and sugar; beat into cocoa mixture. Beat in eggs and

buttermilk until well blended; stir in vanilla and nuts. Spread onto well-greased 10 x 15-inch pan. Bake at 375 degrees for 20 minutes. Cool. Combine equal parts cocoa and confectioners' sugar with small amount of hot water; blend in 2 tablespoons butter until mixture is smooth and of spreading consistency. Frost cooled brownies; cut into squares. Nuts and frosting may be omitted and batter sprinkled with finely ground pecans before baking, if desired.

Mrs. D. Vincent Andrews, Sec.
Florida State Grange
Sarasota, Florida

THRIFTY BROWNIES

1 c. sugar
1/2 c. (scant) butter
2 oz. melted unsweetened chocolate
1 egg
1/2 c. milk
3/4 c. sifted flour
1/2 tsp. baking powder
1 c. chopped nuts
1 tsp. vanilla

Combine all ingredients in order listed; blend thoroughly. Pour into well-greased 8 x 10 x 2-inch pan. Bake at 350 degrees for 25 to 30 minutes.

Mrs. Dorothy Youngers, Master
Warsaw Grange No. 1088
Warsaw, New York

FUDGE NUT BARS

Margarine
2 c. (packed) brown sugar
3 tsp. vanilla
2 eggs, slightly beaten
2 1/2 c. flour
1 tsp. soda
1 tsp. salt
3 c. quick-cooking oatmeal
1 12-oz. package chocolate bits
1 can sweetened condensed milk
1 c. chopped walnuts

Cream 1 cup margarine and brown sugar together until fluffy. Add 2 teaspoons vanilla. Add eggs, one at a time, beating well after each addition. Sift flour, soda and salt together; blend into creamed mixture well. Add oatmeal. Spread 2/3 of the oatmeal mixture in a greased 15 1/2 x 10 1/2 x 1-inch pan. Reserve remaining oatmeal mixture. Combine chocolate bits, sweetened condensed milk and 2 tablespoons margarine in double boiler; heat until chocolate bits and margarine are melted and mixture is smooth. Stir in remaining vanilla and walnuts. Spoon chocolate mixture over oatmeal mixture in pan. Spoon reserved oatmeal mixture over chocolate layer. Bake in a preheated 325-degree oven for 25 to 30 minutes. Cool. Cut into bars to serve.

Margaret A. Overla, Treas.
Broomfield Grange No. 1715
Mt. Pleasant, Michigan

JUMBO BROWNIES

1/4 c. butter or margarine
1 6-oz. package semisweet chocolate
   bits
2 eggs, beaten
1/2 c. sugar
1 tsp. vanilla
1 c. flour
1/4 tsp. salt
1/2 tsp. baking powder
1/2 c. chopped walnuts

Melt butter and chocolate in large saucepan; stir until smooth. Remove from heat; cool. Stir in remaining ingredients. Line 12 muffin cups with paper baking cups. Spoon batter into cups. Bake in a preheated 350-degree oven for 25 to 30 minutes or until done. Yield: 12 brownies.

Lucy M. Graham, Pomona
Niagara Co. Pomona Grange
Gasport, New York

WALNUT TREASURE BARS

1/2 c. shortening
1 c. (packed) brown sugar
1 egg
1/4 c. milk
1/4 c. sherry
1 2/3 c. sifted all-purpose flour
1 tbsp. instant coffee powder
3/4 tsp. salt
1/2 tsp. baking powder
1/2 tsp. soda
1/2 tsp. cinnamon
1 c. coarsely chopped California
   walnuts
1 c. semisweet chocolate morsels
Icing

Cream shortening, sugar and egg together; mix in milk and sherry. Batter may look curdled. Resift flour with coffee powder, salt, baking powder, soda and cinnamon. Add to creamed mixture; blend to a smooth batter. Stir in walnuts and chocolate morsels; spread in greased 10 x 15-inch pan. Bake at 375 degrees for about 20 minutes or until top springs back when touched lightly. Cool in pan. Spread with Icing; cut into bars. Decorate tops of bars with additional walnuts and chocolate morsels.

Icing

2 1/4 c. sifted powdered sugar
1 1/2 tbsp. soft butter
2 tbsp. sherry
1 tbsp. milk
1 tsp. instant coffee powder

Combine all ingredients; beat until smooth.

MARSHMALLOW-FUDGE BROWNIES

1 c. margarine
3 oz. chocolate
1 3/4 c. sifted flour
1/2 tsp. baking powder
1/2 tsp. salt
4 eggs
2 c. sugar
1 tsp. vanilla
3/4 c. chopped nuts

Combine margarine and chocolate in top of double boiler over hot water; cook, stirring constantly, until chocolate is melted and mixture is well blended. Remove from heat; cool. Sift flour with baking powder and salt. Beat eggs in mixer bowl until thick and lemony, adding sugar gradually. Beat in chocolate mixture and vanilla; stir in dry ingredients and nuts. Pour mixture into 9 x 13-inch pan. Bake at 350 degrees for 30 minutes; remove from oven. Turn off oven. Spread top of brownies with miniature marshmallows; return to oven for 2 minutes. Remove from oven; spread marshmallows evenly to frost brownies. Cool. Spread with favorite chocolate frosting, if desired. Cut into squares.

Mrs. Shirley Van Buren, Ceres
Kahlotus Grange No. 939
Pasco, Washington

CHOCOLATE-CREAM CHEESE BROWNIES

1 4-oz. package cooking chocolate
5 tbsp. butter
1 3-oz. package cream cheese
1 c. sugar
3 eggs
Flour
1 1/2 tsp. vanilla
1/2 tsp. baking powder
1/4 tsp. salt
1/2 c. coarsely chopped nuts
1/4 tsp. almond extract

Combine chocolate and 3 tablespoons butter in small heavy saucepan. Cook, stirring constantly, over low heat until chocolate is melted and mixture is smooth; cool. Cream remaining butter with cream cheese until fluffy and smooth, adding 1/4 cup sugar gradually. Beat in 1 egg, 1 tablespoon flour and 1/2 teaspoon vanilla until smooth. Beat remaining eggs until fluffy and lemony; beat in 1/2 cup flour, baking powder, salt and chocolate mixture. Stir in nuts, almond extract and remaining vanilla; blend well. Reserve 1 cup batter; spread remaining batter in greased 9-inch square pan. Spoon cheese mixture evenly over batter. Drop reserved batter from spoon over cheese mixture; swirl with spatula. Bake at 350 degrees for 35 to 40 minutes.

Mrs. Frank Conrad, Lecturer
University Grange No. 335, Vermont
Lebanon, New Hampshire
Mrs. John McConnel
Lake Vista Grange No. 336
Cortez, Colorado

MARBLED BROWNIES

2 3-oz. packages cream cheese
5 tbsp. butter or margarine
1/3 c. sugar
2 eggs
2 tbsp. flour
3/4 tsp. vanilla
1 family-sized pkg. brownie mix

Combine cream cheese and butter in mixer bowl; beat until smooth and well blended. Beat in sugar, eggs, flour and vanilla until mixed well. Prepare cakelike brownie batter according to package directions. Pour half the batter into greased 13 x 9-inch pan. Pour cream cheese mixture over batter. Spoon remaining batter over cheese mixture; swirl with spatula. Bake at 350 degrees for 35 to 40 minutes. Cool.

Easy Milk Chocolate Frosting

3 tbsp. butter or margarine
2 tbsp. cocoa
1 1/2 c. sifted confectioners' sugar
2 tbsp. milk
1 tsp. vanilla

Melt butter in medium saucepan; stir in cocoa until dissolved. Beat in confectioners' sugar, milk and vanilla until smooth and of spreading consistency. Milk may be added if icing becomes too thick. Frost cooled brownies; cut into squares. Yield: 24 Brownies.

Robin Lindsey Quist, Ceres, Youth Com.
Boylston Grange No. 111
Boylston, Massachusetts

CARAMEL-CHOCOLATE SQUARES

1 14-oz. package light caramels
2/3 c. evaporated milk
1 pkg. German chocolate cake mix
3/4 c. melted butter
1 c. chopped nuts
1 c. semisweet chocolate chips

Combine caramels and 1/3 cup evaporated milk in heavy saucepan. Cook, stirring constantly, over low heat until caramels are melted and mixture is smooth; set aside. Combine cake mix, butter, remaining evaporated milk and nuts in large bowl; stir until dough holds shape. Press half the dough into greased and floured 13 x 9-inch pan; reserve remaining dough. Bake at 350 degrees for 6 minutes. Sprinkle chocolate chips over baked crust; spread caramel mixture over chocolate chips. Crumble reserved dough over creamed mixture; return to oven. Bake for 15 to 18 minutes longer; cool slightly. Chill for at least 30 minutes. Cut into squares.

Edward Andersen, Master
Nebraska State Grange
Waterloo, Nebraska
Hazel Swanson, Past CWA Chm.
Pleasant Valley Grange No. 537
Tillamook, Oregon

CHOCOLATE-COFFEE BARS

3 c. flour
1 tsp. soda
1 tsp. salt
2 2/3 c. (packed) light brown sugar
2 eggs
1 c. coffee
1 c. salad oil
1 tsp. vanilla
1/2 c. chocolate bits
1/2 c. chopped nuts

Sift flour with soda and salt into large bowl; stir in brown sugar. Beat eggs until light and lemony; beat in coffee. Add egg mixture to flour mixture; blend well. Stir in oil and vanilla. Spread dough onto well-greased cookie sheet; sprinkle with chocolate bits and nuts. Bake at 375 degrees for 30 to 35 minutes.

Mrs. Josephine E. Shorey, Sec.
Branch Mills Grange No. 336
Palermo, Maine

CHERRI-CHOC BROWNIES

1 box brownie mix
1/2 c. sour cream
1 can cherry pie filling

Prepare brownies according to package directions, adding sour cream. Spoon half the batter into brownie pan; cover with pie filling. Spread remaining batter over pie filling. Bake in a preheated 350-degree oven for about 30 minutes.

Nancy Chandler
Quinnatissett Grange No. 65
North Grosvenordale, Connecticut

CHOCOLATE-WHEAT GERM BARS

1/2 c. shortening
2 oz. bitter chocolate
2 eggs
1 c. sugar
1 tsp. vanilla
3/4 c. sifted flour
1/2 tsp. baking powder
1/2 tsp. salt
1 c. wheat germ
1/2 c. nuts

Melt shortening and chocolate in saucepan over low heat; cool. Beat eggs until light and lemony; beat in sugar, chocolate mixture and vanilla. Sift flour, baking powder and salt; add to chocolate mixture. Stir in wheat germ and nuts. Spread mixture in greased 8 x 8 x 2-inch pan. Bake at 350 degrees for 30 to 35 minutes. Cool. Cut into squares.

Mrs. Charles Huff, Master's Wife
Leitersburg Grange No. 361
Smithsburg, Maryland

CONGO COOKIES

2 2/3 c. (packed) light brown sugar
1 c. softened margarine
1 tsp. vanilla
4 eggs
3 c. flour
Dash of salt
1/2 tsp. soda
1 1/2 tsp. baking powder
1 c. chopped nuts
1   12-oz. package chocolate chips

Combine brown sugar and margarine in heavy saucepan; cook over low heat until sugar is dissolved. Stir in vanilla. Cool; add eggs, one at a time, beating well after each addition. Sift flour, salt, soda and baking powder; beat into egg mixture. Stir in nuts and chocolate chips. Pour into 13 x 9-inch greased baking pan. Bake at 350 degrees for 25 to 30 minutes. Cut when cool. Yield: 60 cookies.

Barbara Hansen, Lady Assistant Steward
Wilbraham Grange
North Wilbraham, Massachusetts

FIVE-CUP SURPRISE COOKIES

1/2 c. margarine
1 c. graham cracker crumbs
1 c. flaked coconut
1 c. chopped nuts
1 c. butterscotch or chocolate bits
1 can sweetened condensed milk

Melt margarine in 9 x 13-inch pan. Sprinkle cracker crumbs over margarine. Add layers of coconut, chopped nuts and butterscotch bits. Pour milk over layers; do not stir. Bake in a preheated 300-degree oven for 30 minutes. Cool for several minutes; cut into squares.

Ella Mae Miller
Kincaid Grange
Kincaid, Kansas

HUSBAND'S DELIGHT

1 c. margarine
3 1/2 c. (packed) brown sugar
Flour

4 eggs, beaten
2 c. chopped nuts
2 c. flaked coconut
1 tsp. baking powder
2 tsp. vanilla
Confectioners' sugar

Cream margarine and 1/2 cup brown sugar together until fluffy. Mix in 2 cups flour gradually until mixture is crumbly. Pat crumb mixture into bottom of 14 x 12-inch pan. Bake in a preheated 350-degree oven for 10 minutes. Combine beaten eggs, remaining brown sugar, nuts, coconut, baking powder, 2 tablespoons flour and vanilla. Mix well. Spoon coconut mixture over crumbs in pan. Bake for 25 minutes; cool. Sprinkle with confectioners' sugar.

Mrs. Betty Lampten, Women's Activity Chm.
Franklin Grange No. 1798
Mount Perry, Ohio

LEMON BARS

1/2 c. butter
Flour
1/4 c. confectioners' sugar
2 eggs, beaten
2 tbsp. lemon juice
1 c. sugar
Frosting

Combine butter, 1 cup flour and confectioners' sugar, blending until crumbly. Press crumb mixture into greased 9-inch pan. Bake in a preheated 350-degree oven for 15 to 20 minutes. Cool. Combine eggs, lemon juice, sugar and 2 tablespoons flour. Spoon into prepared pan. Bake for 25 to 30 minutes. Cool. Spread with Frosting; cut into squares to serve.

Frosting

3/4 c. confectioners' sugar
1 1/2 tsp. milk
1 tbsp. butter
1/2 tsp. vanilla

Combine all ingredients, mixing well.

Mrs. Ester Leighton, Sec.
Mt. Forist Grange
Berlin, New Hampshire

LEMON DREAMS

1 c. flour
1/4 c. confectioners' sugar
1/2 c. butter
2 eggs
1 c. sugar
1/2 tsp. baking powder
1/4 tsp. salt
2 tsp. lemon juice

Combine flour, confectioners' sugar and butter; spread in 8-inch square pan. Bake at 350 degrees for 20 minutes. Beat eggs, sugar, baking powder, salt and lemon juice in bowl until well blended. Pour over baked layer; return to oven. Bake for 20 minutes longer. Cool; cut into squares.

Dorothy Wagoner, WA Chm.
Pleasant Grove Grange No. 475
Summerville, Oregon

PUMPKIN SQUARES

1/2 c. butter
1 c. (packed) brown sugar
1 egg, beaten
1/2 c. canned pumpkin
1 1/2 c. sifted flour
1 tsp. cinnamon
1/2 tsp. ginger
1/2 tsp. allspice
1/4 tsp. soda
1/2 c. chopped dates
1/2 c. chopped nuts
Orange Glaze

Cream butter and brown sugar until light and fluffy. Add egg and pumpkin; beat well. Sift flour, spices and soda together; stir into creamed mixture. Add dates and nuts. Spread batter evenly in greased 10 x 15-inch rimmed cookie sheet. Bake in a preheated 350-degree oven for 15 to 18 minutes. Remove from oven; spread with Orange Glaze. Cool; cut into squares.

Orange Glaze

1 c. powdered sugar
1 to 2 tbsp. orange juice
1 tsp. grated orange rind
Dash of salt

Blend sugar and orange juice together; stir in orange rind and salt.

Mrs. Shirley Van Buren, Ceres
Kahlotus Grange No. 939
Pasco, Washington

MAGIC COOKIE BARS

1/2 c. butter or margarine
1 1/2 c. graham cracker crumbs
1 c. chopped nuts
1 c. semisweet chocolate bits
1 1/3 c. flaked coconut
1   15-oz. can sweetened condensed milk

Melt butter in 9 x 13-inch pan; sprinkle crumbs evenly over butter. Add layers of nuts, chocolate bits and coconut. Pour milk over layers; do not stir. Bake in a preheated 350-degree oven for 25 minutes or until lightly browned. Cut into squares to serve.

Beryl Hines, CWA
Rockemeka Grange No. 109
East Peru, Maine

THREE-WAY COCONUT BARS

1 1/2 c. sifted all-purpose flour
1/2 c. sugar
1 tsp. baking powder
1/4 tsp. salt
1/2 c. butter or margarine, softened
2 beaten eggs
1/4 tsp. almond extract
1 c. fruit jam
1 pkg. fluffy white frosting mix
1 1/3 c. flaked coconut

Sift flour with sugar, baking powder, and salt. Add butter, eggs, 1 tablespoon water and almond extract; beat until smooth. Spread in greased and floured 13 x 9 x 2-inch pan; spread jam over dough. Prepare frosting mix according to package directions; fold in 1 cup coconut. Spread over jam; top with remaining coconut. Bake in 350-degree oven for 30 to 35 minutes. Cool; cut into bars. One cup semisweet chocolate or butterscotch bits may be substituted for jam, if desired. Yield: 30 bars.

Grace R. Lord, Master
Crooked River Grange No. 32
Harrison, Maine

OLD-FASHIONED WALNUT-SOUR CREAM COOKIES

2/3 c. butter
1 c. sugar
2 eggs
1 tsp. grated lemon rind
1 tsp. grated orange rind
1 tbsp. lemon juice
2 c. sifted all-purpose flour
1 tsp. baking powder
1/2 tsp. soda
Salt to taste
1/2 c. sour cream
3/4 c. chopped California walnuts
California walnut halves

Cream butter and sugar together. Add eggs, lemon rind, orange rind and lemon juice; cream until light and fluffy. Resift flour with baking powder, soda and salt; add to creamed mixture alternately with sour cream. Stir in chopped walnuts; mix well. Drop by tablespoonfuls onto greased cookie sheet; sprinkle with additional sugar and decorate with walnut halves. Bake at 350 degrees for 15 to 18 minutes. Yield: 2 dozen cookies.

BANANA DROP COOKIES

2 1/4 c. flour
Sugar
2 tsp. baking powder
1/4 tsp. soda
3/4 tsp. salt
2/3 c. shortening
2 eggs
1 c. mashed ripe bananas
1 tsp. vanilla
1/4 tsp. cinnamon

Sift flour, 1 cup sugar, baking powder, soda and salt together. Cut in shortening. Add eggs, bananas and vanilla. Beat until well blended. Drop by teaspoonfuls about 1 1/2 inches apart on ungreased cookie sheet. Combine 1 tablespoon sugar and cinnamon; sprinkle over each cookie. Bake at 350 degrees for 10 to 12 minutes. Remove from pan at once. Yield: 5 dozen cookies.

Mrs. H. R. Failor, Lecturer
Pleasant Run Grange No. 418
Lyndon, Kansas

BROWN SUGAR LACE COOKIES

1/2 c. shortening
1/2 c. (packed) dark brown sugar
1/2 c. sugar
1 egg, beaten
1/2 c. flour, sifted
1/4 tsp. soda
1/2 tsp. salt
1 c. quick-cooking oats
1 c. flaked coconut
1/2 c. chopped nuts
1 tsp. vanilla

Cream shortening and sugars until smooth; add egg. Beat until blended. Add flour, soda and salt; blend well. Add oats, coconut and nuts; mix well. Add vanilla. Drop by teaspoonfuls on greased cookie sheet; flatten with bottom of cold glass. Bake at 350 degrees for 12 minutes. Remove from cookie sheet immediately.

Frances Leary, Master
Rye Grange No. 233
Rye, New Hampshire

BUTTERSCOTCH DROP COOKIES

2 c. (packed) dark brown sugar
2/3 c. butter
2 eggs

2/3 c. buttermilk
1 tsp. vanilla
1 c. chopped nuts
3 c. flour
1 tsp. baking powder
1/2 tsp. soda
1 tsp. salt
1/2 tsp. cinnamon

Cream brown sugar and butter together until fluffy; beat in eggs, buttermilk and vanilla. Stir in nuts. Sift remaining ingredients together; blend into creamed mixture. Drop from a teaspoon onto greased cookie sheet. Bake in a preheated 350-degree oven for 8 to 12 minutes.

Evelyn H. Pressey, Ceres
Deering Grange No. 535
Portland, Maine

BUTTERSCOTCH CRISPS

1/2 c. shortening
1 c. (packed) light brown sugar
1 egg
1 tsp. vanilla
1 c. sifted flour
1/2 tsp. soda
1/2 tsp. salt
1 c. quick-cooking oats
1/2 c. chopped nuts
1 c. shredded coconut

Blend shortening, sugar, egg and vanilla together until fluffy. Sift flour, soda and salt together; add to creamed mixture. Stir in oats, nuts and coconut. Drop from a teaspoon onto greased cookie sheet; flatten to 1/8 inch thickness with flour-covered glass bottom. Bake in a preheated 325-degree oven for 12 to 15 minutes; remove from pan immediately.

Mrs. George F. Farr
Indian River Grange No. 73
Milford, Connecticut

CHOCOLATE CRINKLES

1/2 c. vegetable oil
4 sq. unsweetened chocolate, melted
2 c. sugar
4 eggs

2 tsp. vanilla
2 c. flour
2 tsp. baking powder
1/2 tsp. salt
1 c. confectioners' sugar

Combine oil, chocolate and sugar; stir until well mixed. Blend in eggs and vanilla. Stir flour, baking powder, and salt into oil mixture. Chill for several hours or overnight. Drop by teaspoonfuls into confectioners' sugar. Roll in sugar; shape into balls. Place 2 inches apart on greased baking sheet. Bake at 350 degrees for 10 to 12 minutes. Do not overbake.

Mrs. Russell Albrecht, S and H Com.
Wide Awake Grange No. 747
Phelps, New York

DATE DROP COOKIES

3/4 c. butter
2 c. brown sugar
2 eggs, beaten
3 1/2 c. flour
1 tsp. salt
1 tsp. soda
1/4 tsp. cinnamon
1 tsp. vanilla
1/2 c. buttermilk
2 c. dates
3/4 c. sugar
3/4 c. water
1/2 c. chopped nuts

Cream butter until light; add brown sugar and eggs. Beat until smooth. Sift flour, salt, soda, and cinnamon together; add to creamed mixture. Add vanilla and buttermilk. Combine dates, sugar and water in saucepan. Cook, stirring constantly, until thickened; add nuts. Place 1 tablespoon cookie mixture for each cookie on greased cookie sheet. Add 1 teaspoon date mixture in middle of each cookie. Top with 1 teaspoon cookie mixture. Bake at 375 degrees for 15 minutes.

Mrs. Robert Northrop, Asst. Steward
Delhi Grange No. 1192
Delhi, New York
Mrs. Russell F. Borst, Master
Worthington Grange No. 90
Huntington, Massachusetts

MINCEMEAT COOKIES DELUXE

1 c. shortening
1 1/2 c. sugar
3 eggs
2 c. mincemeat
3 c. flour
1 tsp. soda
1 tsp. cinnamon

Cream shortening with sugar; beat in eggs. Stir in mincemeat; add dry ingredients. Blend well. Drop from spoon onto greased baking sheet. Bake at 350 degrees for 8 to 10 minutes or until cookies are golden.

Mrs. H. E. Wilds, CWA Chm.
Dorris Grange No. 393
Dorris, California

OLD-FASHIONED MINCE COOKIES

1 c. butter or margarine
2 c. (firmly packed) brown sugar
2 eggs, beaten
1 1/3 c. mincemeat
1 tsp. grated lemon rind
4 c. sifted flour
1 tsp. soda
1 tsp. salt

Cream butter until fluffy, adding sugar gradually; beat until light. Stir in eggs, mincemeat and lemon rind; blend well. Sift flour, soda and salt; blend into egg mixture. Drop from teaspoon onto buttered baking sheet 2 inches apart. Bake at 375 degrees for 10 minutes or until golden brown. Remove from baking sheets immediately; cool on wire racks.

Mrs. Mary Rockhill, Ceres
Westville Grange No. 1047
Constable, New York
Mrs. Larry Hicks
West Oshtemo Grange
Kalamazoo, Michigan

ORANGE DROP COOKIES

3/4 c. lard
2 c. sugar
2 eggs
1 tsp. soda

1 c. sour milk
Juice of 1 orange
4 c. flour
Pinch of salt
1 tsp. baking powder

Cream lard and sugar together until fluffy. Beat in eggs, one at a time, beating well after each addition. Dissolve soda in milk; add soda mixture and juice to creamed mixture. Sift flour, salt and baking powder together; add to creamed mixture. Drop from a tablespoon onto greased cookie sheet. Bake in a preheated 350-degree oven for 10 to 15 minutes.

Icing

2 c. powdered sugar
1 tbsp. melted butter
2 tbsp. orange juice

Combine all ingredients with 2 tablespoons boiling water. Spread over warm cookies.

Carrie E. Baumbarger, Past Master
Providence Grange
Grand Rapids, Ohio

ORANGE-NUT COOKIES

2/3 c. shortening
1 c. sugar
2 eggs, slightly beaten
1 tbsp. grated orange rind
2 1/4 c. sifted flour
1/2 tsp. salt
1/2 tsp. soda
1/2 c. orange juice
1/2 c. chopped nuts

Cream shortening and sugar together until fluffy. Combine eggs, creamed mixture and grated rind. Sift flour, salt and soda together. Add dry ingredients to creamed mixture alternately with orange juice; mix until blended. Add nuts. Drop from tablespoon onto greased baking sheet. Bake in a preheated 375-degree oven for 10 minutes or until golden brown. Yield: 3 dozen cookies.

Mrs. Donald Pickinpaugh, LA Steward
Sharon Grange No. 1561
Caldwell, Ohio

PEANUT BUTTER CRISSCROSSES

1 c. margarine
3/4 c. sugar
1 1/2 c. (firmly packed) brown sugar
2 eggs, beaten
1 tsp. vanilla
1 1/2 c. peanut butter
2 3/4 c. sifted all-purpose flour
2 tsp. soda

Cream margarine, sugars, eggs, and vanilla until smooth. Stir in peanut butter. Sift dry ingredients; stir into creamed mixture. Drop by rounded teaspoonfuls onto ungreased cookie sheet. Press with back of floured fork to make crisscrosses. Bake at 350 degrees for about 10 minutes. Yield: About 5 dozen cookies.

Nancy Chandler
Quinnatissett Grange No. 65
North Grosvenordale, Connecticut

PECAN CREAMS

1/2 c. margarine
1/2 c. light corn syrup
1/2 c. (packed) brown sugar
Pinch of salt
1 tsp. vanilla
1 1/2 c. all-purpose flour
1 c. chopped pecans

Combine margarine, syrup and sugar in saucepan; bring to a boil. Remove from heat; add salt, vanilla, flour and pecans. Beat well. Drop by teaspoonfuls on foil-covered cookie sheet. Bake for 8 to 10 minutes at 350 degrees.

Mrs. Wylie E. Heasley, Flora
Shenango Twp. Grange No. 2057
Pulaski, Pennsylvania

NO-BAKE BROWNIES

1 c. evaporated milk
2 c. miniature marshmallows
1 6-oz. package chocolate chips
1/2 c. light corn syrup
1/4 tsp. salt
1 tbsp. butter
1 tsp. vanilla
3 1/4 c. graham cracker crumbs
1 c. chopped nuts

Combine milk, marshmallows, chocolate chips, corn syrup and salt in heavy saucepan; blend well. Bring to a boil; boil, stirring constantly, for 5 minutes. Remove from heat. Stir in butter, vanilla, crumbs and nuts; blend well. Press mixture into greased 9-inch square pan. Chill thoroughly; cut into squares.

Mrs. Thomas Latterner, Lady Asst. Steward
West Oshtemo Grange
Kalamazoo, Michigan

CRUNCHY SNACK COOKIES

1/2 c. crunchy peanut butter
1/4 c. honey
3 c. oven-toasted rice cereal

Combine peanut butter and honey; blend well. Form into small balls; roll in cereal. Serve immediately.

Mrs. John Hook
Greenwood Grange No. 1615
Pomona, Kansas

NO-BAKE CHOCOLATE MACAROONS

1/2 c. milk
1/2 c. butter
2 c. sugar
3 c. oats
6 tbsp. cocoa
1 tsp. vanilla
1 c. coconut
1/2 c. walnuts

Combine milk, butter and sugar in heavy saucepan; blend well. Bring to a boil; boil for 3 to 5 minutes or to 234 degrees on candy thermometer. Remove from heat; stir in oats, cocoa, vanilla, coconut and walnuts just to blend. Drop from teaspoon onto waxed paper; cool.

Mrs. Kenneth Palmer, Sec.
Adirondack Grange No. 1019
St. Regis Falls, New York

FROZEN CANDIED FRUIT COOKIES

1 c. butter or margarine
1 c. sifted confectioners' sugar
1 egg
2 1/2 c. flour
1/2 c. chopped pecans
1/2 c. chopped candied fruit
1 c. whole candied cherries
1/4 tsp. cream of tartar

Cream butter and sugar together; beat in egg. Stir in flour; blend in pecans, fruit, cherries and cream of tartar. Form in rolls 1 1/2 inches in diameter. Wrap in plastic wrap; freeze. Slice very thinly. Place on greased baking sheet. Bake at 375 degrees for 6 to 8 minutes. Yield: 10 dozen cookies.

Mrs. John Engelhardt, Past CWA Chm.
Richland, Holmes Co. Grange No. 2544
Brinkhaven, Ohio

COCONUT-PECAN COOKIES

1 pkg. yellow cake mix
1 pkg. coconut-pecan frosting mix
3/4 c. margarine, melted
2 eggs

Preheat oven to 350 degrees. Combine all ingredients in large bowl; stir until just moistened. Roll into balls the size of walnuts; place on greased cookie sheets 1 1/2 inches apart. Bake for 10 to 15 minutes or until light golden brown. Yield: 4 dozen cookies.

Mrs. Willa Wurm
Harlem Grange, Delaware Co.
Galena, Ohio

BANANA COOKIES

1 c. shortening
1 1/2 c. sugar
2 eggs
3 c. sifted flour
1 tsp. salt
2 1/2 c. milk
2 bananas, mashed
1 tsp. vanilla

Cream shortening, adding sugar gradually, until mixture is light and fluffy. Beat in eggs, one at a time, beating well after each addition. Sift flour with salt. Add flour mixture alternately with milk to egg mixture, beating well after each addition. Stir in bananas and vanilla. Roll paper thin; cut into desired shapes. Place on greased baking sheets. Sprinkle with sugar. Bake at 400 degrees for 5 minutes or until cookies are golden.

Mrs. Harry Brazlan, Master
Bolton Grange No. 142
Bolton, Massachusetts

AUNT MYRTLE'S HONEY COOKIES

2 c. sugar
1 1/2 c. shortening
2 eggs
1/4 c. honey
1/4 c. buttermilk or sour milk
1 tsp. vanilla
5 c. (about) flour
3 tsp. soda
1 tsp. salt

Cream sugar and shortening; beat in eggs. Add honey, milk and vanilla; mix well. Add flour, soda, and salt; mix well. Shape into balls the size of walnuts; roll in sugar. Place on greased cookie sheets. Bake at 350 degrees for 10 to 15 minutes or until golden. Yield: 80 cookies

Sharon Buehrer
Asst., Home Ec. Chm., Master's Wife
Aetna Grange No. 310
Delta, Ohio

COTTAGE CHEESE ROLLS

1 c. cottage cheese
1 c. butter or margarine
2 c. all-purpose flour
1/2 tsp. vanilla
Melted butter
Brown sugar
Chopped nuts

Cream cottage cheese and butter in large mixer bowl; beat in flour and vanilla to a stiff dough. Chill for several hours. Divide dough in half. Roll each half into 1/8-inch thick circle. Brush dough with melted butter; sprinkle with brown sugar and nuts. Cut each circle into 16 wedges; roll up each wedge crescent fashion, starting with wide end. Place on greased cookie sheets. Bake at 400 degrees for 20 to 25 minutes or until golden brown. Roll in sifted confectioners' sugar while still warm, if desired. Store in airtight container.

Doris Southard, Sec.
Lysander Grange No. 1391
Cato, New York

COOKIE THAT WENT TO MARKET

2 c. sugar
1 c. shortening
2 eggs
4 c. (about) flour
1 tsp. soda
1 tsp. baking powder
1/2 tsp. nutmeg
1 c. milk
1 tsp. vanilla
Raisins

Cream sugar and shortening until smooth; beat in eggs until fluffy. Sift flour, soda, baking powder and nutmeg together; add to creamed mixture alternately with milk and vanilla. Mix thoroughly. Let set in refrigerator for 2 hours or overnight. Roll out on floured surface to about 1/4-inch thick; cut. Place raisin in top of each cookie. Sprinkle with additional sugar. Place on cookie sheet. Bake at 400 degrees until lightly browned. Dough freezes well. Cookies may be frosted for holiday occasions.

Mrs. Lewis Lent, Treas.
Prudence Grange No. 1204
Coudersport, Pennsylvania

FAVORITE CHRISTMAS COOKIES

1 tsp. soda
3/4 c. buttermilk
2 c. sugar
1 1/4 c. shortening
3 eggs
1 tsp. baking powder
1 tsp. salt
1/2 tsp. almond or lemon extract
1 tsp. vanilla
6 c. (about) flour

Combine soda and buttermilk. Cream sugar and shortening until light; beat in eggs, baking powder, salt, almond extract and vanilla. Blend well. Beat in buttermilk alternately with enough flour to form soft dough. Beat well after each addition. Refrigerate, covered, for several hours or overnight. Roll out on lightly floured surface; cut into desired shapes. Place on greased cookie sheets. Bake at 375 degrees for 10 to 12 minutes or until lightly browned.

Mrs. Wilbur G. Emo, Treas.
Oak Hill Grange No. 574
Arkport, New York

PEANUT BLOSSOMS

1/2 c. shortening
1/2 c. peanut butter
1/2 c. sugar
1/2 c. (packed) brown sugar
1 unbeaten egg
2 tbsp. milk
1 tsp. vanilla
3/4 c. sifted flour
1 tsp. soda
1/2 tsp. salt
1 8-oz. package milk chocolate candy kisses

Cream shortening and peanut butter together well. Add sugars gradually, blending until fluffy. Add egg, milk and vanilla; beat well. Sift flour, soda and salt together; add to creamed mixture, blending thoroughly. Shape dough into balls; roll in additional sugar. Place balls on ungreased cookie sheets. Bake in a preheated 375-degree oven for 8 minutes. Remove from oven. Place a candy kiss on each cookie, pressing down so cookie cracks around edge. Bake for 2 to 5 minutes longer. Yield: 3 dozen cookies.

Mrs. Paul F. Vogel, Ceres
McCutchen Grange No. 2360
Fostoria, Ohio

DAD'S OLD-FASHIONED SUGAR COOKIES

2 c. sugar
1 c. lard
4 eggs
1 tsp. soda
5 tsp. baking powder
8 c. flour
1/2 c. milk
1 tsp. vanilla

Cream sugar and lard together until fluffy. Add eggs, one at a time, beating well after each addition. Sift soda, baking powder and flour together; add to creamed mixture alternately with milk and vanilla. Roll dough out to 1/4-inch thickness on lightly floured surface. Cut into desired shapes; place on ungreased cookie sheets. Bake in a preheated 350-degree oven for about 9 minutes or until lightly browned.

Mrs. Woodrow Valentine
Wife of State Master
Indiana State Grange
Portland, Indiana

EASY SUGAR COOKIES

1 c. powdered sugar
1 c. sugar
1 c. margarine
1 c. vegetable oil
2 eggs, beaten
1 tsp. vanilla
4 1/2 c. flour
1 tsp. salt
1 tsp. soda
1 tsp. cream of tartar

Cream sugars, margarine and oil together until fluffy. Beat in eggs and vanilla. Sift flour, salt, soda and cream of tartar together. Add dry ingredients to creamed mixture, blending well. Shape dough into small balls; place on ungreased cookie sheet. Flatten balls with sugar-coated glass bottom. Bake in a preheated 375-degree oven for 10 minutes or just until edges start to brown.

Doris Pearson, WAC
Cloverdale Grange No. 752
Hinckley, Minnesota

BUTTERMILK SUGAR COOKIES

1/2 c. shortening
1/2 c. butter
2 c. sugar
3 egg yolks
1 tsp. vanilla
1 tsp. almond extract
1 1/4 c. buttermilk
4 c. flour
4 tsp. baking powder
1 tsp. soda
1/2 tsp. salt

Cream shortening and butter until fluffy; add sugar gradually, creaming well. Beat in egg yolks, flavorings and buttermilk. Sift flour, baking powder, soda and salt together into mixing bowl. Make well in center of dry ingredients; spoon batter into well. Mix well. Chill dough overnight. Roll out to desired thickness on lightly floured surface; cut with cookie cutter. Place cookies on greased cookie sheet; sprinkle with additional sugar. Bake in a preheated 450-degree oven for 8 minutes.

Mrs. Gertrude Risch, Pomona
Oak Harbor Grange No. 2218
Oak Harbor, Ohio

GRAMP'S SUGAR COOKIES

1/4 c. shortening
1/2 c. sugar
1 egg
1 3/4 c. packaged biscuit mix
1 tsp. almond extract
1/2 tsp. lemon extract
1/2 tsp. vanilla extract

Cream shortening and sugar until fluffy in large mixer bowl; beat in egg until mixture is smooth. Beat in remaining ingredients to form smooth soft dough. Shape dough into 1-inch balls; place on greased cookie sheets. Bake at 350 degrees for 12 to 15 minutes or until lightly browned. Yield: 2 1/2 dozen cookies.

Irving W. Seeley, Sterling Master
Great Falls Grange No. 738
Sterling, Virginia

GRANNY'S SUGAR COOKIES

1 1/2 c. sugar
1 c. butter or margarine
3 eggs
1 c. sour cream
1/2 tsp. nutmeg
1/2 tsp. vanilla
4 c. flour
1 tsp. soda
3 tsp. baking powder
1/2 tsp. salt

Cream sugar and butter together until fluffy. Add eggs, one at a time, beating well after each addition. Stir in sour cream, nutmeg and vanilla. Sift flour, soda, baking powder and salt together. Add to creamed mixture, blending well. Chill for 2 hours. Roll dough out on lightly floured surface, small amounts at a time. Roll out to 1/4-inch thickness. Cut into desired shapes. Sprinkle with additional sugar. Place cookies on ungreased cookie sheets. Bake in a preheated 350-degree oven for 8 to 10 minutes.

Lillian M. Overmyer, Fund Raising
Cleon Grange No. 633
Copemish, Michigan

SOUR CREAM-SUGAR COOKIES

1 c. butter or margarine
2 c. sugar
3 eggs
1 c. sour cream
1 tsp. soda
1 tsp. vanilla
1 tsp. lemon extract
4 c. flour

Cream butter and sugar; add eggs, sour cream, soda, vanilla and lemon extract. Add flour; blend well. Additional flour may be used to form easy to handle dough, if necessary. Roll out on lightly floured surface; cut into desired shapes. Place on greased cookie sheets. Bake at 375 degrees for 8 to 10 minutes or until lightly browned.

Mrs. Jesse I. Hawkins, Chm., Cookbook Sales
Alpha Grange No. 154, Lewis Co.
Chehalis, Washington

NO-ROLL SUGAR COOKIES

1/2 c. butter
1/2 c. shortening
1/2 c. sugar
1/2 c. powdered sugar
1 egg
1 tsp. vanilla
2 1/4 c. sifted flour
1/2 tsp. soda
1/2 tsp. salt
1/2 tsp. cream of tartar

Cream butter, shortening and sugars together until light and fluffy. Beat in egg and vanilla. Sift flour, soda, salt and cream of tartar together; add to creamed mixture. Chill dough thoroughly. Shape dough into small walnut-sized balls. Place balls on ungreased cookie sheet; flatten with sugar-coated glass bottom. Bake in a preheated 350-degree oven for 6 to 9 minutes or until lightly browned.

Mrs. Donald E. Morton
Wife of Pomona Master
Lamont Grange No. 889
Lamont, Washington

LOVELY COOKIES

3 c. flour
1/2 tsp. soda
1/2 tsp. baking powder
1 c. shortening
2 beaten eggs
1 c. sugar
1 tsp. salt
Dash of nutmeg
1 tsp. vanilla

Sift flour with soda and baking powder into large bowl; blend in shortening with pastry blender. Beat eggs, adding sugar gradually, until light and fluffy. Combine egg mixture with flour mixture; blend well. Add salt, nutmeg and vanilla; mix thoroughly. Roll dough into small balls; place on greased cookie sheets. Flatten with bottom of glass dipped in sugar. Bake at 350 degrees for 10 to 12 minutes or until lightly browned.

Minnie Jennings, Past Flora
Springville Grange No. 713
Porterville, California

Dessert Breads ——————

Dessert breads are delicious whatever the occasion. A perfect complement to coffee, a dessert bread is an ideal choice for a brunch dessert, flavorful snack, or companion for an after-dinner demitasse.

Coffee cakes, doughnuts, fruit loaves, pancakes and rolls are among the entries in this chapter. Most of the dessert breads may be kept for several days (if properly wrapped and stored) to be brought out at a moment's notice for unexpected guests . . . or family members who come home impatient for a snack.

RAISIN-ORANGE COFFEE CAKE

2 c. sifted flour
1 tbsp. baking powder
3/4 tsp. salt
1/3 c. sugar
1/4 c. shortening
1 c. California seedless raisins
1 egg, lightly beaten
3/4 c. milk
1/3 c. frozen orange juice
   concentrate
1/2 c. (packed) brown sugar
1 tsp. cinnamon
1 tbsp. butter

Resift flour with baking powder, salt and sugar. Cut in shortening; mix in raisins. Combine egg, milk and orange juice; pour into raisin mixture, stirring just enough to moisten flour. Spread in greased 8-inch square pan. Mix brown sugar, cinnamon and butter together until crumbly; sprinkle over top. Bake in 425-degree oven for 25 to 30 minutes or until done.

Photograph for this recipe on page 156.

EASY APPLE COFFEE CAKE

1 pkg. yellow cake mix
1 pkg. instant vanilla pudding mix
4 eggs
1 c. sour cream
1/2 c. salad oil
1/2 c. chopped walnuts
1/2 c. sugar
2 tsp. cinnamon
2 apples, pared and sliced

Combine cake and pudding mixes, eggs, sour cream and salad oil in large mixer bowl; beat for 5 minutes. Combine walnuts, sugar and cinnamon in small bowl; mix well. Pour half the batter into greased 10-inch tube pan; arrange half the apple slices over batter. Top with half the walnut mixture. Repeat layers. Bake at 350 degrees for 1 hour or until cake tests done. Cool in pan for 30 minutes on wire rack. May be frozen for later use, if desired.

Irene F. Alvord
Shetucket Grange No. 69
Hampton, Connecticut

APPLE-CREAM COFFEE CAKE

1/2 c. chopped walnuts
2 tsp. cinnamon
1 1/2 c. sugar
1/2 c. butter or margarine
2 unbeaten eggs
1 tsp. vanilla
2 c. all-purpose flour
1 tsp. baking powder
1 tsp. soda
1/2 tsp. salt
1 c. sour cream
1 med. apple, thinly sliced

Combine walnuts, cinnamon and 1/2 cup sugar. Beat butter with electric mixer until creamy; add remaining sugar, beating at high speed until light and fluffy. Scrape bowl and beaters occasionally. Add eggs, one at a time, beating well after each addition. Add vanilla; beat until blended. Sift flour, baking powder, soda and salt together; add to creamed mixture alternately with sour cream. Spread half the batter in greased 9-inch tube pan. Top with thinly sliced apple; sprinkle with half the walnut mixture. Top with remaining batter; sprinkle with remaining walnut mixture. Bake in a preheated 375-degree oven for 40 minutes or until cake tests done. Remove from oven; let stand in pan on wire rack for 30 minutes. Loosen cake around side with metal spatula. Lift out by tube; let cool on rack. Loosen from tube and base; transfer to serving plate. Cut into wedges; serve warm or cold.

Mrs. Philip Isaman, Color Bearer
Hunt Grange No. 1512
Dalton, New York

DELICIOUS APPLE COFFEE CAKE

1/2 c. margarine
1 c. sugar
2 eggs, well beaten
2 tsp. vanilla
2 c. all-purpose flour
1 tsp. soda
1 tsp. baking powder
1/2 tsp. salt

1 c. sour cream
2 c. finely chopped apples
1 c. (packed) brown sugar
1/2 c. chopped nuts
2 tbsp. butter, softened
2 tsp. cinnamon

Cream margarine in large mixer bowl, adding sugar gradually, until light and fluffy; beat in eggs and vanilla. Sift flour, soda, baking powder and salt; add alternately with sour cream to egg mixture. Mix well. Fold in apples. Spread batter in 13 x 9 x 2-inch pan. Combine brown sugar, nuts, butter and cinnamon; mix well. Sprinkle evenly over batter. Bake at 350 degrees for 45 to 50 minutes or until cake tests done.

Mrs. Stanley E. DeForest, Overseer
Ogden Grange No. 111
Spencerport, New York

GERMAN COFFEE CAKE

3/4 c. butter or margarine
2 c. sugar
3 eggs
1 1/2 tsp. vanilla
1 1/2 c. sour cream
3 c. flour
1 1/2 tsp. baking powder
1 1/2 tsp. soda
1/2 tsp. salt
1/2 c. beer
2/3 c. chopped nuts
2 tsp. cinnamon

Cream butter in large mixer bowl, adding 1 1/2 cups sugar gradually, until light and fluffy. Beat in eggs, one at a time, beating well after each addition; stir in vanilla and sour cream. Sift flour with baking powder, soda and salt; add to egg mixture alternately with beer. Beat until smooth and well blended. Combine remaining sugar with nuts and cinnamon; mix well. Layer 1/3 of the batter with 1/3 of the nut mixture alternately in well-greased 10-inch tube pan. Bake at 350 degrees for 1 hour or until cake tests done. Cool cake in pan on wire rack.

Mrs. John Vosburgh
Florida Grange No. 1543
Amsterdam, New York

COMPANY COFFEE CAKE

1 box white cake mix
1 pkg. instant vanilla pudding mix
1/2 c. salad oil
4 unbeaten eggs
1 c. sour cream
2 tsp. vanilla
1/3 c. sugar
1 c. crushed pecans
1 tsp. cinnamon

Combine cake mix, pudding mix, oil, eggs, sour cream and vanilla in mixer bowl. Beat with electric mixer for 4 minutes. Combine sugar, pecans and cinnamon. Spoon cake batter into greased and floured tube pan alternately with cinnamon mixture. Reserve small amount cinnamon mixture for topping. Swirl through batter with fork; sprinkle with remaining cinnamon mixture. Bake in a preheated 350-degree oven for 50 to 55 minutes. Cool for 15 to 20 minutes; remove from pan.

Mrs. John Hook
Greenwood Grange No. 1615
Pomona, Kansas

QUICK BLUEBERRY COFFEE CAKE

1/2 c. shortening
1 c. sugar
2 eggs
2 c. flour
1/2 tsp. salt
2 1/4 tsp. baking powder
1 c. milk
1 can blueberry pie filling

Cream shortening and sugar until fluffy. Add eggs, one at a time, beating well after each addition. Sift flour, salt and baking powder together. Add to creamed mixture alternately with milk. Spoon batter into large greased loaf pan. Pour pie filling over batter. Bake in a preheated 350-degree oven for about 40 minutes or until cake tests done. May frost with latticed confectioners' frosting, if desired.

Beryl R. Chrisfield, Lady Asst. Steward
Halsey Valley Grange No. 1318
Spencer, New York

FILLED COFFEE CAKE

1/2 c. (packed) brown sugar
2 tsp. cinnamon
Flour
2 tbsp. melted butter
1/2 c. chopped nuts
1 1/2 c. flour
3 tsp. baking powder
3/4 c. sugar
1/4 c. shortening
1 egg
1/2 c. milk

Combine brown sugar, cinnamon, 2 table-spoons flour, melted butter and nuts, mixing well. Set aside. Sift 1 1/2 cups flour, baking powder and sugar together; cut in shortening with pastry blender to crumbly consistency. Beat egg and milk together; blend into crumbly mixture. Spread half the batter in greased 6 x 10-inch pan. Sprinkle with half the brown sugar mixture. Spoon remaining batter over brown sugar layer; sprinkle with remaining brown sugar mixture. Bake in a preheated 350-degree oven for 25 to 30 minutes.

Mrs. Harry Horton, WAC Chm.
Jackson Grange No. 228
Findlay, Ohio

KATHERYN'S COFFEE BREAD

1 pkg. dry yeast
1/2 c. margarine
1/2 c. sugar
1/2 c. milk
Dash of salt
2 beaten eggs
3 1/4 c. flour, sifted

Dissolve yeast in 1/2 cup warm water. Combine margarine, sugar, milk and salt in saucepan. Cook over low heat, stirring, until blended; cool well. Stir in eggs, flour and yeast mixture, blending well. Place dough in greased bowl. Let rise in warm place until doubled in bulk. Divide dough in half; cut each half into 3 long strips. Braid strips; arrange in 2 circles on baking sheets, pinching ends together. Let rise for 1 hour. Bake in a preheated 375-degree oven for 15 minutes.

Frosting

1/4 c. shortening
1/2 box confectioners' sugar
Milk
Pinch of salt
1/2 tsp. vanilla

Cream shortening and sugar, adding small amount of milk to make of spreading consistency. Add salt and vanilla. Spread over cakes. Garnish with cherries and chopped nuts.

Katheryn Robinson, Sec.
Acorn Grange No. 418
Cushing, Maine

PINCH ME CAKE

1 pkg. dry yeast
Sugar
1 c. milk
1 c. margarine
1 tsp. salt
4 c. flour
2 eggs, beaten
1 1/2 c. (packed) brown sugar
5 tsp. cinnamon
3/4 c. chopped nuts

Dissolve yeast in 1/2 cup warm water; add 1 teaspoon sugar. Set aside. Scald milk in 3-quart saucepan; add 1/2 cup sugar, 1/4 cup margarine, salt and 1 1/2 cups flour. Cool to lukewarm. Blend in eggs, yeast mixture and remaining flour. Shape dough into ball; place in greased bowl. Let rise in warm place until doubled in bulk. Melt remaining margarine in small saucepan. Combine brown sugar, cinnamon and nuts in separate bowl. Turn dough out on lightly floured surface; shape into walnut-sized balls. Dip balls in melted margarine; roll in cinnamon mixture. Place balls in greased tube pan in staggered layers. Let rise until almost doubled in bulk. Bake in a preheated 375-degree oven for 35 to 40 minutes. Let stand for 20 minutes before removing from pan.

Martha Beck, Women's Act.
Salem Grange No. 964
Sykesville, Pennsylvania

FROSTED PINEAPPLE COFFEE CAKE

Sugar
3 tbsp. cornstarch
1/4 tsp. salt
5 egg yolks
1 No. 2 1/2 can crushed pineapple
2/3 c. milk
1 pkg. yeast
4 c. flour
1 c. butter
1 recipe confectioners' sugar icing

Combine 1/2 cup sugar, cornstarch and salt in saucepan; stir in 1 slightly beaten egg yolk and pineapple. Cook, stirring constantly, over medium heat until smooth and thickened; cool to lukewarm. Scald milk with 1 teaspoon sugar; cool to lukewarm. Dissolve yeast in 1/4 cup lukewarm water; add to milk mixture. Beat remaining egg yolks slightly; add to yeast mixture. Measure flour into large bowl; cut in butter with pastry blender. Beat in yeast mixture; blend thoroughly to soft, moist dough. Divide dough in half. Roll out half on lightly floured surface to line jelly roll pan and overlap edges. Spread pineapple filling over dough. Roll out remaining dough in rectangle to cover filling; arrange over filling. Turn overlapping edges over top crust; seal and flute edges. Cut vents in top crust. Let rise, covered, in warm place until doubled in bulk. Bake at 375 degrees for 35 to 40 minutes. Frost with confectioners' sugar icing; cut into squares. Serve warm.

Mrs. Kenneth Palmer, Sec.
Adirondack Grange No. 1019
St. Regis Falls, New York

SOUR CREAM COFFEE CAKE

1 c. butter
1 1/2 c. sugar
2 eggs, well beaten
1 c. sour cream
1 tsp. vanilla
1 tsp. baking powder
1/2 tsp. salt
1/2 tsp. soda

2 c. flour
3/4 c. chopped nuts
1 tsp. cinnamon

Cream butter and 1 1/4 cups sugar in large mixer bowl until light; beat in eggs, sour cream and vanilla thoroughly. Sift baking powder, salt and soda with flour; blend into egg mixture. Combine remaining sugar, nuts and cinnamon; mix well. Pour half the batter into well-greased tube pan; sprinkle with half the cinnamon mixture. Pour remaining batter over cinnamon mixture; sprinkle remaining cinnamon mixture over top. Bake at 350 degrees for 50 minutes or until cake tests done. May be sprinkled with confectioners' sugar while warm, if desired.

Mrs. Hazel Haier, WAC
Kirtland Grange No. 1245
Kirtland, Ohio

SPICY DOUGHNUTS

4 eggs
Sugar
1/3 c. milk
1/3 c. melted shortening
3 1/2 c. sifted flour
3 tsp. baking powder
3/4 tsp. salt
2 tsp. cinnamon
1/2 tsp. nutmeg

Beat eggs in large mixer bowl; add 2/3 cup sugar gradually, beating until light. Beat in milk and shortening. Sift flour with baking powder, salt, 1 teaspoon cinnamon and nutmeg; beat into egg mixture until smooth and well blended. Chill for several hours. Roll out on lightly floured surface to 3/8-inch thickness. Cut with floured doughnut cutter; let stand for 15 minutes. Fry in deep hot fat at 375 degrees, turning once, until golden; drain on absorbent toweling. Combine 1/2 cup sugar and remaining cinnamon in paper bag. Shake doughnuts in cinnamon mixture while warm. Yield: 18-24 doughnuts.

Mrs. Mildred Turner, WAC, Flora, Pomona
North Star Grange No. 671
Pomona Grange No. 71
Geneva, Ohio

AFTERNOON TEA DOUGHNUTS

1 egg, well beaten
2 tbsp. sugar
1/2 tsp. salt
3 tbsp. milk
1 tbsp. melted shortening
1 c. flour
2 tsp. baking powder

Combine egg, sugar, salt, milk and shortening in large mixer bowl; beat until well blended. Sift flour with baking powder; beat into egg mixture until smooth and well blended. Force batter through pastry bag with 1/2-inch tip directly into deep hot fat at 370 degrees. Fry until golden; drain well on absorbent toweling. Yield: 24 doughnuts.

Mrs. Mckee Speer, Master
North Washington Grange No. 1826
Apollo, Pennsylvania

BAKER'S DOUGHNUTS

3 pkg. yeast
1/2 c. oil
1/2 c. sugar
1 tbsp. salt
1 egg
7 to 8 c. flour
3 c. confectioners' sugar
2 tsp. vanilla

Dissolve yeast in 2 cups lukewarm water in large bowl; let stand for 1 minute. Cream oil, sugar, salt and egg until well blended; add to yeast mixture, blending well. Add flour gradually, mixing well to a soft smooth dough; knead lightly. Place in greased bowl, turning to grease top; let rise, covered, for 1 hour or until doubled in bulk. Roll out on lightly floured surface to 1/2-inch thickness; cut with floured cutter. Let rise for 10 minutes. Fry in deep hot fat at 400 degrees until golden; drain on absorbent toweling. Combine confectioners' sugar, 1/4 cup water and vanilla; beat until smooth and well blended. Glaze doughnuts. Yield: 50 doughnuts.

Shirley J. Engler, Matron
Mt. Allison Jr. Grange No. 58
Ignacio, Colorado

BAKED DOUGHNUTS

1/2 c. sugar
3/4 c. shortening
1 egg
3 c. flour
1/2 tsp. soda
1 1/2 tsp. mace
1/2 tsp. salt
3/4 c. milk

Cream sugar and shortening in large mixer bowl until smooth and fluffy; beat in egg. Sift flour with soda, mace and salt. Add flour mixture alternately with milk to egg mixture, beating well after each addition. Roll out dough on lightly floured surface to 3/4-inch thickness; cut with floured cutter. Place on greased baking sheets; sprinkle with additional sugar, if desired. Bake at 400 degrees for 10 to 15 minutes or until golden brown.

Theresa Caliendo, CWA
Southington Grange No. 25
Southington, Connecticut

NEVER-FAIL DOUGHNUTS

1 c. sugar
2 eggs
2 tbsp. salad oil
1 c. milk
2 tbsp. vinegar
3 c. flour
3 tsp. baking powder
1 tsp. salt
1 tsp. ginger
1 tsp. nutmeg
1 tbsp. vanilla

Combine sugar, eggs and oil in large mixer bowl; cream until fluffy. Beat in milk and vinegar. Sift flour, baking powder, salt, ginger and nutmeg; beat into egg mixture. Stir in vanilla; mix to a smooth soft dough. Roll out on lightly floured surface; cut with doughnut cutter. Fry in deep hot fat until golden; drain on absorbent toweling.

Hazel Libby, Lady Asst. Steward
Somerset Grange No. 18
Norridgewock, Maine

BANANA-WALNUT BREAD

2 1/4 c. sifted flour
1 c. sugar
1 tsp. baking powder
1 tsp. soda
3/4 tsp. salt
1/2 c. chopped walnuts
1/2 c. chopped dates
1/2 c. shortening
1 c. mashed bananas
2 tbsp. milk
1 tsp. vanilla

Sift flour, sugar, baking powder, soda and salt together; dust walnuts and dates with small amount of sifted ingredients. Combine dry ingredients, shortening and 1/2 cup bananas; beat for 2 minutes. Add remaining bananas, milk and vanilla; beat for 1 minute. Fold in walnuts and dates. Pour in greased 9 x 5 x 3-inch pan. Bake at 350 degrees for 35 minutes.

Mrs. Carrie Baumbarger
Providence Grange No. 2572
Grand Rapids, Ohio

BANANA-NUT-RAISIN BREAD

1/2 c. shortening
3/4 c. sugar
1 egg
2 c. flour
1/2 tsp. soda
1/2 tsp. baking powder
1/2 tsp. salt
1 c. mashed bananas
1 tbsp. lemon juice
1/2 c. chopped nuts
1/2 c. seedless raisins

Cream shortening, sugar and egg until fluffy. Sift flour, soda, baking powder and salt together. Add flour mixture to creamed mixture; stir until well mixed. Stir in bananas, lemon juice, nuts and raisins. Pour in greased 9 x 5 x 3-inch pan. Bake in preheated 350-degree oven for 1 hour.

Mrs. Mark W. Cheesebrough
Montour Valley Grange No. 2005
Oakdale, Pennsylvania

BAKED WALNUT BROWN BREAD

1 1/4 c. sifted all-purpose flour
2 tsp. baking powder
3/4 tsp. soda
1 1/4 tsp. salt
1 1/4 c. graham flour
1 c. chopped California walnuts
1 egg
1/3 c. (packed) brown sugar
1/2 c. light molasses
3/4 c. buttermilk
3 tbsp. melted shortening

Resift all-purpose flour with baking powder, soda and salt; stir in graham flour and walnuts. Beat egg lightly; beat in brown sugar, molasses, buttermilk and shortening. Stir into dry mixture just until flour is moistened. Spoon into 3 greased 1-pound cans. Bake at 350 degrees for 45 minutes or until bread tests done. Let stand for 10 minutes; turn out onto wire rack. Serve warm or cold. Batter may be spooned into 9 x 5 x 3-inch pan and baked at 350 degrees for 50 to 55 minutes, if desired.

JIFFY ORANGE-NUT BREAD

2 c. sifted all-purpose flour
1 tsp. soda
1 tsp. baking powder
1/2 tsp. salt
2 tbsp. butter or margarine
1/2 c. boiling water
2 tbsp. grated orange rind
1/3 c. orange juice
1 c. sugar
2 tbsp. vanilla
1 egg, slightly beaten
1/2 c. coarsely chopped walnuts
6 walnut halves

Sift flour, soda, baking powder and salt together. Melt butter in boiling water in medium bowl; add orange rind and juice, sugar, vanilla and egg. Stir in flour mixture and chopped walnuts; mix just until dry ingredients are moistened. Batter will be lumpy. Pour batter into greased loaf pan; arrange walnut halves down center of loaf. Bake at 350 degrees for 1 hour or until loaf tests done. Remove from pan; cool on wire rack. Day-old loaf slices more easily than fresh.

Mrs. William C. Daniel, Women's Act. Chm.
Hanover Grange No. 1698
Bethlehem, Pennsylvania

SPICY PUMPKIN BREAD

4 c. sifted flour
3 c. sugar
2 tsp. soda
1/2 tsp. salt
1 tsp. baking powder
1 tsp. cinnamon
1 tsp. nutmeg
1 tsp. allspice
1/2 tsp. cloves
1 c. salad oil
1   14 1/2-oz. can pumpkin pie mix
2/3 c. cold water
4 eggs

Sift flour, sugar, soda, salt, baking powder and spices together into large bowl; make well in center. Add oil, pumpkin and water; blend well with beater. Add eggs, one at a time, beating well after each addition. Pour

into well-greased and floured loaf pans. Bake at 350 degrees for 1 hour. Freezes well wrapped in foil.

Barbara Hansen, Lady Asst. Steward
Wilbraham Grange
North Wilbraham, Massachusetts

PINEAPPLE-PECAN BREAD

2 c. flour
3 tsp. baking powder
1 tsp. salt
1/3 c. sugar
2 eggs, well beaten
1/3 c. butter or margarine, melted
1 c. drained crushed pineapple
1 c. broken pecans

Sift flour, baking powder, salt and sugar together. Combine eggs, butter and pineapple in large bowl; add dry ingredients and pecans to the egg mixture, stirring just enough to moisten. Pour in a greased loaf pan. Bake at 350 degrees for 1 hour or until loaf tests done.

Rosamond Harding, Chaplain
Sauhegan Grange No. 10, Amherst
Merimack, New Hampshire

RHUBARB BREAD

1 1/2 c. (packed) light brown sugar
2/3 c. cooking oil
1 egg
1 c. buttermilk
1 tsp. soda
2 tsp. vanilla
2 1/2 c. sifted flour
1 1/2 c. thinly sliced rhubarb
1/2 c. chopped walnuts
1 tsp. salt
1 tbsp. melted margarine
1/3 c. sugar

Combine brown sugar, oil and egg in bowl. Combine buttermilk, soda and vanilla in another bowl. Add buttermilk mixture to brown sugar mixture alternately with flour; mix well. Fold in rhubarb, walnuts and salt. Pour into greased loaf pans. Bake at 325 degrees for 45 to 55 minutes. Combine margarine and sugar for glaze. Remove loaves from oven. Spread with glaze.

Judy Fernald, Ceres
Wonder Grange
Medway, Maine

LIGHT BLUEBERRY MUFFINS

2 c. flour
4 tsp. baking powder
1/2 tsp. salt
1/4 c. sugar
1 egg, beaten
1/4 c. melted shortening or oil
1 c. milk
1 c. blueberries

Sift dry ingredients together; mix egg, shortening and milk together thoroughly. Combine mixtures, stirring just enough to dampen flour. Fold in blueberries. Fill greased muffin pans 2/3 full. Bake in a preheated 400-degree oven for 25 minutes. Yield: 12-15 muffins.

Mrs. Kenneth Palmer, Sec.
Adirondock Grange No. 1019
St. Regis Falls, New York

VI'S BLUEBERRY MUFFINS

1/4 c. sugar
3 tbsp. butter
1 egg
2 c. flour
4 tsp. baking powder
1/2 tsp. salt
1 c. milk
1 c. blueberries

Cream sugar and butter together until fluffy; beat in egg. Sift flour, baking powder and salt together. Add to creamed mixture alternately with milk, mixing well. Dust blueberries with additional flour; fold into batter gently. Fill 12 greased muffin cups 2/3 full. Bake in a preheated 350-degree oven for 25 to 30 minutes. Yield: 12 muffins.

Viola Blake, Home Ec. Chm.
New Hampton Grange No. 123
New Hampton, New Hampshire

FAVORITE SOUR CREAM MUFFINS

1 egg
1 c. sour cream
2 tbsp. sugar
1 tbsp. shortening
1/2 c. chopped dates
1/2 tsp. salt
1 1/3 c. all-purpose flour
1 tsp. baking powder
1/2 tsp. soda

Beat egg until light. Blend in sour cream, sugar, shortening and dates. Sift dry ingredients together; add to egg mixture, blending just to moisten dry ingredients. Spoon batter into greased muffin cups, filling 2/3 full. Bake in a preheated 400-degree oven for 20 to 25 minutes or until golden brown. Yield: 8 muffins.

Marion B. Comstock, Pomona CWA Chm.
New Haven Co. Grange No. 5
Cheshire Grange No. 23
Yalesville, Connecticut

FRENCH MUFFINS

1 c. sugar
1/3 c. shortening
1 egg
1 1/2 c. sifted all-purpose flour
1 1/2 tsp. baking powder
1/2 tsp. salt
1/4 tsp. ground nutmeg
1/2 c. milk
1 tsp. ground cinnamon
6 tbsp. butter, melted

Combine half the sugar, shortening and egg in mixer bowl; cream well. Sift flour, baking powder, salt and nutmeg together. Add to creamed mixture alternately with milk, beating well after each addition. Fill 12 greased muffin cups 2/3 full. Bake in a preheated 350-degree oven for 20 to 25 minutes. Combine remaining sugar and cinnamon. Remove muffins from cups. Dip into melted butter; roll in sugar mixture until coated. Serve warm. Yield: 12 servings.

Mrs. Edward Hoene, Sec.
Kennedy Grange No. 496
Kennedy, New York

SEVEN-WEEK MUFFINS

2 c. 40% bran cereal
4 c. All-Bran
4 eggs, beaten
1 c. oil
2 1/2 c. sugar
1 qt. buttermilk
5 c. flour
5 tsp. soda
1 tsp. salt
1 1/2 c. raisins

Pour 2 cups boiling water over cereals. Cool. Combine eggs, oil, sugar and buttermilk; add bran cereals, mixing well. Add flour, soda and salt; mix well. Stir in raisins. Store in refrigerator in tightly covered containers. Use as needed. Batter will keep in refrigerator for 7 weeks. Spoon into greased muffin cups. Bake in a preheated 350-degree oven for 20 minutes.

Margaret Thomson, Master
El Camino Grange No. 462
Gerber, California

CHEESE BLINTZES

1 8-oz. package farmer cheese,
   softened
1 8-oz. carton cottage cheese
Sugar
2 tsp. grated lemon rind
1 tsp. vanilla
3/4 c. flour
1/4 tsp. salt
4 eggs
2 c. milk
1 tbsp. brandy
Melted butter

Combine cheeses, 2 tablespoons sugar, lemon rind and vanilla; set aside. Combine flour and salt in mixer bowl; add eggs, beating to smooth paste with electric mixer. Stir in milk gradually, mixing to heavy cream consistency. Add 1/2 teaspoon sugar, brandy and 2 tablespoons cooled butter. Beat for 2 to 3 minutes. Heat greased 7-inch crepe pan until drop of water sizzles when dropped on pan. Spoon 2 tablespoons batter into pan for each crepe; tilt pan until batter covers bot-

tom. Cook on 1 side for 1 minute. Spoon mound of cheese mixture on uncooked side of each crepe; roll halfway up. Fold edges in; continue rolling. Pour 1/2 cup butter into large skillet. Brown blintzes on each side over medium heat. May serve with sour cream, if desired.

Marjorie H. Campbell, Home and Comm.
Guiding Star Grange No. 1
Greenfield, Massachusetts

SOURDOUGH PANCAKES

1 c. sifted all-purpose flour
2 tbsp. sugar
1 1/2 tsp. baking powder
1/2 tsp. salt
1/2 tsp. soda
1 beaten egg
1 c. sourdough starter
1/2 c. milk
2 tbsp. cooking oil

Combine flour, sugar, baking powder, salt and soda. Blend egg, sourdough starter, milk and oil together. Stir into flour mixture. Drop batter on hot greased skillet, using 2 tablespoons for each pancake. Bake until golden brown on each side. Yield: 24 pancakes.

Rita P. Armstrong, Lecturer
Nute Ridge Grange No. 316
Farmington, New Hampshire

CINNAMON ROLLS

3/4 c. milk
3 tbsp. margarine
3 tsp. sugar
1/4 tsp. salt
1/2 c. cold water
1 cake yeast
1 egg
3 1/2 c. flour
5 tbsp. melted margarine
1 1/4 c. (firmly packed) brown sugar
2 tbsp. cinnamon
3/4 c. chopped nuts (opt.)

Scald milk; add margarine, stirring until melted. Add sugar, salt, and cold water; crumble yeast into mixture. Beat egg; add to mixture. Add flour; beat with fork. Place on floured board. Cover; let rise for 15 to 20 minutes. Roll thin in oblong form. Combine margarine, brown sugar, cinnamon and nuts. Spread over dough; roll as for jelly roll. Cut in 1 1/2-inch thick slices. Place on greased cookie sheet; press each roll flat. Let rise for 15 to 20 minutes. Bake at 350 degrees for 10 to 15 minutes.

Mrs. Larry Betts
Youth Chm. and Pomona Officer
North Star Grange No. 671, Pomona Grange No. 71
Geneva, Ohio

RICH SWEET ROLLS

3/4 c. milk
1/2 c. sugar
1/2 tsp. salt
1/3 c. margarine
2 env. yeast
1/2 c. warm water
3 eggs
4 c. flour

Heat milk to lukewarm; add sugar, salt and margarine. Dissolve yeast in warm water in large mixing bowl. Add milk mixture, 2 eggs and flour to yeast mixture; stir until all flour is absorbed. Turn out on floured cloth. Divide into 3 equal pieces; form into rectangles. Cover with cloth; refrigerate for at least 30 minutes. Shape as desired. Place in muffin pans or on baking sheet. Let rise until dough holds fingerprint. Brush with 1 beaten egg. Bake at 425 degrees until brown. Ice with powdered sugar icing, if desired.

Blanche Engle, CWA Chm.
Mulino Grange No. 40
Mulino, Oregon

CHERRY REFRIGERATOR BUNS

1 c. butter
4 1/2 c. sifted all-purpose flour
1 pkg. dry yeast
1/4 c. warm water
Sugar
2 eggs, slightly beaten
1/2 tsp. salt
1 lg. can evaporated milk
1 tbsp. lemon juice

1 1-lb. can tart red pitted cherries
3 tbsp. cornstarch
1/2 tsp. nutmeg
Red food coloring (opt.)
Confectioners' sugar

Cut butter into flour in large mixing bowl until mixture resembles coarse meal. Sprinkle yeast over warm water in medium mixing bowl; let stand for 5 minutes to dissolve. Combine 3 tablespoons sugar, eggs, salt, 1 cup evaporated milk and lemon juice; add to flour mixture, stirring to blend. Cover tightly; chill overnight in refrigerator. Drain cherries, reserving 2/3 cup liquid. Combine 1/2 cup sugar, cornstarch and nutmeg in small saucepan; stir in reserved cherry liquid and food coloring. Cook over medium heat until thickened, stirring constantly. Stir in cherries; cook for 1 minute longer. Set aside. Roll out half the dough on lightly floured board to 1/4-inch thickness. Cut into circles, using 3-inch cookie cutter; place on ungreased cookie sheet about 2 inches apart. Spoon 1 teaspoon cherry filling on center of circles; brush circle edges with evaporated milk. Cut remaining dough with 3-inch doughnut cutter; place doughnut circles over filling. Press edges together with floured tines of fork. Bake in preheated 375-degree oven for 10 to 15 minutes or until lightly browned. Combine remaining evaporated milk and enough confectioners' sugar to make icing of desired consistency. Drizzle over warm buns. Yield: 2 dozen buns.

Beverages ———————

Beverages can cool the tongue, warm the body, quicken the spirit,
calm the nerves, set or change a mood, make or break a dinner!
No meal or snack is complete without one, yet the beverage is often
a last-minute consideration . . . more an after-thought than
the integral part of the meal it should be.

Our chapter on beverages has drinks to complement any food,
punches for parties, and beverages that can stand alone on
their own flavor merit.

Also included are desserts for dieters . . . so delicious no one
would suspect they are low calorie. These recipes will help provide
your family with dessert courses that will not add
unwanted pounds.

EGGNOG

12 eggs, separated
2 c. powdered sugar
1 pt. milk
1 pt. whipped cream
Nutmeg to taste (opt.)

Beat egg yolks until light; stir in sugar until dissolved. Stir in milk; fold in whipped cream. Add nutmeg; fold in beaten egg whites. Serve in punch cups.

Mrs. Ruth E. Myers, CWA Chm.
North Stonington Grange No. 138
Gales Ferry, Connecticut

APRICOT TEA

4 c. water
1 c. sugar
1 tea bag
3 sticks cinnamon
8 whole cloves
Juice of 1 lemon
4 c. apricot juice

Mix water, sugar, tea, cinnamon, cloves and lemon juice; bring to a boil. Boil for 5 minutes. Add apricot juice; bring just to a boil. Serve hot. Yield: 12 servings.

Mrs. William Brite, Sec.
Gardner Grange No. 68
Gardner, Kansas

MULLED CRANBERRY DRINK

2 c. low-calorie cranberry juice
   cocktail
1 1/2 c. water
1/3 c. unsweetened grapefruit juice
2 tsp. liquid sweetener
1/4 tsp. cinnamon
1/4 tsp. cloves
1/8 tsp. allspice
1/8 tsp. salt
Cinnamon sticks

Combine all ingredients in saucepan; heat to boiling point. Pour into mugs. Serve with cinnamon sticks. Yield: 1 quart.

Photograph for this recipe on page 168.

HOT APPLE CIDER NOG

2 eggs, beaten
1/2 c. sugar
1 c. apple cider or juice
1/4 tsp. salt
1/4 tsp. cinnamon
1/8 tsp. nutmeg
3 c. scalded milk
1/2 c. whipping cream, whipped

Combine eggs, sugar, apple cider, salt and spices in saucepan. Add scalded milk gradually; heat almost to boiling point, stirring constantly. Pour into mugs; top with whipped cream. Garnish with cinnamon sticks, if desired. Yield: 4 1/2 cups.

FRIENDSHIP TEA

2/3 c. instant tea
1 13-oz. jar orange-flavored
   instant breakfast drink
2 pkg. lemonade mix
2 1/2 c. sugar
2 tbsp. cinnamon
2 tbsp. ground cloves

Mix all ingredients thoroughly. Store in covered container. Use 2 teaspoons tea mixture for each cup of boiling water.

Mrs. Eileen Devore, Home Ec. Chm.
Chester Grange
Wooster, Ohio

SPICED CIDER

1 gal. cider
1/2 lb. brown sugar
3 sticks cinnamon
1 tbsp. allspice
1/2 tsp. salt
1 orange
Whole cloves

Place cider, sugar, cinnamon, allspice and salt in an enamel, Teflon-lined or stainless steel kettle. Stud orange with cloves; add to cider mixture. Simmer for about 30 minutes or until desired spiciness has been reached. Remove orange and spices; serve hot in mugs.

Mrs. Frank Conrad, Lecturer
University Grange No. 335, Vermont
Lebanon, New Hampshire

BASIC PUNCH

2 oz. citric acid
3 lb. sugar
2 qt. boiling water
2 gal. water
1 lg. can pineapple juice
1 lg. can orange juice
Food coloring

Mix first 3 ingredients; let stand overnight. Add remaining ingredients, using desired amount of food coloring. Fruits and more fruit juices may be added, if desired. Yield: 50 servings.

Mrs. LaVerne Eagan, Master
Clinton Grange No. 77
Clinton, Connecticut

DELICIOUS FRUIT PUNCH

1 6-oz. can frozen orange juice
   concentrate
2 6-oz. cans frozen limeade
   concentrate
1 6-oz. can frozen lemonade
   concentrate
1 46-oz. can pineapple juice
1 pt. cranberry juice cocktail
3 c. cold water
2 qt. ginger ale, chilled
Fruit ice ring

Mix concentrates, juices and water in large container; pour into punch bowl. Add ginger ale just before serving; float ice ring on top. Yield: About 30 servings.

Janice N. Going, Lecturer
Coventry Grange No. 75
Coventry, Connecticut

EASY FRUIT PUNCH

1 lg. can unsweetened grapefruit
   juice
1 lg. can red mixed fruit punch
1 qt. ginger ale, chilled

Mix first 2 ingredients in gallon container; chill. Add ginger ale just before serving.

Catherine S. Pulling
Skaneateles Grange No. 458
Skaneateles, New York

GOLDEN PUNCH DELIGHT

3 lg. cans unsweetened pineapple
   juice
1 lg. can unsweetened orange juice
1 can frozen lemon juice
2 pkg. orange drink powder mix
4 1/2 c. sugar
2 qt. water
3 qt. club soda or lemon soda

Combine all ingredients except club soda; add soda just before serving. Yield: Eighty 1/2-cup servings.

Mrs. William Brite, Sec.
Gardner Grange No. 68
Gardner, Kansas

WEDDING PUNCH

4 16-oz. cans frozen orange juice
2 lg. cans pineapple juice
2 lg. bottles club soda
3 16-oz. bottles lemon-lime
   carbonated drink
5 qt. water

Mix all ingredients; add ice just before serving. Yield: 100 servings.

Agnes Stewart, State Secretary's Wife
Cadmus Grange
Meriden, Kansas

INSTANT APPLE TINGLER

2 c. apple juice
1 c. grape juice
1 c. orange juice
2 tbsp. lemon juice

Combine juices in saucepan; heat to boiling point. Serve hot with cinnamon sticks for stirrers. May chill all ingredients and serve over ice, if desired.

APPLE-APRICOT COOLER

2 qt. chilled apple juice
1 qt. chilled apricot nectar
1 qt. chilled club soda
1/4 c. lime juice
1/2 tsp. peppermint extract

Combine all ingredients; pour over ice in tall glasses. Garnish with strips of citrus peel. Yield: 4 quarts.

SURPRISE SPICY REFRESHER

1 c. sugar
11 c. apple juice
1 1/2 tsp. cinnamon
1/2 tsp. cloves
1/4 tsp. ginger
1 qt. chilled pineapple juice
1/4 c. lemon juice

Combine sugar, 1 cup apple juice and spices in saucepan. Boil for 3 minutes; let cool. Combine all ingredients; pour over ice in punch bowl. Garnish with lemon slices, if desired. Yield: 4 quarts.

FROTHY APPLE JUICE COOLER

1 qt. chilled apple juice
1 pt. vanilla ice cream, softened
1 8 3/4-oz. can crushed pineapple
1/2 tsp. cinnamon

Combine apple juice, ice cream and pineapple in blender container; blend until frothy. Serve in tall glasses. Garnish each serving with cinnamon. May be combined using rotary beater, if desired. Yield: 2 quarts.

GRAPE PUNCH

Lemon slices
1 qt. water
1 c. sugar
1 pt. grape juice
Juice of 2 lemons
Juice of 1 orange

Place lemon slice in each compartment of refrigerator trays; fill trays with water. Freeze until hard. Mix water and sugar; heat, stirring, until dissolved. Cool. Stir in remaining ingredients; chill well. Serve with ice cubes.

Oral McKenney
Westvisalia Grange
Tulare, California

GOLDEN FRUIT PUNCH

4 6-oz. cans frozen orange juice
4 6-oz. cans frozen grapefruit
   juice
4 6-oz. cans frozen pineapple
   juice
5 qt. water
Thin orange slices
Hulled fresh strawberries

Combine fruit juices in large pitcher; dilute with 1 quart water. Stir to blend. Pour juice mixture and remaining water over ice cubes in punch bowl; stir to blend. Float orange slices and strawberries on punch. Yield: 50 punch-cup servings.

Mrs. John Cannon, Sec.
Marshall Grange No. 1840
Washington Court House, Ohio

RHUBARB PUNCH

1 1/2 lb. sliced rhubarb
1 qt. water
1 c. sugar
1/3 c. orange juice
1/4 c. lemon juice
Dash of salt
1 qt. ginger ale or soda water

Cook rhubarb in water until tender; strain liquid. Discard rhubarb. Stir sugar into liquid; cool. Add orange juice, lemon juice and salt; place in refrigerator until chilled. Pour over ice cubes; stir in ginger ale.

Mrs. William Balcom
Souhegan Grange No. 10
Amherst, New Hampshire

OUR CHRISTMAS PUNCH

1 1/2 c. sugar
1 1/2 c. lemon juice
3/4 c. orange juice
1 qt. grape juice
1 pt. pineapple juice
3 qt. cold water
1 lg. bottle ginger ale

Mix first 5 ingredients; chill until ready to serve. Add water and ginger ale; mix well. Add ice; serve immediately.

Mrs. Daisie L. Mardin, Master
Campton Grange No. 93
Plymouth, New Hampshire

LEMON-LIME CHRISTMAS PUNCH

3 pkg. presweetened lemon-lime
  drink powder mix
2 qt. milk
1 lg. bottle lemon-lime carbonated
  drink or ginger ale
1 pt. vanilla ice cream

Mix drink powder mix and milk in large container; stir in carbonated drink. Add scoops of ice cream; serve immediately.

Mrs. Nedra Shepard
Sec., Colorado State Grange
Maple Grove Grange No. 154
Wheat Ridge, Colorado

PINK PUNCH

2   3-oz. packages raspberry gelatin
1 lg. can pineapple juice
1 lg. can frozen lemon juice
2 c. sugar
1 qt. ginger ale

Prepare gelatin according to package directions; cool. Add pineapple juice, lemon juice, sugar and 5 cups water; stir until lemon juice is melted and sugar is dissolved. Add ginger ale and ice just before serving.

Mrs. Mae Long, DWA
Lafayette Grange No. 773
Elliston, Virginia

VERY GOOD FRUIT PUNCH

1 qt. orange juice
1 qt. pineapple juice
1 qt. apple juice
2 qt. ginger ale
2 qt. lemon or orange sherbet (opt.)

Mix juices; stir in ginger ale. Place scoops of sherbet in punch; serve immediately. May place ice mold made of fruit juices in punch, if desired. Yield: 40-45 servings.

Mrs. Glenn Lowe, Sec.
Chester Grange No. 1930
West Salem, Ohio

MIXED FRUIT PUNCH

4 lg. cans mixed fruit punch
1 lg. bottle ginger ale
2 pt. lime sherbet

Pour punch into punch bowl; stir in ginger ale. Add ice cubes; place scoops of sherbet in punch. Serve immediately.

Coramae C. Bailey, S and H Com., Treas.
East Bloomfield Grange No. 94
Holcomb, New York

LOW-CALORIE NO-BAKE CHEESECAKE

2 env. unflavored gelatin
3/4 c. sugar
1/4 tsp. salt
3 eggs, separated
1 1/2 c. skim milk
1 tsp. grated lemon rind
3 c. creamed cottage cheese
1 tbsp. lemon juice
1 tsp. vanilla
1/3 c. graham cracker crumbs

Combine gelatin, 6 tablespoons sugar and salt in top of double boiler. Beat egg yolks with skim milk; stir into gelatin mixture. Cook, stirring constantly, over boiling water for 6 minutes or until gelatin dissolves and mixture is slightly thickened; remove from heat. Stir in lemon rind. Chill until syrupy. Beat cottage cheese in large mixer bowl on high speed for 3 minutes; stir in lemon juice and vanilla. Fold in gelatin mixture. Beat egg whites until soft peaks form; add remaining sugar gradually, beating until stiff peaks form. Fold into gelatin mixture. Turn into 8-inch springform pan; sprinkle top with crumbs. Chill until firm. Yield: 12 servings.

Mrs. Elizabeth Dalton, Adv. Chm.
Kapowsin Grange No. 804
Tacoma, Washington

COFFEE-MINT FLOAT

1 tbsp. instant coffee
1/4 c. sugar
1 qt. cold milk
Dash of salt
Few drops of mint extract
1 qt. vanilla ice cream

Combine instant coffee and sugar in large pitcher. Add a small amount of milk; stir until coffee and sugar are dissolved. Add remaining milk, salt and mint extract; stir to blend well. Spoon ice cream into milk mixture; stir lightly. Milk mixture may be poured into tall glasses and topped with scoops of ice cream, if desired. Yield: 6 to 7 servings.

DIETER'S CHEESECAKE

1 env. unflavored gelatin
2 1/2 c. skim milk
1 pkg. instant vanilla pudding mix
1 c. low-fat sm.-curd cottage
   cheese
3 tbsp. lemon juice
2 tbsp. sugar or substitute
Pinch of grated orange rind (opt.)
4 graham crackers, coarsely crumbled

Place gelatin in blender container with 1/4 cup boiling water; blend, covered, at high speed until gelatin is dissolved. Add milk and pudding mix; blend thoroughly on high speed. Add cottage cheese, lemon juice, sugar and orange rind; blend on low speed to mix. Blend on high speed until smooth and thoroughly blended. Place blender container in refrigerator for 20 minutes or until mixture is slightly set. Swirl into 8 sherbet glasses; top with crumbs. Chill for several hours before serving. Yield: 8 servings.

Lucy M. Graham, Pomona
Niagara County Pomona Grange
Gasport, New York

BAKED APPLES

2 apples
2 tsp. artificial brown sugar
Dash of cinnamon
Dash of nutmeg
1 tsp. lemon juice
Hot Lemon Custard

Core apples; place in baking pan. Combine brown sugar and spices; sprinkle over apples. Blend lemon juice and 1/4 cup hot water together; pour around apples. Bake in a preheated 450-degree oven for 25 minutes or until apples are tender. Serve with Hot Lemon Custard.

Hot Lemon Custard

2 eggs, beaten
6 drops of artificial sweetener
1/4 tsp. lemon extract
1/3 c. instant nonfat milk powder

Combine eggs, sweetener and lemon extract; mix well. Combine milk powder and 1 cup water in double boiler; heat until small bubbles form around edge. Add small amount of hot milk mixture to egg mixture, beating well. Return egg mixture to milk mixture. Cook, stirring, until thickened. Yield: 2 servings.

Eugenia Eash, Lady Asst.
Broomfield Grange No. 1757
Coleman, Michigan

CALORIE WATCHER'S DESSERT

1 env. unflavored gelatin
1/4 c. cold water
3/4 c. boiling water
2/3 c. instant nonfat dry milk
Sweetener to equal 4 tbsp. sugar

1/2 tsp. cherry flavoring
1/4 tsp. almond flavoring
1/4 tsp. brandy flavoring

Soften gelatin in cold water. Add to boiling water, stirring until dissolved. Add dry milk, sweetener and flavorings. Chill until almost set. Beat with electric beater at high speed for about 10 minutes or until tripled in bulk and smooth. Spoon into bowl or sherbet dishes immediately.

Rose Michalek, Sec.
Fairfield Grange No. 720
Gervais, Oregon

DIETER'S DELIGHT

1 carton low-fat cottage cheese
1 3-oz. package flavored gelatin
1 lg. can crushed pineapple, drained
1 carton frozen dessert topping

Empty cottage cheese into large bowl. Sprinkle dry gelatin over cottage cheese; mix well. Add pineapple; mix well. Fold in dessert topping. Let stand in refrigerator for 1 hour or until set.

Sophie Potempo, Master
Reseda Grange No. 703
Sepulveda, California

LOW-CALORIE CHOCOLATE PUDDING

1 env. unflavored gelatin
1/4 c. cold water
4 packets sugar substitute
2/3 c. instant nonfat dry milk
1 tbsp. chocolate extract
1/2 tsp. instant coffee
1 c. boiling water

Sprinkle gelatin over cold water in blender container. Add remaining ingredients; blend for several seconds until fluffy. Drop ice cubes in blender, one at a time, letting blender run on medium speed until ice melts. Spoon in dessert dishes.

Gertrude Perron, Past Master
Swansea Grange No. 148
Swansea, Massachusetts

ORANGE-BANANA JELL

1 env. unflavored gelatin
1 tbsp. sugar
1 c. orange juice
2 tsp. lemon juice
1 tsp. vanilla
1 banana, sliced

Soften gelatin in 1/4 cup cold water; dissolve in 1/2 cup hot water. Stir in sugar until dissolved. Add orange juice, lemon juice and vanilla; blend well. Chill until almost set; beat with rotary beater until light and fluffy. Fold in banana; pour into mold. Chill until firm. Yield: 4 servings.

Wilma G. Hoch, Past CWA Chm.
Ostrom Grange
Yuba City, California

PINEAPPLE-COCONUT DELIGHT

1 2/3 c. crushed pineapple
1 env. unflavored gelatin
1/4 tsp. vanilla
1/2 c. instant nonfat milk powder
2 tbsp. lemon juice
1/4 c. sugar
1/2 c. flaked coconut

Drain pineapple, reserving juice. Add enough water to reserved juice to make 1 cup liquid. Soften gelatin in pineapple liquid. Place over low heat, stirring, until gelatin is dissolved. Remove from heat; add pineapple and vanilla. Chill until slightly thickened. Combine milk powder and 1/2 cup ice water in bowl; beat until soft peaks form. Add lemon juice; beat until stiff peaks form. Add sugar gradually, beating well. Fold gelatin mixture and coconut into milk mixture. Spoon into individual dessert dishes; chill until set. Yield: 6-8 servings.

Helen Penhiter, Past Chaplain
Center Grange No. 714
Merrifield, Minnesota

LOW-CALORIE PINEAPPLE CHIFFON CAKE

1 env. unflavored gelatin
1/4 c. sugar
1/4 tsp. salt
3 eggs, separated
1 1/4 c. crushed pineapple and syrup
1 tbsp. lemon juice
1/2 c. ice water
1/2 c. nonfat dry milk solids
6 lg. thin chocolate cookies

Combine gelatin, sugar and salt in top of double boiler; add beaten egg yolks, pineapple and syrup. Cook over boiling water, stirring constantly, until gelatin is dissolved. Remove from heat; add lemon juice. Chill to unbeaten egg white consistency. Fold in stiffly beaten egg whites. Beat ice water and dry milk solids together with rotary beater until stiff peaks form; fold into gelatin mixture. Spoon 1/4 of the mixture into 9 x 5 x 3-inch pan; top with 2 chocolate cookies. Repeat 2 more times; finish with chiffon mixture. Chill until firm.

Mrs. Elizabeth Dalton, Adv. Chm.
Kapowsin Grange No. 804
Tacoma, Washington

RIBBON FUDGE PARFAIT

1 env. chocolate low-calorie
   pudding mix
1 tbsp. instant coffee
2 1/4 c. skim milk
2 egg whites
1   2-oz. package dessert topping
   mix
1/2 tsp. vanilla
1 1/2 tsp. toasted flaked coconut

Combine pudding mix and coffee in saucepan; stir in 1 3/4 cups skim milk. Cook, stirring, until mixture comes to a boil. Remove from heat; cool thoroughly. Beat until smooth. Fold in stiffly beaten egg whites. Prepare topping mix according to package directions, substituting remaining skim milk for whole milk. Stir in vanilla. Fold 1/2 cup topping mix into chocolate mixture. Spoon chocolate mixture and remaining dessert topping alternately into 6 parfait glasses. Sprinkle each parfait with 1/4 teaspoon coconut. Yield: 6 servings.

Irene F. Alvord
Shetucket Grange No. 69
Hampton, Connecticut

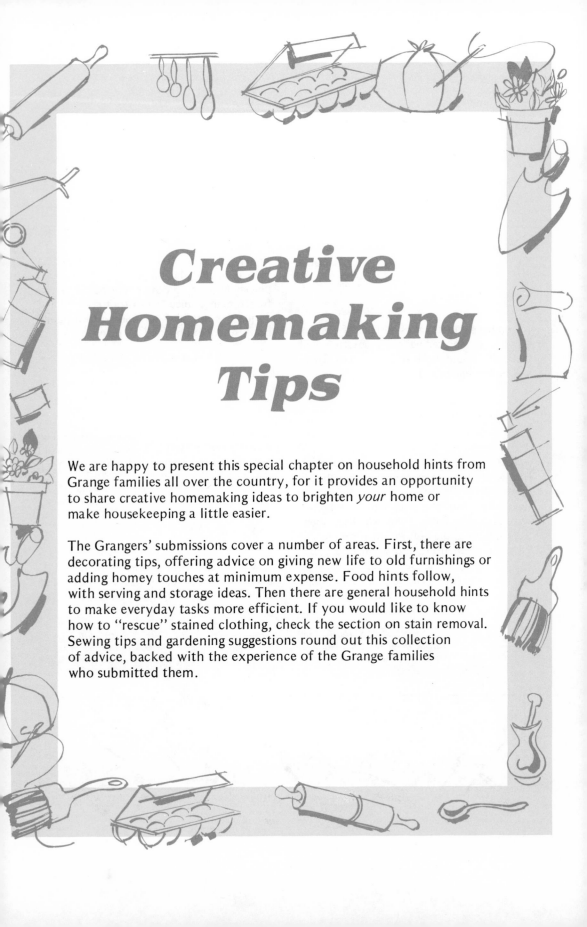

Creative Homemaking Tips

We are happy to present this special chapter on household hints from Grange families all over the country, for it provides an opportunity to share creative homemaking ideas to brighten *your* home or make housekeeping a little easier.

The Grangers' submissions cover a number of areas. First, there are decorating tips, offering advice on giving new life to old furnishings or adding homey touches at minimum expense. Food hints follow, with serving and storage ideas. Then there are general household hints to make everyday tasks more efficient. If you would like to know how to "rescue" stained clothing, check the section on stain removal. Sewing tips and gardening suggestions round out this collection of advice, backed with the experience of the Grange families who submitted them.

For a plate and pot scraper, cut nylon mesh citrus bags into 4-inch lengths and gather into a bundle. Either tie or wrap a bread tie tightly around the middle. This scraper will last longer than nylon net.

Mrs. Luther Mylander, WA Chm.
Oak Harbor Grange No. 2218
Oak Harbor, Ohio

Bake apples in muffin tins to keep their shape.

Helen Saunders, Master
Pleasant Valley Grange No. 136
West Bethel, Maine

If you bake griddle cakes, instead of greasing griddle with shortening, cut a potato in half and rub on griddle, then bake cakes. There will be less smoke and no grease.

Grace Krach, Treas.
Salem Grange No. 964
Dubois, Pennsylvania

It is easier to pare pineapple if you slice it first.
Cover dried fruit and nuts with flour before adding to cake batter. This will keep them from sinking to the bottom when baking.
To ripen green fruits, put them in a paper bag in a dark place for several days.
If grapefruit is unusually sour, a pinch of salt will do more to mellow the flavor than a teaspoon of sugar.

Mary S. Harris, Sec.
Taft Settlement Grange No. 973
Mattydale, New York

Canned or packaged coconut should be refrigerated, tightly covered, after it has been opened.
If shelled nuts are refrigerated in tightly covered containers, they stay fresh-tasting for as long as 9 months.

Mrs. Elizabeth P. Coleman
Home and Comm. Serv. Com. Chm.
Chesterfield Grange No. 83
Chesterfield, Massachusetts

Fixing a beverage for 18 grandchildren can be a problem. Make a punch of 1 large can pineapple juice, 1 can apricot nectar, 1 can frozen orange juice, 1 can fruit cocktail and 1 quart ginger ale and pour into a punch bowl. Add ice cubes and it's ready.

Lillian M. Overmyer, Fund-Raising Chm.
Cleon Grange No. 633
Copemish, Michigan

When making fudge or frosting, add 1/4 teaspoon cream of tartar before removing from heat. This will keep candy from getting hard.

Mrs. Russell Albrecht, S and H Com.
Wide Awake Grange No. 747
Phelps, New York

A white facial tissue placed in the basket of a coffee percolator makes an inexpensive filter and helps in neat removal of the grounds.

Mrs. Wilbur G. Emo, Treas.
Oak Hill Grange No. 574
Arkport, New York

When making ginger puff cookies, use a pastry blender. It works better than a mixer.

Mrs. Russell Albrecht, S and H Com.
Wide Awake Grange No. 747
Phelps, New York

Grease the inside of a pie shell with butter or margarine. It will keep the pie shell from soaking.

Mrs. Marion Schilliger, Home Ec. Chm.
Ashley Grange
Ashley, Ohio

To make pie crust flaky, try adding 1/2 spoon vinegar to cold water when mixing.

Mrs. Earl Mutchler, WACC
Hanover Grange No. 2465, Ashland Co.
Loudonville, Ohio

When cutting a meringue-topped pie, grease the knife and the meringue doesn't tear.

Gertrude Failor, Home Ec. Chm.
Pleasant Run Grange No. 418
Lyndon, Kansas

To keep any soft pie filling from soaking into the bottom crust, brush the crust thoroughly with white of egg before adding the filling.
Add a small amount of sugar to squash and small amount of cream to turnips when cooking; more flavor is obtained.

Evelyn H. Pressey, Ceres
Deering Grange No. 535
Portland, Maine

When baking or cooking, prepare extra pie shells or casseroles to place in the freezer for when time to prepare a meal runs short.

Marion Altemus, CWA Chm.
Rocksburgh Grange No. 116, Warren Co.
Phillipsburg, New Jersey

Prepare a mixture of 1/2 pound butter or margarine, 3 cups sugar, 1 cup quick-cooking oats and 2 cups flour and keep in the refrigerator. A working wife can take a frozen pie crust from the freezer, use a can of prepared pie filling and top with this mixture. Bake at 375 degrees for 30 to 35 minutes and have a quick, warm pie for supper.

Mrs. John O. Smith, WAC
Fairview Grange No. 2177
Goshen, Indiana

Do you bake with your oven light on? If so, the light puts extra heat into that side and could cause uneven baking.
A pound of wieners has nearly as much protein as a pound of T-bone steak — 50 grams compared to 59 in the steak.

Mrs. Walter Davis, WAC
Goehnor Grange No. 371
Seward, Nebraska

To keep raisins from drying out after being opened, keep them in an airtight jar or a covered plastic container.

Nellie DeWitt, Lecturer
Wonder Grange No. 448
Medway, Maine

Rub a small amount of salad oil in gelatin molds. The salads will be easier to remove.

Mrs. H. R. Failor, Lecturer
Pleasant Run Grange No. 418
Lyndon, Kansas

Add several drops of lemon juice to water in which cauliflower is cooked. It will help to preserve the whiteness.

Lucille Hamann, CWA Chm.
Blue Mt. Grange No. 345
LaGrande, Oregon

Freeze leftover gravy in an ice tray to have the exact amount needed for individual hot sandwiches at a later date.

Rosamond Harding, Chaplain
Sauhegan Grange No. 10, Amherst
Merrimac, New Hampshire

After peeling onions, wash hands in cold water and sprinkle small amount of salt on hands to remove odor.

Ruth Holst, CWA Chm.
Thurston Grange
Springfield, Oregon

When boiling eggs, always add 1 teaspoon salt to the water. If the egg should crack, it will not come pouring out of the shell.

Mrs. LaVerne Eagan, Master
Clinton Grange No. 77
Clinton, Connecticut

Grease only the bottoms of layer cake pans. Never grease the side of a tube pan used to bake angel or sponge cakes which must hang inverted after they are baked. Greased sides may hinder the batter from rising to its best volume.

Mrs. Rhoda W. Fennell, WA Chm.
Marshall Grange No. 539, Armstrong Co.
Ford City, Pennsylvania

Keep homemade biscuit mix and pie mix at a cottage for unexpected company. The mixes will keep indefinitely in a cool place; no need to place in refrigerator if kept in jars.

Mrs. Genieva T. Wakely, Flora
Riverview Grange No. 449
Lisbon Falls, Maine

To keep Grange cookbooks from getting soiled while in use, open to recipe and slip book into a 9 x 3 x 18-inch freezer bag.

Ruby Hannigan, Sec.
Westmond Grange No. 302
Sagle, Idaho

Tear off the top of an egg carton and fill with parsley and water. Freeze. When making soup, pop out a cup and place in soup.

Mrs. William C. Daniel
Women's Activity Com.
Hanover Grange No. 1698
Bethlehem, Pennsylvania

When using whipped cream or other whipped topping for the top of gelatin or other desserts, place the topping in a pastry bag and use a cake decorating tube such as one used to make shell borders. Decorate dessert with a border and rosettes of whipped topping.

Doris Southard, Sec.
Lysander Grange No. 1391
Cato, New York

Use a blender for chopping ingredients such as onions, peppers, cabbage and carrots for coleslaw, bread crumbs, nuts, cheese and many others. This saves time and is so easy.

Mrs. Merrill L. Going, CWA Chm.
Coventry Grange No. 75
Andover, Connecticut

Three tablespoons soda in a small dish placed in refrigerator will banish all odors for about 6 weeks. Replace with new soda when soda doesn't work anymore.

Mrs. Willard J. Beckley
Washington Hall Grange No. 2216
Carrolton, Ohio

Place moistened paper towel on dirty rack in hot oven broiler. Steam softens food and grease.

Margaret A. DeForest, Lecturer
Ogden Grange No. 111
Spencerport, New York

To remove an angel food cake from a tube pan and transfer, right side up, to serving dish, slide 2 thin pieces of cardboard down side of cake. Lift cake from pan.

Mrs. Stanley E. DeForest, Overseer
Ogden Grange No. 111
Spencerport, New York

Before using raisins in a cake, put raisins in a sieve; pour boiling water over them. Drain well. Raisins do not need to be floured; they will mix all through the cake.

Eugenia V. Smith, LAS, HE Chm.
Contoocook Grange No. 216
Contoocook, New Hampshire

To remove fish odors from hands or pan, wash with vinegar.
Vinegar will remove tom cat odors from walls or floors.
Combine 1 teaspoon hot vinegar with 1 teaspoon salt in 1/4 cup water for relief of sore throat.

Mrs. Mary Engelhardt, Master
Petaluma Grange No. 23
Petaluma, California

Keep quart freezer container in freezer; add those 2 or 3 tablespoons leftover vegetables. This gives a variety of vegetables when making a pot of soup or stew.

Mrs. Joe French, Chm., Home Ec.
Lincoln Grange No. 237
Wellsburg, New York

I plant tansy, chives and nasturtiums all through the garden; they keep garden pests away. Never need to use any sprays.

Rita P. Armstrong, Lecturer
Nute Ridge Grange No. 316
Farmington, New Hampshire

Fill an empty seasoning jar with salt and about 1 tablespoon pepper. This mixture comes in handy when cooking.

Mrs. Catherine S. Pulling
Skaneateles Grange No. 458
Skaneateles, New York

Parboil potatoes and pour water off when preparing scalloped potatoes; baked mixture will not curdle.

Mrs. Thomas Latterner, Lady Asst. Steward
W. Oshtemo Grange
Kalamazoo, Michigan

When cutting out quilts, make the patterns out of firm pliable plastic. These patterns may be purchased from Quilters Newsletter, Box 394, Wheat Ridge, Colorado. They have hundreds of precut patterns to choose from.

Rebecca Stiff, Pres., Women's Aux.
East Spokane Grange No. 148
Spokane, Washington

To renew bedroom drapes, add ball fringe in color to match bedspread.

Mrs. John Vosburgh
Florida Grange No. 1543
Amsterdam, New York

Knit or sew 8 plastic egg carton bottoms together with inside of cartons turned outside. Using two colors of yarn, sew from bottom up; tie at top. When ready to sew the last one, slip pie pan 1 notch up inside to make bottom.

Mrs. Mae Long, DWA
Lafayette Grange No. 773
Elliston, Virginia

To display pictures of grandchildren, place the oldest child's first picture in the middle of a large picture frame. Make a border around center picture with small pictures of other grandchildren.

Lillian M. Overmyer, Fund Raising
Cleon Grange No. 633
Copemish, Michigan

Unusual, boldly patterned paper may be placed in panels made from half round moldings. This wall treatment would be attractive in a dining room, hall or living room.

Mrs. Justin Price, Treas.
Price's Fork Grange No. 786
Blacksburg, Virginia

For practical, easy-care curtains for the bathroom, use towels to suit your taste. When ready to discard, rip out casings. Use for towels.

Mrs. Charles Lewis, HEC
New York Valley Grange
Yates Center, Kansas

For a holiday wall plaque, cut a 1 1/2-foot circle from plywood. Cut a 6-inch circle out of center. Cover plywood circle with nuts in shells and artificial fruit. Trim edges with pine cone petals. Use Elmers Glue to hold the pieces. Spray with lacquer.

Rosanna Mitchell, CWA Com.
Somerset Grange No. 18
Norridgewock, Maine

Cut decorative wrapping paper 2/3 the height of the fireplace and 4 times the width. Fold this strip in 1-inch pleats; staple folds at bottom. Spread out top and sides to form fan. Place fan inside the fireplace, letting edges touch both sides of opening. Tension holds fan in place.

Mrs. John Cannon, Sec.
Marshall Grange No. 1840
Washington Court House, Ohio

To make an Easter picture cross, place 1 styrofoam egg carton on flat surface, bottom side up. Cut another egg carton into 2 pieces, having 4 egg sections of carton for 1 piece and 8 egg sections for remaining piece. Place short section, bottom side up, along middle of long side of whole egg carton; place long section along middle of other side of egg carton to form cross. Adhere with glue. Color with spray paint; decorate with artificial flowers. Sew ribbon around edge of cross. Hang on wall.

Mrs. Arthur Shaddick, Home Ec. Chm.
Paw Paw Grange No. 1884
Paw Paw, Illinois

The white eggs that Leggs panty hose come in make perfect containers for buttons waiting to be sewed on and sewing supplies such as elastic, rickrack and needles. The eggs also make good containers for that inquisitive 4 year-old that loves to put play things in little spaces. They also come in handy when you can't find a box to wrap that small gift in. The egg wrapped makes an unusual looking present.

Robin Lindsey Quist, Pres., Youth Com.
Boylston Grange No. 111
Boylston, Massachusetts

Cut kitchen towel in half; sew matching colored cotton cloth on cut edge. Make a buttonhole on top. Hang on sink door knob. Towel will be handy to wipe hands on.

Caroline Minegar
Trowbridge Grange No. 296
Allegan, Michigan

To dress up a room, stick adhesive paper on the inside of window shades. Adhesive paper comes in different designs and colors.

Betty Behn, Flora
Cromwell Grange No. 67
Middleton, Connecticut

Cut nylon hose in strips and braid mats. Cut out parts of newspaper colored pictures, paste on old lamp shades.

Marjorie H. Campbell, Home and Community
Guiding Star Grange No. 1
Greenfield, Massachusetts

To refurbish old milk cans, soften with kerosene. Rub with fine steel wool. Be sure the rust is all gone or more will form. Wash in hot suds; rinse and dry well. Apply a coat or two of rust-preventive paint before decorating.

Lucy M. Graham, Ceres
Lockport Grange No. 1262
Gasport, New York

Cut a sponge in desired design; glue sponge on a block of wood. Dip into wall paint, rubbing off excess paint. Press sponge on walls evenly to make a design.

Mrs. William Balcom
Souhegan Grange No. 10
Amherst, New Hampshire

To make a kitchen bulletin board, cut a piece of tin of desired size; fasten to wall with tile cement. Paint to match wall; attach memos with magnets.

Mrs. Albert J. Halsey
Sub. Sec., Pomona Lecturer
Southampton Grange No. 1281
Southampton, New York

Put your plastic flowers and vines in the top rack of your dishwasher to be washed. Be sure they cannot come in contact with heating coil.

Mrs. Donald Pickinpaugh, Lady Asst. Steward
Sharon Grange No. 1561
Caldwell, Ohio

Place 1/2 cup salt, sugar or beach sand in a paper bag; place soiled artificial flowers in the bag upside down. Close bag firmly; shake well. When you remove flowers, they will be sparkling clean again.

Mrs. Norene G. Cox, DWA
Virginia State Grange
Mouth of Wilson, Virginia

Cover an empty ice cream carton with your favorite color felt or other material to make a wastebasket for your room.

Wilma G. Hoch, Past CWA Chm.
Ostrom Grange
Yuba City, California

Cut a smiling face four inches in diameter of foam rubber in different colors for each child in family; glue to small magnets. Leave notes for them under their magnet on the refrigerator door as that is the first place they stop when arriving home.

Lenora Geenen, Flora
Westmond Grange No. 83813
Cocolalla, Idaho

Combine 1 teaspoon citric acid, 1 teaspoon soda, 1 quart water and 1 cup mothballs in large bowl. In a short time, balls will bounce up and down. When they stop, add more citric acid. They will start again.

Mrs. Carrie Baumbarger
Providence Grange No. 2572
Grand Rapids, Ohio

If you burn many candles in your home, save all small pieces or short candles. Melt down in a coffee can. Coat inside of any size tin can with salad oil. Make sure can is smooth without ridges. Pour in melted wax; insert wick as it begins to harden to make a new large candle.

Janice N. Going, Lecturer
Coventry Grange No. 75
Coventry, Connecticut

To make clay dough, combine 1 cup flour, 1 cup salt, 1 tablespoon alum and 1/2 cup water in saucepan; cook until thick. Tint with food coloring as desired. Store in airtight container.

Mrs. Carrie Baumbarger
Providence Grange No. 2572
Grand Rapids, Ohio

Make beautiful pictures using buttons for flowers and old pieces of jewelry, crewel design and whatever odds and ends will work into the picture. Use Swiss straw for stems. May use sequins and beads.

Mrs. Wanda Honn
Exec. Com., Sec. & Treas., CWA
Winchester Bag Grange No. 906
North Bend, Oregon

Combine crushed egg shells, chopped banana and vegetable peels and coffee grounds to mulch soil with good nutrients. The sediment from the bottom of aquarium tank has good nutrients also.

To feed wild birds use half an orange spiked on a tree branch and peanut butter mixed with raisins, cracked corn and seed, shaped into a firm ball on a tree. Place ball in freezer until firm.

Mrs. Maurice Linder, Sec.
Lake Katrine Grange No. 1065
Lake Katrine, New York

When making hills for cucumbers or squash, make holes with a can opener in large tin juice cans all around the bottom outside edge of can. Sink on top of fertilizer; fill around with soil. Plant seed around cans. When they need water fill the cans.

Eugenie R. de Groff, WA Chm.
Nobleboro Grange No. 369
Waldoboro, Maine

To remove white spots on TV cabinet due to interior heat, rub with vaseline. Repeat every 6 to 8 months.

Agnes Stewart, State Sec. Wife
Cadmus Grange
Meriden, Kansas

Use lemon juice for stained and rough hands; makes them smooth and removes stain.
For a sick house plant, put several empty egg shells into a bottle or jar; fill with water. Let stand for several days; water plant.
For a low-calorie rhubarb pie, instead of using sugar, add 1 package low-calorie strawberry gelatin for 8-inch pie.

Edith M. Nail, Vice Chm., CWA
Central Union Grange No. 559
Lemoore, California

To remove grease from clothing, rub with unsalted fat. Rub well into material so all grease stains are gone before washing.

Eunice Blackmer, Flora
Broomfield Grange No. 9757
Remus, Michigan

To remove grass stains from clothing, rub lard well into stain. Wash with soap by hand before laundering.

Lillian Globun, Pomona
Schyrock Grange
Cherrytree, Pennsylvania

To remove ball-point pen ink, spray fabric with hair spray. Let dry; launder as usual.

Florence M. Evans, Lady Asst. Steward
Floyd Grange No. 665
Rome, New York

When doing hand sewing with double thread, tie a knot in each thread instead of tying them together and the thread will not tangle.

Mrs. Glenn Carter, Treas.
Texas Valley Grange No. 972
Marathon, New York

Make braid for dresses out of washable yarn by embroidering. Chain stitch, lazy daisy and French knots are effective.

Mrs. Lewis Lent, Treas.
Prudence Grange No. 1204
Coudersport, Pennsylvania

Knit 4 1/2-inch squares of different colored yarn using garter stitch for an afghan. Join strips together with single crochet of yarn. Crochet a scalloped border of shell pattern around afghan.

Edna I. Everingham, Lecturer
LaFayette Grange No. 1330
LaFayette, New York

Use the widest gauze bandage for facing for a dress. It is easy to sew even on the knitted materials and is never bulky.

Mrs. Hannah E. Williams, Sec.
Wapping Grange No. 30
Manchester, Connecticut

Turn 84-inch drapes which have faded or gotten old into drapes for a smaller window by measuring and cutting off from the bottom. At the cutting line, turn up and hem. Open the ends at the original hem in the bottom to run a rod through and you have drapes for smaller windows.

Wanda Wagner, Lecturer
Fulton Grange No. 2421
Canal Fulton, Ohio

Save money by making neckties and shirts for your husband and sons. They are originals, too.

Mrs. G. T. Wallbillich, Lecturer
Rocksburgh Grange No. 110
Phillipsburg, New Jersey

When sewing on snap fasteners, sew all the snaps on one side first. Rub chalk over them and press against the opposite side. This marks the correct place for the other half of the fasteners and also assures a correct fit.

Minnie Lampard, Flora
Ney Grange No. 1845
Genoa, Illinois

If thread breaks, it may be dry and brittle. Place spool in refrigerator for 12 hours and thread will not break so easily.

Mrs. Larry Hicks
West Oshtema Grange
Kalamazoo, Michigan

To evenly distribute wear on sheets, place the same hem at the top of the bed at least half the time.
Sew the upper and lower hems of plain curtains the same width; reverse ends at each laundering to insure longer and more even wear.

Mrs. Marion Judd, Master
Lake Harbor Grange No. 1185
Muskegon, Michigan

To cut buttonholes, place the fabric in a small embroidery hoop to hold tightly; cut with a single-edged razor blade.

Mrs. Thomas Goshe
Home Ec. Chm. of Womens Activities
McCutchen Grange No. 2360
New Riegel, Ohio

After pressing dress seams open, an easy way to put a finished look is to overcast edge with the zig-zag stitch of sewing machine.

Evelyn H. Pressey, Ceres
Deering Grange No. 5
Portland, Maine

Sew 2 washcloths together, leaving one end opened. Cut yarn four inches or longer. Double yarn; pull through washcloth with crochet hook and loop over. Fill with foam and finish the other side.

Ruth Masceau, Sec.
Danville Grange No. 520
Groton, Vermont

Tea stains on china cups may be removed by rubbing salt on them.
To have liver go through a food chopper easily, cover with boiling water; let stand for ten minutes before grinding.

Viola Blake, Home Ec. Chm.
New Hampton Grange No. 123
New Hampton, New Hampshire

Use rubbing alcohol on paper toweling to clean the bathroom mirror and fixtures. It removes soap film and leaves no water spots, and is usually in the bathroom cabinet.

Mrs. George J. Lee, WAC, Sec.
Priest Lake Grange No. 447
Priest River, Idaho

To remove odor from a bottle, put a table-spoon dry mustard into bottle; fill half full of cold water. Shake well, let stand for 30 minutes. Rinse with clear water.

Get last bit of catsup from nearly empty bottle by pouring some milk or water into bottle and using thinned mixture in making meat loaf.

Viola Blake, Home Ec. Chm.
New Hampton Grange No. 123
New Hampton, New Hampshire

Stuff your wet shoes with newspapers; they will absorb the moisture so shoes will dry and remain soft. Change papers once or twice, if necessary.

Mrs. Elva L. Benner, Chaplain
Acorn Grange No. 418
Friendship, Maine

Save small empty safety type match boxes; bind 6 or 8 together with gummed paper for small chest in which to keep pins, needles, buttons, snap fasteners and other small items in sewing kit.

Pearl Estabrook, Pomona
Bolton Grange No. 142, P of H
Bolton, Massachusetts

To open a clogged drain if no plunger is handy, place palm of the hand over drain. Move palm up and down. If not clogged too badly it will open.

Mrs. Willa Wurm
Harlem Grange, Delaware Co.
Galena, Ohio

For shiny, lint-free windows, use a paper towel to wipe them.

Mrs. Ralph Tornes, Jr.
Jr. Matron, Co. CWA Com.
Waterford Grange No. 231
Waterford, Ohio

For too many shoes on the floor, fasten a curtain rod to your closet door; hang shoes by the heels. Place hooks on the door to hang handbags.

Mrs. Harry Brazlan
Bolton Grange No. 142
Bolton, Massachusetts

Never water house plants until stirring the top dirt with a finger to be sure they are really dry. Most house plants are killed by too much watering.

Mrs. Carrie Baumburger
Providence Grange No. 2572
Grand Rapids, Ohio

Use mothballs in small paper sacks in cupboards to keep ants away.

Mrs. Paul F. Vogel, Ceres
McCutchen Grange No. 2360
Fostoria, Ohio

Remove sticky labels from jars, windows, walls, counters or tables by sponging or soaking with vinegar.

Della Grove, WAC Chm.
Blackhawk Grange
Leaf River, Illinois

Tape a chart of poison antidotes with the telephone number of your local poison control center inside your medicine cupboard so it will be available if such an emergency should arise.

Mrs. John U. Cannon, Sec.
Marshall Grange No. 1840
Jeffersonville, Ohio

When cleaning windows, instead of using paper towels, use crumpled pieces of newspaper. There is no lint; something about the paper and ink gives the best shine ever.

Mrs. Frank Conrad, Lecturer
University Grange No. 335, Vermont
Lebanon, New Hampshire

Place a telephone extension in the garage or barn where the menfolk are most of the time. It will save you untold running and yelling.

Mrs. John O. Smith, WAC
Fairview Grange No. 2177
Goshen, Indiana

To clean silver quickly, combine 1 tablespoon salt and 1 teaspoon soda with hot water in large aluminum kettle. Place silver to be cleaned in solution for a minute or until tarnish disappears. Rinse and dry thoroughly.

Mrs. Floyd Milburn, Women's Activity Chm.
Clear Creek Grange No. 233
DeSoto, Kansas

Use leftover cold tea or coffee to water house plants occasionally.

Sandra Pearce, Sec.
Golden Gate Grange No. 451
Golden, Colorado

To eliminate odor of marigolds, place 1 teaspoon sugar in water in vase holding the arrangement.

Dorothy Wagoner, WA Chm.
Pleasant Grove Grange No. 475
Summerville, Oregon

Wash windows with 1 gallon warm water to which has been added 2 tablespoons cornstarch.

Dorothy Wagoner, WA Chm.
Pleasant Grove Grange No. 475
Summerville, Oregon

To make pot handle sleeves, cut 3 x 6-inch strips from old towels. Sew three sides, leaving one 3-inch side open. Turn inside out; slip over hot pot handles.

Mrs. Lloyd Belden, Lady Asst. Steward
Trowbridge Grange No. 296
Allegan, Michigan

To remove odor from refrigerator, place 3 tablespoons vanilla in a cup; place in lower part of refrigerator for several hours.

Irene F. Alvord
Shetucket Grange No. 69
Hampton, Connecticut

When terrycloth tablecloths or towels wear thin in spots leaving good material, cut round kitchen hand towels. Bind with bias tape; sew 16-inch piece of tape to center of circle, leaving two 8-inch ties. Towel may be tied to cabinet or refrigerator door.

Mrs. W. J. Waterson, Ceres
Pine River Grange No. 197
Bayfield, Colorado

Sew two thicknesses of nylon net on one side of new dishcloths. This saves reaching for a scouring pad. Net may be replaced if worn out before dishcloth.

Edrice McLean, CWA Chm., Sec.
Freshwater Grange No. 499
Eureka, California

Keep a clean metal sponge in a small plastic bag with your rolling pin. A few rubs with this sponge and your rolling pin is clean. Wipe with a cloth and it is ready to store. No washing is necessary.

Ruth L. Lord, Pomona, Ceres
Essex Grange
Ipswich, Massachusetts

Rotate the linens in the linen closet so that the same ones do not get used each week. Place freshly laundered items on the top; use from the bottom or vice versa. If you have several stacks of one item, place a marker under the stack to be used next. Use from left to right.

Mrs. William A. Steel
Sec., CWA Chm., Arlington, Virginia
Potomac Grange No. 1
Washington, D. C.

Mason jar rings sewn in corner of small scatter rugs prevents slipping on polished floors.

Irving W. Seeley, Sterling Master
Great Falls Grange No. 738
Sterling, Virginia

To remove tea or coffee stains from cups, sprinkle soda in cups and rub well with damp cloth. They will be like new again.

Mrs. Wylie E. Heasley, Flora
Shenango Township Grange No. 2057
Pulaski, Pennsylvania

To make a good cleaning solution for walls, woodwork and bathtubs, combine 1/2 cup vinegar and 1/4 cup soda with 1 gallon water.

Frances Leary, Master
Rye Grange No. 233
Rye, New Hampshire

A marvelous formula for washing walls is 1/4 cup soda, 1/2 cup vinegar and 1 cup ammonia to 1 gallon water. Apply with a coarse sponge. Usually, no rinsing is needed.

Lucy M. Graham, Pomona
Niagara Co. Pomona Grange
Gasport, New York

Meat tenderizer mixed with water and rubbed into an insect bite will take away the pain within seconds. Mix 1/4 teaspoon tenderizer with 1 tablespoon water.

Mrs. Diane Doyle
Holland Grange No. 1023
Holland, New York

When drying clothes in the dryer, set timer for 15 minutes or less. Remove clothes to be ironed. They are evenly dampened and easy to iron.

Rose Michalek, Sec.
Fairfield Grange No. 720
Gervais, Oregon

Tie small pieces of soap in an old nylon stocking. Use to wash the bathtub out.
Use a small amount of alcohol when washing windows in cool weather.

Mrs. Elsie Dingus, Lecturer
Kincaid Grange No. 1482
Kincaid, Kansas

If tap water has clogged your steam iron, fill it with 1/4 cup vinegar and 1 cup water; let stand overnight. Heat iron; remove mixture. Rinse with clear water; iron will work like new.

Frances Hirsch, CWA
Quillisascut Grange No. 378
Rice, Washington

Wrap rubber bands around the ends of unpadded wooden coathangers. Clothes won't slip off so easily.
Buy hand towels to match your kitchen colors. Fold in half crossways; cut into 2 pieces. Gather or pleat the cut edges to about 4 inches. Make a 7-inch tab with a piece of leftover material. Set one end to gathered towel. Put a gripper on to fasten to drawer pull or handle.

Marion B. Comstock, Pomona CWA Chm.
Chesnere Grange No. 23
Yalesville, Connecticut

Boil potatoes or carrot peelings in the tea kettle to remove lime from kettle.

Mrs. Robert Latterner, WA Chm.
West Oshtemo Grange
Kalamazoo, Michigan

Use a long handled sponge mop dipped in 1/3 cup sudsy ammonia to 1 gallon of warm water to wash outside windows. Rinse off with hose. Windows sparkle.

Blanche Engle, CWA Chm.
Mulino Grange No. 40
Mulino, Oregon

Don't shake the dust mop out the window if you want your neighbor to love you. Tie a bag around the mop head and shake vigorously. Throw bag and dust away.

Mrs. Leon Hoffman
Adams Grange No. 286
North Adams, Michigan

Plastic bags may be used over again by washing them. Keep a large bag pinned to a towel rod with a clothes pin. Tuck the clean bags in the large bag. They are handy for many uses.

Ruth E. Steger, Pianist
Scotts Mills Grange No. 938
Scotts Mills, Oregon

If bothered with roaches, sprinkle boric acid powder around infested area. Roaches will disappear.

Mrs. Nellore Rice, Master
Terre Haute Grange No. 2480
Urbana, Ohio

Index

COLOR ILLUSTRATIONS

PHOTOGRAPHY CREDITS: Filbert/Hazelnut Institute; National Kraut Packers Association; California Strawberry Advisory Board; Proctor & Gamble Company: Crisco Division; International Tuna Fish Association; Florida Citrus Commission; American Lamb Council; Accent International; Olive Administrative Committee; The Quaker Oats Company; National Cherry Growers & Industries Foundation; Carnation Evaporated Milk; National Red Cherry Institute; Standard Brands Products: Fleischmann's Yeast, Royal Puddings & Gelatins, Fleischmann's Margarine, Planter's Nuts; Pineapple Growers Association; California Raisin Advisory Board; McCormick & Company; United Fresh Fruit and Vegetable Association; Knox Gelatine; The Nestle Company; North American Blueberry Council; Apple Pantry: Washington State Apple Commission; C & H Sugar Company; Processed Apples Institute; Best Foods, a Division of CPC International, Inc.; National Dairy Council; Evaporated Milk Association; DIAMOND Walnut Growers, Inc.; Pillsbury Company.

Complete Your Cooking And Entertainment Library With The Grange Cookbooks!

New Desserts Cookbook — The crowning complements to every meal — scrumptious and beautiful desserts! This brand new, never before published collection of favorite dessert recipes is sure to bring smiles of delight to young and old alike. And a new glow to your everyday meals.

Meats Cookbook — The way to a man's heart? Nothing beats roast beef, lamb, pork, veal ... or any other meat dish. Plain or fancy, mouth watering main dishes for every taste and occasion are included in this valuable recipe book.

Holiday Cookbook — Prepare delicious and festive meals for all those special holiday events. Recipes are included for not only Christmas, Thanksgiving and New Year's Eve and Day ... but for Halloween, Fourth of July, St. Patrick's Day ... every exciting occasion.

All-Purpose Cookbook — Desserts, main dishes, salads, snacks ... recipes for every meal you can imagine. This happy combination cookbook makes meal planning and preparation fun and easy, and guarantees success — every time.

American Cooking Cookbook — Yankee Pot Roast, Southern Pecan Pie, New England Clam Chowder ... favorite American dishes the whole family will enjoy. Handed down by families through the years ... these are foods that best reflect our great heritage.

Grange Members Are Proud To Share With You All The Fun And Excitement Of Cooking

Make your cooking library come alive with all five editions of *The Grange Cookbooks*. You'll find thousands of just-right recipes for every taste and occasion at your fingertips. And they're all so easy to prepare!

Each recipe has been personally tested and tasted by Grange members from all across the country . . . and each has the enthusiastic approval of their families. We're so proud of these recipes, and want you and your family to enjoy them as much as we do.

Order the complete library of *The Grange Cookbooks* today. Remember, these books make perfect gifts for birthdays, weddings, showers, anniversaries, etc. Don't miss this great opportunity to really show off your cooking talents . . . with *The Grange Cookbook* series.

GRANGE COOKBOOKS

Use these handy order forms to order books for yourself and for friends.

Grange Cookbooks
Order Form 30890

PLEASE SEND ME THE FOLLOWING BOOKS:

Name

Address

City   State   Zip

☐ Please Bill Me — Plus Postage and Handling

☐ Enclosed is payment for full amount. No charge for postage and handling.

Quan.	Cookbook Title	Item No.	Price Each	Total
	New Desserts	124008	3.95	
	Holiday	124006	3.95	
	Meats	124002	3.95	
	All-Purpose	124005	3.95	
	American Cooking	124007	3.95	
			Total Order	

MAIL TO: FAVORITE RECIPES PRESS ●BOX 3396 ●MONTGOMERY, ALABAMA 36109

Grange Cookbooks
Order Form 30890

PLEASE SEND ME THE FOLLOWING BOOKS:

Name

Address

City   State   Zip

☐ Please Bill Me — Plus Postage and Handling

☐ Enclosed is payment for full amount. No charge for postage and handling.

Quan.	Cookbook Title	Item No.	Price Each	Total
	New Desserts	124008	3.95	
	Holiday	124006	3.95	
	Meats	124002	3.95	
	All-Purpose	124005	3.95	
	American Cooking	124007	3.95	
			Total Order	

MAIL TO: FAVORITE RECIPES PRESS ●BOX 3396 ●MONTGOMERY, ALABAMA 36109

Grange Cookbooks
Order Form 30890

PLEASE SEND ME THE FOLLOWING BOOKS:

Name

Address

City   State   Zip

☐ Please Bill Me — Plus Postage and Handling

☐ Enclosed is payment for full amount. No charge for postage and handling.

Quan.	Cookbook Title	Item No.	Price Each	Total
	New Desserts	124008	3.95	
	Holiday	124006	3.95	
	Meats	124002	3.95	
	All-Purpose	124005	3.95	
	American Cooking	124007	3.95	
			Total Order	

MAIL TO: FAVORITE RECIPES PRESS ●BOX 3396 ●MONTGOMERY, ALABAMA 36109